Suicide

C000157102

In an original and provocative study of suicide, Ian Marsh examines the historical and cultural forces that have influenced contemporary thought, practices and policy in relation to this serious public health problem. Drawing on the work of French philosopher Michel Foucault, the book tells the story of how suicide has come to be seen as first and foremost a matter of psychiatric concern. Marsh sets out to challenge the assumptions and certainties embedded in our beliefs, attitudes and practices concerning suicide and the suicidal, and the resulting account unsettles and informs in equal measure. The book will be of particular interest to researchers, professionals and students in psychology, history, sociology and the health sciences.

IAN MARSH is a Senior Lecturer at Canterbury Christ Church University. He previously worked in an NHS Community Mental Health Team and continues to facilitate suicide prevention training.

Suicide

Foucault, History and Truth

Ian Marsh

Canterbury Christ Church University

CAMBRIDGE UNIVERSITY PRESS
Cambridge, New York, Melbourne, Madrid, Cape Town, Singapore,
São Paulo, Delhi

Cambridge University Press
The Edinburgh Building, Cambridge CB2 8RU, UK

Published in the United States of America by Cambridge University Press,
New York

www.cambridge.org
Information on this title: www.cambridge.org/9780521130011

First published 2010

Printed in the United Kingdom at the University Press, Cambridge

A catalogue record for this publication is available from the British Library

Library of Congress Cataloguing in Publication data
Marsh, Ian, 1952–
Suicide : Foucault, history and truth / Ian Marsh.
   p.   cm.
ISBN 978-0-521-11254-3 (hardback)
1. Suicide.   2. Suicide–History.   3. Foucault, Michel, 1926–1984.   I. Title.
HV6545.M274   2010
362.28–dc22
                                                                        2009039348

ISBN 978-0-521-11254-3 Hardback
ISBN 978-0-521-13001-1 Paperback

For Rosarii, Cara and Connor

Contents

Contents ix

Figures

Acknowledgements

Many people are owed a very large debt of thanks for their help and support in the writing of this book. At the University of Brighton Gaynor Sadlo and Alec Grant were generous in their support as supervisors during my doctoral studies there, and Ann Moore, Marilia Vasquet-Whittome, Tracey Harrison and Jayne Ingles were all tremendously helpful at the Clinical Research Centre. Jon Wright deserves special mention for his kindness, guidance and support over many years. East Kent Mental Health NHS Trust initially supported the research, and the whole project was inspired by my colleagues and clients from the ten years I worked there. Canterbury Christ Church University supported the research from May 2002, and Kate Springett was instrumental in providing me with sufficient study leave to complete the project. Colleagues at Christ Church have been very supportive and encouraging and I would like to thank in particular Simon Hannaford, Jan Jenson, Julie Taylor, Pat Chung, Doug MacInnes, Angela Wilson, Hilary Bungay, Lee Bolton and Anita Volkert. Rayya Ghul deserves special thanks for not only covering a significant part of my teaching while I was on study leave, but also for her encouragement and inspiration – I feel lucky to have such a generous colleague and friend.

Peter Watts very carefully critiqued the various drafts he has been presented with over the last couple of years and I am very grateful for the help and support he has provided. He has been a wonderfully patient and intelligent mentor (and the phrase 'compulsory ontology of pathology' is rightly his). Liz Hoult read through the whole book and her comments helped clarify my thinking and provided many, many useful suggestions. She is another valuable friend and colleague. Tom Osborne and Chris Stevenson were generous examiners of my PhD thesis, as well as being inspirational with their own work. I would also like to thank Timothy Hill for kindly reading and commenting on chapter 5, and for the anonymous reviewers at Cambridge University Press for their helpful suggestions. Heidi Rimke helped enormously (without being aware of it) with the overall organisation and structure of the book as well as with the development of many ideas. Others have also contributed a great deal (again without their awareness let alone approval) and here the writings of Derek Hook, Nikolas Rose, Judith Butler and Arnold Davidson stand out. All the mistakes and misunderstandings are mine, however.

I would also like to thank Jayne Curran and Athene Lane-Martin from the East Kent Health Promotion Service, and all the participants of the many Understanding and Managing Suicidal Behaviour training days, for their ideas and suggestions but mostly for keeping me 'grounded' as to the realities of suicide prevention work (many might say they have not quite succeeded but if true that would be my fault not theirs).

The friendliness and helpfulness of the staff at the East Kent Archives Centre, Whitfield, made the summer I spent trawling through the records of the local County Lunatic Asylum a very enjoyable experience.

At Cambridge University Press commissioning editors John Haslam and Hetty Reid have been as helpful and supportive as I could have hoped.

My parents and sister have always been supportive of me, and I am extremely grateful to them. Finally, my partner Rosarii Harte, and our children Cara and Connor, have had to live with this project for a long time, but have done so with great good grace and humour. I am eternally grateful for their love and support.

Part I

Introduction and analytic strategy

My aim will be to show you how social practices may engender domains of knowledge that not only bring new objects, new concepts, and new techniques to light, but also give rise to totally new forms of subjects and subjects of knowledge. The subject of knowledge itself has a history; the relation of the subject to the object; or, more clearly, truth itself has a history.   Michel Foucault (2002a)

A critique is not a matter of saying that things are not right as they are. It is a matter of pointing out on what kinds of assumptions, what kinds of familiar, unchallenged, unconsidered modes of thought the practices that we accept rest.   Michel Foucault (1988a)

1 Introduction

Foucault, critique and the study of suicide

This book, which is for the most part influenced by the work of Michel Foucault, critically examines contemporary approaches to the problem of suicide. From Foucault comes a focus on relations of power, knowledge and the subject, and it is argued that it is possible to identify certain principles and strategies of analysis from Foucault's own studies (e.g. *Madness and Civilization*, 1965; *Discipline and Punish*, 1977 and *The History of Sexuality*, vol. I: *An Introduction*, 1981) that can usefully be employed to interrogate the assumptions and certainties embedded in our beliefs, attitudes and practices concerning suicide and the suicidal.

One way of characterising Foucault's work (and there are many ways of so doing it must be admitted, as even a brief survey of the secondary literature will confirm) would be to say that it concerned itself with mapping the often complex relationships between the production, dissemination and circulation of authoritative knowledge, particular relations of power-to-knowledge and knowledge-to-power, and certain 'truth effects' in terms of the constitution of objects and subjects of knowledge. This book looks to map such relations with regard to the ways in which suicide and the suicidal are most commonly conceptualised and responded to in practice.

Foucault's writings were also forms of critique – they sought to call into question the 'taken-for-granted', and to cast light on and challenge the necessity of the 'kinds of familiar, unchallenged, unconsidered modes of thought [on which] the practices that we accept rest' (Foucault, 1988a, p. 155). Foucault's book-length studies of madness, discipline and punishment, and sexuality could be said to be, in part, attempts to trace the ways in which certain 'authoritative knowledges' were produced, circulated and organised, how particular 'regimes of truth' (Foucault, 2002a, p. 131) could come to be formed, and, importantly, as kinds of critical analyses, to map the 'truth effects' that followed. Analysis of the possibilities for thought and action opened up by particular 'truth-telling'

3

practices proceeded alongside consideration of the ways in which they could be said to be problematic.

Such a critical approach can usefully be brought to bear, I believe, on the study of suicide. Suicide is now read, almost always, as a tragedy, one caused primarily by pathological processes internal to the individual that require expert diagnosis and management. Such is the dominance of this position that it is possible to speak here of a contemporary 'regime of truth', one centring on a compulsory ontology of pathology in relation to suicide. Obviously, attempts to understand suicide and to prevent its occurrence by focusing on questions of illness and pathology possess an obvious rationale but the assumptions embedded within these approaches, and their effects (in terms of both intended and unintended consequences) have not themselves been the subject of any sustained critical analysis (with one or two notable exceptions, e.g. Szasz, 1999; Stevenson and Cutcliffe, 2006). One aim of this book is, therefore, to explore the possibilities for thought and action that the insistence on reading suicide as pathological opens up, as well as to examine the limitations imposed by the dominance and hegemonising tendencies of this particular 'regime' (evidenced, perhaps, by the marginalisation of other meanings of self-accomplished death – an act of protest or resistance, of self-determination, choice or will, an event of moral, criminal or political concern, even as a subject of philosophical debate).

In many of his writings Foucault made strategic use of historical analysis as a means of unsettling contemporary claims to truth by drawing attention to the numerous contingencies that underlay the certainties of the present, but also by mapping the vested (but often veiled) interests at work in the making of such claims (again, as examples, 1965, 1977, and 1981). The central idea is that particular truths have a history that can usefully be traced in the service of critique. In an interview in 1983, Foucault commented on how certain forms of historical analysis could allow an understanding of the contingencies of contemporary truths and practices to emerge, and how this could, in turn, open up a conceptual space, freed from 'necessities' imposed by the present, where other ways of thinking and acting become possible. Foucault explicitly linked the use of a historicist approach to addressing concerns in the present, and the opening up of possibilities for the future. For Foucault, a 'diagnosing' of the present

does not consist in simply characterizing what we are, but in following the lines of fragility of the present, in coming to grasp in what way that which is and how that which is could no longer be that which is. And it is in this sense that the description should be made according to that kind of virtual rupture that opens a space of freedom, understood as a space of concrete freedom, that is to say, of possible transformation. (In Davidson, 2001, p. 189)

It can be by means of the 'recourse to history' that such possibilities can come to be realised, for

what different forms of rationality present as their necessary condition one can perfectly well do the history of, and recover the network of contingencies from which it has emerged; which does not mean however that these forms of rationality were irrational; it means that they rest on a base of human practice and of human history and since these things have been made, they can, provided one knows how they were made, be unmade. (Davidson, 2001, p. 189)

In a similar vein, Nikolas Rose (1998) speaks of 'a critical history' that 'helps us think about the nature and limits of our present, about the conditions under which that which we take for truth and reality has been established' (p. 18). For Rose, such a critical history 'disturbs and fragments, it reveals the fragility of that which seems solid, the contingency of that which seems necessary ... [i]t enables us to think *against* the present, in the sense of exploring its horizons and conditions of possibility' (p. 18).

A similarly historicist approach can be useful, it is argued, as a way of 'diagnosing' the present and of unsettling 'taken-for-granted' truths so as to open up possibilities for thinking and acting differently with regard to suicide and the suicidal. There have, of course, been many histories of suicide published (e.g. Anderson, 1987; MacDonald and Murphy, 1990; Murray, 1998, 2000; Minois, 1999) but analysis in terms of relations of power, knowledge and the subject has been partial at most (perhaps certain chapters in Ian Hacking's *The Taming of Chance* (1990) come closest, despite this not being the book's primary aim by any means). So a 'Foucauldian' analysis is employed here in order to map the formation, consolidation and expansion of a 'regime of truth' centring on a compulsory ontology of pathology in relation to suicide that has come to be so dominant. The conditions of possibility for such a regime, the site of its formation, the means by which relations of power and of power-knowledge acted to produce its truths and justify its practices, and its effects in terms of the objects, concepts and subjects formed, are the broad targets for analysis. The analytic strategy employed in the book will be considered in more detail in chapter 2, but perhaps before then it is necessary, given the sensitivity of the subject matter, to speak a little more about the possible utility of taking such a critical approach.

Rationale

As discussed above, this book can be thought of as an attempt to critically analyse the workings of a contemporary 'regime of truth' in relation to suicide. Unfortunately, such a task is not easy, for governing or dominant rationalities of any period tend to be self-justifying. If we seek to pass judgement on 'accepted' ways of talking and doing we are often faced with setting out a case using a vocabulary and concepts that, for the most part, already effectively constrain what can be said in general about a topic, and more particularly what can be truthfully stated. Strong normative forces tend to be at work here. But Foucault's primary concern in his own work was not really with opening up the present to criticism – as in a passing of judgement – but more of making strange, or unfamiliar, that which had come to feel most true, most natural, most necessary and most real. Again, this task is rendered difficult with respect to the current subject, as the 'truths' of suicide tend to feel particularly real – after all there are dead bodies and grief; to describe people who take their own lives as having acted 'while the balance of their minds was disturbed' appears a natural, almost self-evident, truth. To seek to prevent suicide by any means available, given the above, would seem to be an absolute necessity. Critique can thus be met by recourse to 'the real', 'the true', 'the natural', and 'the necessary', and fears can be raised that any loosening of the 'conventional' grip will lead to more suicides.

So what leverage can a critical analysis, or critique, hope to have if what can be stated is already normatively and forcibly constrained? Judith Butler asserts, following Foucault, that 'the primary task of critique will not be to evaluate whether its objects – social conditions, practices, forms of knowledge, power, and discourse – are good or bad, valued highly or demeaned, but to bring into relief the very framework of evaluation itself' (in Salih, 2004, pp. 306–7). Through the engagement in such a task – the interrogation of the constitution and limits of normatively organised discursive formations (an unsettling of our 'most sure ways of knowing' (p. 307)) – a space may be created where new possibilities for thought and action can emerge. But, it might be asked, how can we be sure that such a project will be beneficial? Butler provides an answer (drawing on more of a deconstructionist argument than a Foucauldian one) that points to an inherent incompleteness in our ways of categorising the world that can lead to a crisis of knowing:

One asks about the limits of ways of knowing because one has already run up against a crisis within the epistemological field in which one lives. The categories by which social life are ordered produce a certain incoherence or entire realms of unspeakability. And it is from this condition, the tear in the fabric of our epistemological web, that the practice of critique emerges, with the awareness that no discourse is adequate here or that our reigning discourses have produced an impasse. (pp. 307–8)

For Butler such is the instability of discourse that hegemonic foreclosure will never be complete. From this perspective suicide, as a discursively constituted phenomenon, will always resist complete description, if for no other reason than as a cultural product it lacks any unchanging essence that could act as a stabilising centre by which to secure such a description. The last 200 years have seen concerted efforts to find such a centre, through related medical and scientific investigations, and in the process 'a certain incoherence or entire realms of unspeakability' may have arisen, and it is to these areas that a critical analysis may productively focus.

Such a critical practice can also uncover the means by which that which is productive, formative and ideologically saturated comes to be read as merely representational and ideologically neutral. For if dominant or governing discourses and practices act to form over time, at least in part, 'suicide' and 'suicidal subjectivities', rather than simply responding to them in order to contain or eradicate them, then this can cast them in a new light. Analysis of the constituting effects of dominant discursive practices offers the possibility of opening up a new field of enquiry rather than just seeking to contest one that is already foreclosed to criticism.

Critique, then, looks to the fissures and fragilities of governing, compulsory discursive formations, not in order to pass judgement on them, but to uncover the assumptions embedded within them and the ways by which they in part constitute the very acts and subjectivities they claim only to name. That such an approach is itself open to criticism – to charges of, in Butler's words, 'immorality, evil, aestheticism' (p. 313) – is perhaps inevitable, for

the critical attitude is not moral according to the rules whose limits that very critical relation seeks to interrogate. But how else can critique do its job without risking the denunciations of those who naturalize and render hegemonic the very moral terms put into question by critique itself? (pp. 313–14)

By interrogating the well guarded certainties of suicide it may be possible to approach the subject in such a way that the cultural and historical forces that act to form 'suicide' and 'suicidal subjectivities' are not concealed by reference to universal 'truths', but are instead opened up to scrutiny. The results of such an enquiry will not take the form of a prescriptive list of solutions that have somehow been overlooked by the experts. Rather, as noted earlier, what is sought is more an unsettling of the terms upon which certainties are based, by recourse to historical analysis of the discursive elements and practices that come together to form these 'truths' and of the constituting effects of such discursive practices, in order to locate the places and moments where their contingency may be revealed.

The principal focus of the book is on the assumptions embedded within accepted ways of thinking and practices with regard to suicide and suicide prevention in the clinical field, the means by which certain truths of suicide have been formed and disseminated over time, and the effects of these truths on groups and individuals. This book is therefore not intended as a general work of social theory or medical sociology nor as a traditional history of suicide. It is, for the most part, an attempt to understand how suicide came to be read as arising from some form of internal pathology and has thus come to be taken as primarily a matter of medical/ psychiatric concern. So rather than an attempt at a 'complete' genealogy (if such a thing were possible), a narrower focus is maintained, for the most part tracing those ways of thinking and acting that produced and reproduced truths of suicide in terms of its pathology. Emphasis is placed on analysis of medical texts and practices over that of the wider context, and as a consequence the economic and political aspects of the 'pathologisation' of suicide are relatively under-examined. However, the comprehensive histories of the medicalisation of madness already available have, arguably, explored similar territory in great detail (see, for instance, Scull, 1981, 1993; or Porter, 1987; and Foucault, 2005), whereas analysis of specific historical texts that relate to suicide are notable by their absence. By maintaining a focus on certain 'styles of thought' (Fleck, 1981; Rose, 2000, 2007) and practices that are seen to relate most directly to contemporary clinical beliefs and ways of working with regard to suicide, it is hoped that these may be problematised in a way that may prove productive. By this it is meant that if we can more fully understand the ways by which contemporary constructions of suicide have come to be formed over time we may be able to change what self-accomplished death is for us now, and move away from the insistence that there is a singular act – suicide – with a singular meaning – pathology. In so doing, new possibilities for thought, actions and experiences in relation to self-accomplished deaths can come to be formed. What is sought is the enabling of new freedoms of thought and action in place of those that have come to be constraining and problematic in themselves – not new freedoms whereby it becomes easier for people to kill themselves, more the creating of a space where a wider framework for understanding and responding to the reality or possibility of such acts could arise.

Plan of the book

The book is divided into four parts. The first concerns itself with the analytic strategy employed throughout the study. In chapter 2 the basic principles of the approach taken are outlined, as are the main domains and forms of analysis. Research questions that address the relationship between the production of scientific truths and the formation of objects and subjects with regard to suicide within certain relations of power are set out.

Part II of the book looks to map and problematise contemporary truths and practices with regard to suicide. Many different sources are drawn upon – from government policy documents to journal articles and books written by experts in the field, as well as media guidelines on the reporting of suicide, newspaper articles and first-person accounts – in order to understand how suicide is most often discursively constituted, by whom, with what authority, by what means and to what effect. It is argued that suicide is most often taken to be pathological in nature, with the suicidal person usually represented as a tragic and tormented figure. The potentially problematic nature of present-day truths and practices are discussed in terms of the objects, concepts and subjects they act to form and the relations of power that constitute and are constituted by such a contemporary 'regime of truth', as well as by reference to possible alternative ways of thinking and acting in relation to self-accomplished deaths that are foreclosed or marginalised by such dominant and authoritative accounts.

Part III looks to understand the cultural and historical forces involved in the formation of present-day truths in relation to suicide. Here, the historicist approach employed in many of Foucault's own studies is adopted. As noted above, historical analysis along the lines pursued by Foucault can call into question contemporary assumptions and practices by uncovering their contingency, as well as allowing an examination of the relationship between the production of truths, 'truth effects' and relations of power.

Contingency is thus a central theme of chapter 5. Here, an attempt is made to understand how self-accomplished deaths were described at other times and other places. Roman and Greek accounts of such acts are interesting as contrasts to present-day formulations, as they allow us to see the possibility of a diversity of acts and a multiplicity of descriptions that are not subsumed under the singular term 'suicide'. An example of a Roman self-accomplished death that could be read as relational, philosophical and political, as opposed to internal, pathological and medical, is analysed in order to call into question the universality of present-day assumptions and practices. For similar reasons, examples of the construction of self-inflicted death as self-killing and thus a sin and a crime are set out in order to illustrate how relations of power-knowledge can vary according to time and place, and produce markedly different effects. After Augustine (late fourth/early fifth century) self-killing increasingly came to be read as a sin (the worst kind as it involved the rejection of God's grace) and later, under canon and common law, self-murder became a crime (the most heinous, more despised even than murder) (MacDonald and Murphy, 1990). As a sin and a crime – a form of transgression against

God and the king – such acts could be punished by the desecration of the body of the deceased, burial outside consecrated ground and the forfeiture of goods from the surviving family. An example of such practices in relation to an act of self-murder is set out in order to illustrate the relationship between authoritative discourse and practices, and to provide a contrast to present-day ways of thinking and acting with regard to suicide.

Chapter 6 looks to understand the conditions of possibility for the formation of contemporary truths of suicide. Here I discuss a number of related historical changes in terms of the constitution of the subject, the coinage and uptake of the word 'suicide' to signify acts of self-inflicted deaths in the seventeenth century, the gradual secularisation of suicide in the 'Classical Age' (roughly the seventeenth and eighteenth centuries), and the ways in which asylums could act as laboratories for the production of medical truths towards the end of the eighteenth and into the nineteenth century. These, it is argued, were prerequisites for the redescription of suicide in medical terms that occurred in the first decades of the nineteenth century. The chapter concludes by drawing on Foucault's (1981) notions of sovereign power and bio-power to cast light on the shift from punishment to prevention during this period.

Chapter 7 offers a detailed analysis of a key text in the 'pathologisation' of suicide. In an entry for the 1821 *Dictionnaire des sciences médicales* (1821), French physician and *aliéniste* (a term coined in late eighteenth-century France to describe a doctor specialising in 'mental maladies' or 'alienation') Jean-Etienne Esquirol declared that suicide was a form of *'pathologie interne'* and was thus 'one of the most important subjects of clinical medicine' (p. 213). At this moment, it is argued, new truths in relation to suicide, based on notions of diseased interiorities (bodily and mental), are set out in detail for the first time. Whereas previously the condemnation of suicide, in the form of judicial and canonical laws, acted as a deterrent through fear, now the 'discovery' of premonitory medical signs of a disposition to suicide opened up the possibility of intervention before a suicidal act could be committed. Medicine not only claimed expertise and authority, but also promised a more effective solution to the problem of suicide through prevention. A circular relationship between the production of knowledge through asylum practices of confinement, observation and examination, and the rationalisation of these practices by reference to the knowledge produced is noted and analysed in terms of the development of a productive power-knowledge nexus.

Such themes are taken up in chapter 8, where the production, dissemination and circulation of medical, later psychiatric, truths of suicide in the nineteenth century, and their effects in terms of practices and the constitution of subjects, are examined in detail. Initially, pathological anatomy was taken to be the cause of suicide; however neither autopsies nor the reading of the signs of internal pathology, said to be written on the surface of the bodies of the suicidal, provided sufficient evidence for these theories and after mid-century focus shifted to notions of diseased instincts and impulses. The effects of these approaches are explored, and it is argued that medical/psychiatric discourses, with the increasing weight of authority afforded to medicine and science as the century wore on, acted to form certain subjects and experiences in relation to suicide. A key argument developed in this chapter is that not only was suicide constituted by reference to contemporary notions of pathology and insanity, but also that suicide acted as a key reference point in the development of new, medicalised formulations of madness that arose in the nineteenth century. Insanity was established as implicitly dangerous by means of repeated allusions to the destructiveness of the madman and thus provided the *raison d'être* for the emerging psychiatric profession; namely, 'the control of dangers hidden in the human behaviour' (Foucault, 2002a, p. 185). Chapter 9 outlines the practices that arose in relation to the prevention and treatment of the suicidal during this period, and also seeks to make sense of the comparatively low numbers of suicides that occurred within the asylums.

Chapter 10 offers an examination of the various ways 'psy' discourses and practices have constituted objects and subjects of knowledge in relation to suicide from the late nineteenth century on. It is argued that psychiatry, and the related disciplines of psychology, psychoanalysis and the psychotherapies have each acted to extend the notion of pathology as the primary cause of suicide and in so doing changed what it means to be suicidal, insane or mentally ill. During the twentieth century clues as to the cause of suicide, or signs of a propensity to self-destructive acts, have been sought 'within' the individual subject by means of reference to a pathologised 'psyche'; in the biographical history of patients through analysis of childhood memories; or in the everyday speech, gestures, moods, acts and behaviours of observed suicidal individuals as well as retrospectively by means of psychological autopsy studies of those who did end their own lives. Knowledge of suicide and the suicidal subject thus comes to be gathered from ever broader and 'deeper' sources. Equally, it becomes possible to extend notions of what it is to be abnormal or mentally ill by drawing on such knowledge – so suicidal thoughts or behaviours can come to indicate the presence of some form of pathology linked to unconscious drives and impulses, biographical details, or through any number of human traits or actions. Such processes are illustrated by examples taken from the psychoanalytic literature on suicide from the 1930s, and from a well-known psychological autopsy study published in 1959.

Also considered in this chapter are those challenges to the dominance of the idea that suicide is necessarily caused by individual pathology. Here, sociological explanations, beginning with Emile Durkheim's *Le suicide* of 1897, and the critiques of psychiatric practices in relation to suicide set out most notably by Thomas Szasz are briefly reviewed, but an argument is put forward that formulations of suicide as an individual and pathological phenomenon have for the most part seen off any serious challenges and come to dominate the field of study and, more importantly, practice.

Chapter 11 further considers the ways in which suicidal subjects are produced in relation to the truths of suicide discussed in earlier chapters. The idea that 'psy' discourse can be read as 'performative' (Butler, 1990; Borch-Jacobsen, 2001) – that authoritative ways of constituting the topic can act to form objects and subjects they purport only to name – is explored by reference to Sarah Kane's play *4.48 Psychosis* (2000). This is taken to be illustrative of the different ways in which a suicidal individual may stand in relation to these truths of suicide – as both subjected to authoritative accounts and practices and, at the same time, resistant to such modes of subjection.

The final chapter offers a summary of the book alongside reflections on the utility of reading suicide from a Foucauldian perspective. It is argued that such a form of critical analysis – one that focuses on relations of power, knowledge and the subject – can productively be employed in order to cast new light on, as well as to challenge, established ways of thinking and acting. For a long time suicide has been taken to be an act consequent upon mental instability or ill-health, and a discourse of pathology has come to not only frame (and largely constitute) the topic but also to determine what counts as responsible practice in preventing such deaths. There is no doubt that the pathologisation of suicide has opened up many possibilities for thought and action over the last two centuries or so, but the increasing dominance of such a reading has also led to the marginalisation or foreclosure of many other ways of understanding and responding to self-accomplished death. In addition, the promises of medical science in relation to suicide – of accurate prediction of risk and the development of effective treatments – have remained largely unfulfilled, but more than this (and more subtly and problematically) the formation and maintenance of a 'regime of truth' (one centring on a compulsory ontology of pathology) has led to 'truth effects' that are complex, often hard to discern and not necessarily benign. These are the main themes addressed in the book.

2   Analytic strategy

Introduction

Summarising a series of lectures he had delivered at the University of Berkeley in 1983 under the title 'Discourse and Truth', Foucault spoke of two aspects of the 'problematization of truth': '[o]ne side is concerned with ensuring that the process of reasoning is correct in determining whether a statement is true (or concerns itself with our ability to gain access to the truth)' (2001, p. 170). This side Foucault calls the 'analytics of truth' and Western philosophical concerns with questions of ontology and epistemology can be situated within this tradition. On the other side – the one 'concerned with the question of the importance of telling the truth, knowing who is able to tell the truth, and knowing why we should tell the truth' – Foucault locates the 'roots of what we could call the "critical" tradition in the West' (p. 170) and certain aspects of Foucault's own work can be understood as exemplary of this 'critical' approach to truth. For it was not so much the veracity, or otherwise, of the claims to truth of the human sciences that interested Foucault, more the ways in which certain groups of people come to be authorised as 'truth-tellers', and the effects of the production and circulation of truths in relation to 'man' as both object and subject of knowledge. To an interviewer in 1982 Foucault had declared:

What I have studied are the three traditional problems: (1) What are the relations we have to truth through scientific knowledge, to those 'truth games' which are so important in civilization and in which we are both subject and objects? (2) What are the relationships we have to others through those strange strategies and power relationships? And (3) what are the relationships between truth, power, and self? (1988b, p. 15)

These concerns – the relationship between the production of scientific truths, relations of power, and the formation of objects and subjects – are taken up in this book with regard to suicide, and what is taken from Foucault is not so much a prescribed method, more a set of guiding principles and strategies for analysing such themes.

Principles of analysis

The first principle could be said to be scepticism towards all 'anthropo-logical universals'

which does not mean rejecting them all from the start, outright and once and for all, but that nothing of that order must be accepted that is not strictly indispensable. In regard to human nature or the categories that may be applied to the subject, everything in our knowledge which is suggested to us as being universally valid must be tested and analysed. (Foucault, 2000b, p. 461)

So claims to truth in relation to suicide are not to be read as universally true and thus beyond questioning, nor rejected outright as invalid, but rather subjected to analysis that casts light on the conditions of their emergence as 'historical constructs' (p. 462), as well as on their constituting effects in relation to the formation of related subjects and objects of knowledge.

From here a second principle follows, one that can be discerned in much of Foucault's work; namely the rejection of the notion of the 'constituent subject' in favour of one that could be said to be 'constituted' in relation to authoritative knowledge:

One must also reverse the philosophical way of proceeding upward to the constituent subject which is asked to account of every possible object of knowledge in general. On the contrary, it is a matter of proceeding back down to the study of the concrete practices by which the subject is constituted in the immanence of a domain of knowledge. (p. 462)

This is not to suggest that Foucault proposed a general theory of the subject, more that the processes by which the subject is formed in relation to particular 'games' or 'regimes' of truth can be analysed without recourse to notions of an ahistorical, acultural self that can act as foundation for all knowledge. However,

these games are not imposed on the subject from the outside according to a necessary causality or structural determination. They open up a field of experience in which the subject and the object are both constituted only under certain simultaneous conditions, but in which they are constantly modified in relation to each other, and so they modify this field of experience itself. (p. 462)

The subject is thus taken to be neither fixed nor fully determined by authoritative knowledge(s); rather such ways of knowing act to create a certain 'field of experience' that is both constraining and open to change. So for the purposes of this book, the nature of the 'suicidal' person is not read as unchanging, and neither is 'suicide' itself as an object of knowledge, but both are conceived as being formed in relation to each other in particular places at specific times in history. As will be argued, certain acts of self-accomplished death were experienced in relation to notions of honour in late Republican Rome in the first century AD, in relation to notions of legality/illegality, sin/innocence in sixteenth-century Europe, and more recently in the West in terms of psychopathology and mental illness. By positing that humans possess an inherent 'plasticity' (Osborne, 1998, p. 72) an analysis can be conducted that casts light on the conditions of possibility of such 'experiences' by mapping the relations between the production of truths and the formation of objects and subjects.

Such an analysis, Foucault argued, would also need to focus on 'practices', that is,

the ensemble of more or less regulated, more or less deliberate, more or less finalized ways of doing things, through which can be seen both what was constituted as real for those who sought to think it and manage it and the way in which the latter constituted themselves as subjects capable of knowing, analysing, and ultimately altering reality. (2000b, p. 463)

By focusing on what was done in relation to suicide and the suicidal, as well as what was thought, the ways in which certain related subjectivities and objects of knowledge came to be formed at different times can be explored. Thus 'practices ... understood as a way of acting and thinking at once ... provide the intelligibility key for the correlative constitution of the subject and the object' (Foucault, 2000b, p. 463)

Finally, Foucault argues that 'since it is a matter of studying the different modes of objectivation of the subject that appear through these practices, one understands how important it is to analyze power relations'. The analysis of relations of power with regard to those 'methods and techniques used in different institutional contexts to act upon the behavior of individuals ... so as to shape, direct, modify their way of conducting themselves' is taken to be central to any analysis of the ways in which 'men are "governed" by one another' (p. 463).

A critical analysis of the relationship between authoritative knowledge and the formation of objects and subjects in relation to self-accomplished death could be said to rest upon the following principles:

- Scepticism towards all 'anthropological universals' (p. 461), or rather the positing of an inherent 'plasticity' or malleability as a feature of human nature (Osborne, 1998, p. 72).
- The rejection of the 'constituting' subject in favour of one that is 'constituted' or formed in relation to particular 'regimes of truth'.
- The necessity of analysing practices and power relations when seeking to account for the formation of subjects and objects.

Certain strategies of analysis could be said to follow from such principles, and these will be considered next.

Analytic strategies

In each of his major books Foucault made use of differing forms of analysis, but these are often grouped into 'archaeological' works (*Madness and Civilization*, 1965, *The Order of Things*, 1970, *The Birth of the Clinic*, 1973 and *The Archaeology of Knowledge*, 2002b); 'genealogies' (*Discipline and Punish*, 1977 and *The History of Sexuality*, vol. I: *An Introduction*, 1981); and later work on ethics and 'subjectivity' (*The Use of Pleasure*, vol. II of *The History of Sexuality*, 1985 and *The Care of the Self*, vol. III of *The History of Sexuality*, 1986) (e.g. Prado, 2000, 2006; Andersen, 2003; O'Farrell, 2005).

Archaeology focuses on systems of knowledge within the human sciences and has as its primary concern

a critical investigation of disciplinary systems of knowledge with the goal of understanding the discursive practices that produce and sustain those systems of knowledge. The archaeologist's interest is in disciplinary discourse, in expert pronouncements and idioms. (Prado, 2006, p. 72)

Foucault studied such 'expert pronouncements' at the level of the 'statement', and the method employed involved describing 'systems of dispersion' (Foucault, 2002b, p. 41) between such statements. Further, '[w]henever one can describe, between a number of statements, such a system of dispersion ... we will say that we are dealing with a *discursive formation*' (p. 41). The rules that govern this dispersion are the 'rules of formation' (p. 42). Foucault was particularly interested in the processes by which new formations appeared and others came to be discarded (cf. *The Order of Things*). For Prado (2006) archaeology can be summarised as

the investigation of discontinuities, and particularly those that reveal abandonment of one conceptual framework and the adoption of another. It also is the unearthing of abandoned frameworks and the comparing of them with presently dominant ones. It is the meticulous mapping of established and excavated frameworks with a view to understanding how they are produced and how they work. (p. 74)

Archaeology involves a search for those 'discontinuities that mark shifts between conceptual frameworks, inventorying the disparate and accidental elements that result in the formation of conceptual frameworks and in the acceptance of something as knowledge' (p. 75). In relation to self-accomplished deaths, an analytic strategy drawing on an archaeological approach would look to map changes in conceptual frameworks with regard to such deaths over time, and would analyse how such 'discursive formations' came to be produced, maintained and possibly abandoned. It could also be utilised as a starting point in any analysis of the types of objects, concepts and subjects produced in relation to the emergence of new formations of authoritative knowledge.

The 'genealogical' works of the 1970s mark something of a shift in Foucault's thinking. The differences between these and his earlier 'archaeologies' mostly concern the relative importance given to those 'practices' discussed earlier, and also to a changing conception of power. For while issues of power were not exactly absent in *Madness and Civilization* (1965) and *The Birth of the Clinic* (1973), Foucault's first book-length 'genealogical' study, *Discipline and Punish* (1977), emphasised to a much greater degree the importance of power relations in changing forms of punishment between the eighteenth and nineteenth centuries, and in *The History of Sexuality*, vol. I: *An Introduction* (1981), relations of power are similarly afforded a position of prominence. In these books, as well as in interviews and lectures during this period, Foucault is at pains to stress that power should not be conceived as merely a 'negative' force that acts to repress, but rather relations of power should be understood as productive in their effects (e.g. Foucault, 1980, pp. 140–2; 1988a, pp. 102–6; 2006, pp. 13–14). In an interview from 1976 (published as 'Truth and Power', 2002a, pp. 111–33) Foucault spoke of the notion of power as repressive as 'insidious':

When I wrote *Madness and Civilization*, I made at least an implicit use of this notion of repression … But it seems to me now that the notion of repression is quite inadequate for capturing what is precisely the productive aspect of power. In defining the effects of power as repression, one adopts a purely juridical conception of such power, one identifies power with a law that says no, power is taken above all as carrying the force of a prohibition. (pp. 119–20)

In place of such a reading of power, Foucault posited 'a productive network which runs through the whole social body' that 'traverses and produces things, it induces pleasure, forms knowledge, produces discourse' (p. 120). *Discipline and Punish* (1977) looked to map an 'economy of power' from the seventeenth and eighteenth centuries onwards which enabled the formation of docile yet productive bodies through various 'disciplinary' techniques and procedures. Volume 1 of *The History of Sexuality* (1981) again dispenses with a conception of power that locates it as a force possessed by the powerful and used to subjugate or control those weaker – a model of power Foucault characterised as 'sovereign':

By power, I do not mean 'Power' as a group of institutions and mechanisms that ensure the subservience of the citizens of a given state. By power, I do not mean, either, a mode of subjugation which, in contrast to violence, has the form of the rule. Finally, I do not have in mind a general system of domination exerted by one group over another, a system whose effects, through successive derivations, pervade the entire social body. (p. 92)

Power, then, 'is not an institution, and not a structure; neither is it a certain strength we are endowed with' (p. 93). Rather, it is dispersed and always relational, and 'must be understood in the first instance as the multiplicity of force relations immanent in the sphere in which they operate and which constitute their own organization, as the process which, through ceaseless struggles and confrontations, transforms, strengthens, or reverse them' (pp. 92–3).

Relations of power, then, must be traced to the 'sphere in which they operate'. Of interest here, with regard to this book, are the 'multiplicity of force relations' that have acted to form, over time, suicide and suicides as objects of knowledge, and related processes or modes of subjectivation. These 'force relations' are to be found in the ways in which expert, authoritative knowledge comes to be produced and disseminated and in the practices that enable and sustain such knowledge, and their effects can be mapped in terms of the objects, concepts and subjects produced in relation to such discursive practices.

Discourse itself can be conceived as an element in any 'relation of forces', for 'the mere fact of speaking, of employing words, of using the words of others (even if it means returning them), words that the others understand and accept (and, possibly, return from their side) – this fact is in itself a force' (in Davidson, 1997, p. 4). For Foucault, '[d]iscourse is, with respect to the relation of forces, not merely a surface inscription, but something that brings about effects' (pp. 4–5). Ways of speaking and writing that are taken to be authoritative, that are given the status of 'truth', carry particular weight in this regard in our society; for truth and power, as is emphasised by Foucault over and over, should not be conceived as somehow operating apart from each other, for

truth isn't outside power or lacking in power: contrary to a myth whose history and functions would repay further study, truth isn't the reward of free spirits, the child of protracted solitude, nor the privilege of those who have succeeded in liberating themselves. Truth is a thing of this world: it is produced only by virtue of multiple forms of constraint. And it induces regular effects of power. (Foucault, 2002a, p. 131)

From such a standpoint – understanding truth and power to be inextricably intertwined – it is possible to study particular 'regimes of truth'; that is, the ways in which truths are produced and maintained, by whom, and with what effects:

Each society has its regime of truth, its 'general politics' of truth – that is, the types of discourse it accepts and makes function as true; the mechanisms and instances that enable one to distinguish true and false statements; the means by which each is sanctioned; the techniques and procedures accorded value in the acquisition of truth; the status of those who are charged with saying what counts as true. (p. 131)

Foucault identifies 'five important traits' of a contemporary 'political economy' of truth:

'Truth' is centered on the form of scientific discourse and the institutions that produce it; it is subject to constant economic and political incitement (the demand for truth, as much for economic production as for political power); it is the object, under diverse forms, of immense diffusion and consumption (circulating through apparatuses of education and information whose extent is relatively broad in the social body, notwithstanding certain strict limitations); it is produced and transmitted under the control, dominant if not exclusive, of a few great political and economic apparatuses (university, army, writing, media); finally, it is the issue of a whole political debate and social confrontation ('ideological' struggles). (p. 131)

Analysis of truth in these terms returns us to the ideas set out at the beginning of this section – that is to the notion of a 'critical' analysis of truth. For Foucault:

'Truth' is to be understood as a system of ordered procedures for the production, regulation, distribution, circulation, and operation of statements.
    'Truth' is linked in a circular relation with systems of power that produce and sustain it, and to effects of power which it induces and which extend it – a 'regime' of truth. (p. 132)

A form of analysis centring on questions concerning the production, regulation and circulation of truths, the relationship between particular 'regimes of truth' and relations of power, as well as on the effects of truth and power in terms of the production of objects and subjects of knowledge is suggested by Foucault's comments, and a similar line of enquiry is pursued here.

    Of particular interest is the relationship between the production of authoritative knowledge and the formation of subjects, and this was dealt with in different ways by Foucault. Writing of his work as it concerned the creation of a 'history of the different modes by which, in our culture, human beings are made subjects', Foucault identifies 'three modes of objectification that transform human beings into subjects':

The first is the modes of inquiry that try to give themselves the status of sciences; for example, the objectivizing of the speaking subject in *grammaire générale*, philology, and linguistics. Or again, in this first mode, the objectivizing of the productive subject, the subject who labors, in the analysis of wealth and of economics. Or, a third example, the objectivizing of the sheer fact of being alive in the natural history of biology.

   In the second part of my work, I have studied the objectivizing of the subject in what I shall call 'dividing practices'. The subject is either divided inside himself or divided from others. This process objectivizes him. Examples are the mad and the sane, the sick and the healthy, the criminals and the 'good boys'.

   Finally, I have sought to study – it is my current work – the way a human being turns him- or herself into a subject. For example, I have chosen the domain of sexuality – how men have learned to recognize themselves as subjects of 'sexuality'. (pp. 326–7).

The relationship between modes of objectivation and subjectivation, understood as arising in relation to particular 'regimes of truth' involving the production and circulation of truths not separate from relations of power, was thus a line of enquiry pursued by Foucault in his work. For him, individuals are formed as subjects – that is both 'subject to someone else by control and dependence, and tied to his own identity by a conscience or self-knowledge' (p. 31) – through the imposition of 'a law of truth' that 'he must recognize and others have to recognize in him' (p. 331). But Foucault did not propose that subjects came to be formed in any singular or uniform way; rather he identified a range of 'technologies' or processes at work at different times within various 'economies of power'. For instance, in *Discipline and Punish* (1977), Foucault traces the emergence of the 'delinquent' as an effect or product of a system that had, supposedly, the elimination of crime as its primary purpose:

For the observation that prison fails to eliminate crime, one should perhaps substitute the hypothesis that prison has succeeded extremely well in producing delinquency, a specific type, a politically or economically less dangerous – and, on occasion, usable – form of illegality; in producing delinquents, in an apparently marginal, but in fact centrally supervised milieu; in producing the delinquent as a pathologized subject. (Foucault, 1977, p. 277)

Similarly, in volume 1 of *The History of Sexuality* (1981) Foucault discusses the invention of the category of 'perversity' in the nineteenth century, and the production of the 'pervert' as an effect of medical discourse and practices. Again, what is suggested in Foucault's analysis in relation to sexuality and the creation and multiplication of 'abnormal' types in the Victorian age is that rather than repressing or eliminating unwanted conduct, or containing or controlling certain kinds of people – the stated aim of the various practices of the prison or asylum – such practices rather acted to produce and multiply such kinds.

   How the subject comes to be constituted in relation to discursive practices has been the subject of some debate (e.g. Butler, 1997). Many have been unhappy with the rather bleak view of subjectivity seemingly espoused by Foucault in his 'genealogical' writings, where individuals are constituted in relation to knowledges and practices that limit their freedom, with Foucault giving little clue as to how subjects could resist the negative effects of power they were 'subjected' to. Foucault himself, in his later works, moved away from understanding subject formation only in terms of an imposition from 'outside', with modes of subjection and subjugation giving way to talk of the formation of subjectivities through 'technologies of the self' – those ways in which the self acts on the self – and the possibility of creating an aesthetic form of existence: life lived as a work of art. For the purposes of this book, however, the emphasis remains primarily on processes of subjection understood as imposed rather than self-chosen or fashioned. One of the primary reasons for this is that a too strong focus on self-formation, on the relationship the individual can have with him- or herself, can lead to a failure to recognise or address those areas where subjection and subjugation predominate. Contemporary forms of suicide and the formation of the 'suicidal subject' are better understood, it is argued, by reference to the constitution of the subject in relation to the scientific truths and practices of psychiatry/medicine, and these are primarily technologies of control and compulsion when dealing with the threat or actuality of self-accomplished death.

However, it is also understood that the subjects thus formed, and those truths concerning such subjects, are not static entities. Ian Hacking, influenced by Foucault's work, explored the ways in which classifications can interact with those classified (1986; 1995a and b; 1998; 1999; 2002):

People think of themselves as of a kind, perhaps, or reject the classification. All our acts are under descriptions, and the acts that are open to us depend, in a purely formal way, on the descriptions available to us. Moreover, classifications do not exist only in the empty space of language but in institutions, practices, material interactions with things and other people. (Hacking 1999, p. 31)

People, under Hacking's scheme, can be conceptualised as 'interactive kinds', for they can 'become aware of how they are classified and modify their behavior accordingly', in contrast to inanimate, unaware, non-interactive 'natural kinds' (p. 32). It follows that the 'classifications of the social sciences are interactive. The classifications of the natural sciences are not' (p. 32). Hacking further proposed that there was a 'looping effect' whereby the changes undergone by people in response to being classified come to affect the systems of classifications themselves. Hacking argued that people come, albeit imperfectly, to resemble descriptions of themselves and their categorisation. Over time the classificatory system (for instance psychiatric nosology) alters to accommodate the differences between existing descriptions and presenting 'signs and symptoms', and a form of dialogue is thus set in motion – a process of construction and co-construction between classification and those classified. Hacking characterised these processes as a form of 'dynamic nominalism' (1986, 1999).

Tracing the interaction between systems of classification and those classified is thus another possible form of analysis open if one works within the principles and domains suggested by Foucault. Such a form of analysis can be one way of illuminating the effects of the production and circulation of truths in relation to the human sciences. Hacking notes that there is a

constant drive in the social and psychological sciences to emulate the natural sciences, and to produce true natural classifications of people. This is evidently true for basic research on pathologies such as schizophrenia, but it is also, at present, true for some but only some investigators who study homosexuality (the search for the homosexual gene) or violent crime (is that an innate or heritable propensity?). (Hacking 1999, p. 11)

Hacking describes, somewhat in the spirit of Wittgenstein, a 'picture' that acts as a guide to such an endeavour:

[t]here is a picture of an object to be searched out, the right classification, the classification that is true to nature, a fixed target if only we can get there. But perhaps it is a moving target, just because of the looping effect of human classi-fications? That is, new knowledge about the 'criminal' or 'the homosexual' becomes known to the people classified, changes the way that individuals behave, looping back to force changes in the classifications and knowledge about them ... creating new names and assessments and apparent truths is eventually enough to create new 'things'. (p. 11)

Those sciences that are concerned with suicide and the suicidal ('suici-dology') may thus not be dealing with static targets, and the knowledges produced in relation to suicide and the suicidal may be said to 'intervene' as part of a dynamic process rather than merely represent an unchanging reality. This process can be mapped by means of tracing the interaction between the formation of objects and subjects of knowledge over time, and that is another aim of this book.

In summary, the main areas of enquiry of this study, as a form of critical analysis, could be said to be how individuals are constituted as subjects in relation to the truths of suicide. Such a focus requires con-sideration of the ways in which authoritative knowledge is produced, by whom, with what relations to power and to what effect. How such concerns translate into specific questions to be addressed in the book will now be considered.

Questions addressed in the book

A number of questions are suggested by the domains and strategies of analysis outlined above:

1 What are held to be contemporary truths of suicide?
   i How is suicide most usually formulated, in government reports, in the media, in professional journals and books?
   ii What descriptions are taken to possess authority with regard to expressing truths of suicide?
2 How are such truths assembled or constituted?
   i What rhetorical devices, vocabularies, metaphors, stories and images are brought to bear in the constitution of truths in relation to suicide?
   ii What assumptions are embedded in such authoritative accounts?
   iii What institutions and social practices support, or are supported by, these ways of talking about suicide?
   iv What professional groups are seen to possess authority with regard to suicide and the suicidal – or, put differently, who gets to tell the truth of suicide?
3 How are the truths of suicide disseminated?
   i How are authoritative accounts distributed and circulated?
   ii More specifically, by what means do 'expert' accounts of suicide come to inform/form 'non-expert' ones?
4 What 'truth effects' can be discerned?
   i What objects and concepts are produced in relation to present-day truths of suicide?
   ii Specifically, what different kinds of self-accomplished death are formed, in part at least, by contemporary, authoritative accounts?
   iii What subjectivities are constituted by such descriptions? How are the suicidal, suicide survivors, the mentally ill, 'high-risk' individuals, and mental health professionals discursively formed in relation to contemporary truths of suicide?
5 In what ways might our accounts of suicide be read as problematic?
   i In what ways might the production and reproduction of certain truths in relation to suicide contribute to the maintenance of such problematic events?
   ii How might such truths also lead to either an exacerbation or a diminution of suffering in relation to self-accomplished death?
   iii What alternative accounts of suicide are foreclosed or marginalised as a consequence of the production and reproduction of contemporary truths?

6 How have our present truths of suicide come into being?
    i What historical and cultural forces can be identified in the forma-
      tion of present-day truths of suicide?
    ii What relations of power-knowledge can be discerned in the con-
      stitution of these truths?
   iii What other ways of thinking and acting in relation to self-
      accomplished deaths have come to be excluded over time?
   iv In what ways might solutions to the problems posed by suicide in
      the past have come now to be problematic themselves?

Questions 1 to 3 address the production, regulation, distribution and
circulation of truths in relation to suicide. Question 4 looks to map the
effects of such truths in terms of the formation of objects and subjects of
authoritative knowledge. Question 5 analyses the ways in which contemporary accounts of suicide may be problematic, and Question 6 histori-
cises the formation of contemporary truths. Throughout the book
relations of power-to-knowledge and knowledge-to-power immanent to
each 'regime of truth' are mapped.

Part II

The present

For much of the twentieth and on into the twenty-first century, thinking about suicide in the West has been normatively monolithic: suicide has come to be seen by the public and particularly by health professionals as primarily a matter of mental illness, perhaps compounded by biochemical factors and social stressors, the sad result of depression or other often treatable disease – a tragedy to be prevented. With the exception of debate over suicide in terminal illness, the only substantive discussions about suicide in current Western culture have concerned whether access to psychotherapy, or improved suicide-prevention programs, or more effective antidepressant medications should form the principal lines of defense.   Margaret Pabst Battin (2005, p. 164)

3   Mapping a contemporary 'regime of truth'
       in relation to suicide

Introduction

Whereas once suicide was considered to be a moral, theological and criminal issue, such acts are now, for the most part, understood and explained by reference to psychopathology and mental illness (Rosen, 1971; Berrios and Mohanna, 1995; Battin, 2005). In professional journals and books, government policy documents and media reports, suicide is frequently represented as the tragic act of a mentally unwell individual (for examples see Department of Health, 2002; Goldney, 2005; Hawton and van Heeringen, 2000; Samaritans, 2002; World Health Organization, 2000a), with the suicidal person characterised as in some way morbid, anguished, isolated and driven to end their life by some 'peculiarly internalized torment' (Hill, 2004, p. 2). The position that suicide arises as a consequence of mental illness is often presented as an indisputable scientific and medical fact. Here is Kay Redfield Jamison, Professor of Psychiatry, Johns Hopkins University:

> Study after study in Europe, the United States, Australia and Asia has shown the *unequivocal* presence of severe psychopathology in those who die by their own hand; indeed, in all the major investigations to date, 90 to 95 per cent of people who committed suicide had a diagnosable psychiatric illness. (Jamison, 1999, p. 100, emphasis added)

This linkage of mental illness and suicide is, on the whole, accepted uncritically within medicine and psychiatry, by government (e.g. Department of Health, 2002), by the media (e.g. Samaritans, 2002), and even by organisations that have traditionally been opposed to such views (for instance the 1997 *Catechism of the Catholic Church* indicated that suicide often arose due to '[g]rave psychological disturbances, anguish, or grave fear of hardship, suffering, or torture' that could thus 'diminish the responsibility of the one committing suicide', no. 2282). Other ways of conceptualising suicide are taken to be of marginal importance or usefulness by comparison with those that emphasise the pathology of suicide:

Philosophical views and assumptions about the causation of suicide, while strongly held and necessarily and importantly debated, are not sufficient to disregard the massive and credible medical, psychological, and scientific research literature about suicide. Ignoring the biological and psychopathological causes and treatments of suicidal behavior is clinically and ethically indefensible. (Jamison, 1999, p. 255)

Mental illness, then, is 'unequivocally' present in those who kill themselves, and further, to ignore this fact is 'clinically and ethically indefensible'. Such a view is now rather commonplace – most writings on the subject assume suicide to be in some way pathological in nature and these views are drawn upon by health professionals, friends and family of patients, and patients themselves, when seeking to make sense of suicide and suicidal behaviour. In addition, in terms of practice, mental health professionals are regularly called on to assess risk of suicide, to treat suicidal patients, and perhaps to assist in the hospitalisation of those who are seen to require in-patient treatment, against the patient's will if necessary – the rationale for intervention resting on the understanding that the patient represents 'a danger to themselves' due to the presence of mental illness.

This constituting of the truth of suicide by reference to notions of pathology involves many elements and has many effects. In line with the analytic strategy outlined previously this chapter seeks to address these by focusing on:

- the means by which authoritative knowledge is produced and circulated;
- the practices that enable the formation of truths and are in turn enabled by such truths;
- the formation of objects and subjects in relation to the truths produced and
- the relations of power immanent to the production and maintenance of such a 'regime of truth'.

Producing and reproducing truths in relation to suicide: a compulsory ontology of pathology in professional accounts of suicide

Margaret Pabst Battin, who has written extensively on ethical matters relating to suicide, notes the 'uniform assumption that suicide is the causal product of mental illness, the normatively monolithic assumption seemingly so prevalent in contemporary times' (2005, p. 173). This section explores the ways by which suicide comes to be constituted as pathological in nature, and looks to understand how certain ways of thinking and acting in relation to such a form of death are positioned as self-evident, 'natural' and necessary, and thus difficult to contest. Questions that are addressed are:

- How, where and by whom, are accounts that assert a link between pathology and suicide constructed? What discursive resources (metaphors, vocabularies, etc.) are drawn upon? How are these rendered as truths of suicide? What practices support or enable the production of truths in relation to suicide, and how are these related to issues of power-knowledge?
- What 'truth effects' can be discerned? That is, in what ways are such accounts productive in terms of forming objects, concepts and subjects? And what forms of action follow on from such truths?

Overview: suicide as pathological and a matter of psychiatric concern

Suicide is an issue taken to be relevant to all mental health professions, and this is reflected in the range and sheer volume of writings produced by and for mental health workers. Psychology (e.g. Shneidman, 1985, 1993, 1996; Williams, 1997; O'Connor and Sheehy, 2000), the various psychotherapies – psychoanalysis (e.g. Maltsberger, 2004), cognitive therapy (e.g. Freeman and Reinecke, 1993), dialectical behaviour therapy (e.g. Miller *et al.*, 2006), problem solving (e.g. Pollock and Williams, 2004) or person-centred therapy (e.g. Leenaars, 2004) – mental health nursing (e.g. Anderson and Jenkins, 2006) and other allied health professionals such as occupational therapy (e.g. Gutman, 2005) all address suicide through profession-specific writings. What links these approaches, in the broadest sense, is an assumption of psychopathology in those who wish, or attempt, to end their own lives. What is also common to these approaches is the assertion of the need for psychiatric assessment and treatment in the event of a person presenting as a danger to themselves. The necessity for medical/psychiatric intervention is often inscribed in law – in England and Wales the Mental Health Act of 1983 gives 'Section 12 Approved' doctors (usually psychiatrists) the power to detain and treat people deemed to be a risk to themselves or others. Psychiatry thus has a central place in contemporary clinical practices in relation to suicide. Psychiatrists also figure prominently as advisors to government on policy in this area, as editors of journals relating to suicide and suicidal behaviour, as heads of research centres and national and international organisations dedicated to suicide prevention, and as authors of journal and conference papers, books and book chapters.

The extent to which suicide could be said to have become primarily an issue of psychiatric concern can be illustrated by reference to *The International Handbook of Suicide and Attempted Suicide* (Hawton and van Heeringen 2000). The editors, both professors in university psychiatric departments (Keith Hawton at the University of Oxford, and Kees van Heeringen the University of Ghent), write in the introduction that, '[s]uicidal behaviour is ... an extremely important health and social issue throughout the world. This was the major reason for producing a comprehensive book with an international focus' (p. 1). Contributions were invited from 'leaders in the field, especially in research and/or development of prevention strategies' (p. xviii), and of the 69 who wrote or co-wrote chapters, 43 were psychiatrists, 10 were psychologists, 8 were medics (but not psychiatrists), and there were 8 others (mostly researchers in medical settings). Thus a publication that sought 'to bring together ... the burgeoning amount of knowledge from research and experience about the causes of suicidal behaviour, and its treatment and prevention' (p. xvii) is, for the most part, the work of psychiatrists, with contributions also from psychologists, doctors and medical researchers – each perhaps articulating slightly different truths in relation to suicide but each drawing upon (and adding to) a discourse of pathology.

Within the book, suicide is constituted in relation to biology, depression, schizophrenia, substance abuse, personality disorders, anxiety disorders and genetics. Treatment of suicidal behaviour is addressed by reference to pharmacotherapy, psychotherapy and general hospital management, and prevention at both individual and population levels. Suicide is thus constituted as primarily a pathological phenomenon, the truths of suicide formed by reference to clinical diagnoses, medically defined populations, genetics and biology. It is an issue to be categorised, managed, controlled and prevented, and solutions to the problem are pharmacological or psychotherapeutic. The contributions from psychologists are also framed in a scientific language similar to that drawn upon by the medics and psychiatrists, and although a small nod is made in the direction of other disciplines ('Sociology and Suicidal Behaviour', 'Ethical and Legal Issues'), it is medicine, in the form of epidemiology or psychiatry, that for the most part predominates. Duffy and Ryan's (2004) *New Approaches to Preventing Suicide*, and Hawton's *Prevention and Treatment of Suicidal Behaviour* (2005) contain similar themes. Of course books aimed at treatment and prevention are inevitably going to be predominantly medical and psychiatric, but it is important to at least note the extent to which suicide has become a clinical issue, one framed almost exclusively in terms of psychopathology, and that these accounts have achieved a certain authoritative status in terms of articulating truths in relation to suicide.

These truths – of the essentially pathological nature of suicide – are produced across a wide range of sites by a variety of means. Two broad approaches to the establishment of the truth of the pathology of suicide can be discerned, however: 'traditional' ones that seek to establish mental illnesses as the primary cause of suicide, and those that seek to explain suicide by reference to specific brain abnormalities. The boundaries between the approaches are rather 'fuzzy' as illness categories and brain states find their way into both accounts, but there is, however, a degree of divergence in terms of the means of their production, the resources they draw upon (assumptions, metaphors and analogies) to construct their accounts, and differing conclusions reached in each as to the nature and causes of suicide. It may be helpful here to talk in terms of differing 'styles of thought' rather than 'approaches'. The phrase 'style of thought' is one used by Nikolas Rose (2000, 2007) (drawing on Ludwik Fleck's (1981) notion of 'thought style'), and it can be of use when trying to identify and isolate distinctive ways of thinking and acting, particularly as they relate to the production of authoritative knowledge. To Rose (2007), a 'style of thought is a particular way of thinking, seeing and practicing. It involves formulating statements that are only possible and intelligible within that way of thinking. Elements – terms, concepts, assertions, references, rela-tions – are organized into configurations of a certain form that count as arguments and explanations' (p. 12). But a style of thought involves not just the production and organisation of statements, as Rose goes on to make clear, but also, certainly in relation to medicine, related practices such as the recruitment of subjects for research trials, the assembling of model systems, the use of inscription devices, the conducting of clinical trials, and membership of a 'thought community' in a discipline.

These elements that come together to constitute a particular style of thought can be mapped in relation to both biological and more traditional psychiatric approaches to the production of truths of suicide, and the next section attempts to do so. To begin, the discursive means by which state-ments are presented as factual in both traditional and biological accounts are analysed, as there are many similarities here. Then, the practices that produce traditional and biological truths of suicide are addressed somewhat separately, as the approaches tend to diverge in this area, and examples are drawn upon as illustrative of the differing processes at work. Also, the elements that are brought together to constitute truth accounts, and those that are in turn constituted by them – those objects and subjects formed in relation to the truths produced – are mapped and analysed in terms of relations of power-to-knowledge and knowledge-to-power.

Constructing a compulsory ontology of pathology in relation to suicide

In this section some common themes in the discursive formation of truths in relation to suicide are explored. Truth, as the term is used here, is not taken to involve the relationship between sentences and 'states of affairs' (Prado, 2006, p. 2) or any sense of correspondence between statements and some notion of *how things really are*. The position taken here is that statements and beliefs are not made true by the world, but rather truth can best be conceived of, following Foucault (1980, p. 118), as wholly discursive, and thus '[i]t is the rules of discourse, not the world, that make a sentence true' (Prado, 2006, p. 143). Those 'rules of discourse' vary historically, and truth can be said, in Prado's phrase, to be the 'highest-order value in a discourse and a set of practices' for any given time and place (p. 81). Statements held to be true are those that are read as possessing 'discursive currency' (p. 2) within certain 'regimes of truth' (Foucault, 1980, p. 131). At the present time approaches to knowledge deemed to be 'scientific' in nature are held to possess much currency as a means to access and speak the truth. 'Empiricist discourse' (Gilbert and Mulkay, 1984) in particular, in presenting statements as factual, objective and independent of any individual speaker (and thus free of bias), has a tendency to imply that 'facts' are able to speak for themselves. It is argued here that such an effect – the presentation of statements as accurate and objective – can be conceived of as a rhetorical achievement, and can be analysed, not in order to show they are not, in fact, true, but rather to highlight how such statements gain currency in part through how they are constructed.

As Jonathon Potter (1996) notes, 'bringing off an utterance as factual' can be conceived of as an activity, a *doing* (p. 204; see also Gergen, 1999, pp. 74–6). Psychiatry (and related 'psy' disciplines) makes claims to truth with regard to suicide and the concern of this section is to map some of the ways this is achieved. A number of papers are drawn upon to illustrate the processes at work here, with particular attention paid to 'Biological aspects of suicidal behaviour' by Lil Träskman-Bendz and J. John Mann (2000), in Hawton and van Heeringen's *International Handbook of Suicide and Attempted Suicide* (selected as representative of biological psychiatric discourse on suicide), and to 'Mental illness and suicide: a case-control study in East Taiwan' by A. T. A. Cheng (1995) from the *Archives of General Psychiatry* (selected as an example of traditional psychiatric discourse on suicide, one that seeks to link mental illness to suicide, most usually in a causal relationship). Both these articles are taken to be illustrative of certain ways claims to truth can be discursively established: they can be conceived as 'empiricist discourse' in that they make use of rhetorical strategies common to scientific writings; it could be said that they make claims to (universal) truths, and have been read by other experts in suicide as authoritative, plausible accounts. Also, as was noted, they diverge a little in terms of their style of thought, as well as in the resources drawn upon in their construction, and these elements will be examined. Finally, certain relations of knowledge-to-power and power-to-knowledge can be discerned in the formation of authoritative accounts of suicide (its causation, prediction and prevention) and these are analysed.

The truths articulated in these and related texts can be summarised fairly succinctly; for biological psychiatry it is that abnormalities in brain anatomy or chemistry can account for suicide and suicidal behaviour (see for examples Asberg *et al.*, 1976; Arango and Mann, 1992; Ordway *et al.*, 1994; Arango *et al.*, 1997; Fawcett *et al.*, 1997; Kunugi *et al.*, 1997; Engstrom *et al.*, 1999; Mann *et al.*, 2001; or Leonard, 2005). More 'traditional' psychiatric approaches emphasise the association between mental illness and suicide, usually suggesting a causal relationship (noted examples of this style of thought can be found in Robins *et al.*, 1959/1996; Rorsman, 1973; Barraclough *et al.*, 1974; Cavanagh *et al.*, 1999; World Health Organization, 2000a). The factual basis of the claims made in relation to suicide is not the issue at stake here, but rather the focus is on those processes by which certain claims come to be constructed as statements of truth.

Achieving authority within texts

Claims to truth involve issues of authority – the focus in this section is on how authority to tell the truth of suicide is 'achieved' by the use of certain rhetorical strategies. Researchers interested in the textual construction of scientific facts (e.g. Gilbert and Mulkay, 1984; Gergen, 1994, 1999; Potter, 1996) have pointed to the use of certain 'tropes, grammatical forms and argumentative styles' (Potter, 1996, p. 151) to achieve credibility and authority in relation to the claims that are made. In 'empiricist discourse', the aim is to present claims as factual, neutral and independent of any individual speaker (Potter, 1996). Statements here tend to be presented as objective, impartial and impersonal, and opinions that could be considered subjective, uncertainties and 'lay' language are generally omitted. Examples of such strategies from the Träskman-Bendz and Mann (2000) chapter and from Cheng's (1995) paper are used to illustrate these processes of 'fact construction' (Potter, 1996), and the building of authority through textual means to enable the authors to position themselves as truth-tellers with regard to suicide. The circular relationship between the production and dissemination of truths and certain relations of power are highlighted. It is argued, following Foucault, that there can be 'no power relation without the correlative constitution of a field of knowledge, nor any knowledge that does not presuppose and constitute at the same time power relations' (1977, p. 27). Relations of power are inherent in the production of knowledge with regards to suicide, and the knowledge produced acts to further constitute relations of power.

As earlier noted in chapter 2, Foucault was at pains to emphasise that 'truth isn't outside power', rather, it is 'a thing of this world: it is produced only by virtue of multiple forms of constraint. And it induces regular effects of power' (Foucault, 2002a, p. 131). Many forms of constraint are at work in the production of truths of suicide, and relations of power are inherent in each and are effected by each. Some strategies of truth production and circulation are discursive in nature – the setting out of credentials, the use of citations to achieve a sense of consensus and corroboration, and the construction of 'out-there-ness' (Potter, 1996, pp. 150–75; Gergen, 1999, pp. 74–5) – but are dependent upon, and further strengthen, certain regulated (and thus constraining) practices:

- That the authors of professional texts on suicide possess authority, that they are experts in the field, is, in part, established through the setting out of the credentials and institutional affiliations of the authors – certainly in articles published in professional journals, or chapters in academic books. In the chapter 'Biological aspects of suicidal behaviour' (Träskman-Bendz and Mann, 2000), from Hawton and van Heeringen's *International Handbook of Suicide and Attempted Suicide*, the authors Lil Träskman-Bendz and J. John Mann are listed as based in a university Department of Psychiatry (University Hospital, Lund, Sweden), and from a university Department of Neuroscience (New York State Psychiatric Institute, Columbia University, New York, USA) respectively. The paper 'Mental illness and suicide: A case-control study in East Taiwan' is by A. T. A. Cheng (1995), affiliated to the Institute of Biomedical Sciences, Academia Sinica, Taipei, Taiwan. Statements made by these authors, as accredited professionals engaged in research at prestigious academic institutions, would thus carry a degree of weight, and contribute to the degree of authority they would hold as 'truth-tellers' in relation to suicide. Such authority would add 'discursive currency' to any subsequent claims to truth. Access to such institutions is regulated through assessment of the adherence to, and competence in, the theory and practices of medical science, in psychiatry (as a form of medical science) as well as to certain codes of conduct (both formal and informal). Not just anybody can make claims to truth in relation to suicide.
- Certain styles of writing also serve to give an impression of objectivity and neutrality in relation to the claims being made. Phrases (here taken from Träskman-Bendz and Mann, 2000) such as 'a variety of studies', 'studies indicate', 'tests have informed us', 'a meta-analysis ... reveals',

'findings were replicated', 'this finding was confirmed', 'most studies find' are used, and work, as Potter (1996) suggests, by giving an impression that findings are arrived at by means of impersonal processes and without partiality of any kind – the product of the tests themselves rather than of a socially situated human endeavour perhaps involving, to varying degrees, assumptions, interpretations, prejudices, politics and professional rivalries. A sense of 'out-there-ness' (Potter, 1996) is achieved by such means – that is, an impression is given that the facts here are speaking for themselves. As Gilbert and Mulkay (in Potter, 1996, p. 154) state, the advantages of such forms of writing are that 'it makes the speaker's scientific conclusions appear entirely unproblematic and in need of no further support'. Absent from such impersonal forms of writing are of course any personal expressions which could be construed as subjective or emotional. To include the personal would raise the possibility of there being biases or distortions in the findings (Gergen, 1999).

- Another means of achieving authority is to make reference to other papers in support of your claims. Träskman-Bendz and Mann (2000) have sixty-one references for an eight-page chapter; Cheng (1995) has forty for an eight-page paper. These have in turn been cited by others as authoritative statements of fact – Cheng's paper, for instance, has been cited by seventeen other papers at the last count. When Kay Redfield Jamison claims that studies have shown the 'unequivocal presence of severe psychopathology' in those that kill themselves, or Robert Goldney, Professor of Psychiatry at the University of Adelaide and past President of the International Association for Suicide Prevention, writes that '[p]sychological autopsy studies have consistently demonstrated, across countries with different cultures, that 80% to 90% of suicides had mental disorders, particularly depression and substance abuse' (Goldney, 2005, pp. 129–30), a number of papers are cited in support of these statements (both draw attention to the paper by Cheng, 1995, for instance). Potter (1996, p. 159) talks of how such strategies provide a sense of corroboration for claims to truth, and how consensus is built through such means. In citing the work of others one is establishing that one has *allies* in one's claim-making (Gergen, 1999, p. 56). The truths articulated in such papers are taken to be have been arrived at by the steady accumulation of knowledge and facts by a disinterested group of authoritative, accredited professionals and scientists rather than the opinions or beliefs of individual authors. As Gergen (1999) notes, rarely are works cited in support of one's claims examined for their 'ambiguities and shortcomings; to question the work would raise doubts about one's own' (p. 56).

Through such means 'knowledge communities', founded, and to an extent dependent upon, certain relations of power (doctor–patient; scientist–research subject; senior–junior researcher, editor–author), establish the truth of their claims, and further strengthen their relative positions of authority by producing truths presented as objective and (for the most part) agreed upon. By reading such truth claims as rhetorical achievements (the outcome of particular discursive practices and relations of power) rather than as statements of discovered facts, it is possible to question the 'givenness' or inevitability of dominant accounts, to contest the claim that facts speak for themselves or that knowledge is value free. Bruno Latour and Steve Woolgar, in their *Laboratory Life: The Social Construction of Scientific Facts* (1979), pursued similar themes in their examination of the social processes that make up the production and circulation of scientific knowledge. The field of science studies, as well as what has been termed 'the sociology of scientific knowledge' (e.g. Bloor, 1976), have explored related territory, for the most part attempting to situate scientific practices and claims within a social, historical and philosophical context. The central premise of each, and of the analysis presented here, is that it is historically and socially situated groups of people and institutions that speak of truth, knowledge and facts, rather than the world, and that the production and circulation of truths, as Foucault (2002a) contended, do not arise outside of relations of power.

Construction of concepts, objects and subjects

Another strand in seeking to understand the means by which a compulsory ontology of pathology in relation to suicide is produced and maintained (as a 'regime of truth') is to examine the concepts and objects that constitute, and are constituted by, contemporary professional accounts. Here, there is a divergence between the traditional and more biologically orientated styles of thought in terms of the practices involved in the production of authoritative knowledge, and the objects and subjects that are formed in relation to these.

Within both forms of account certain objects and concepts are afforded the status of the 'real'. With regard to suicide, descriptions of mental illnesses, physiological processes, personality types and behaviours are drawn upon to make a link between pathology and suicide. In the chapter by Träskman-Bendz and Mann (2000), for example, a large number of objects and concepts are brought together to establish the truth of a link between brain abnormalities and suicide. There are the brain, brain chemicals, brain functions, personality characteristics and associated types of personality, psychiatric disorders and diagnoses, behaviours and types of people categorised according to their behaviour. Such an assortment of elements is not untypical of articles concerning biological psychiatry and suicide (see also Nielsen *et al.*, 1998; Mann *et al.*, 2000; van Heeringen, 2001). Usually, the goal of research in this field is to identify dysfunctions or abnormalities in a region of the brain and to map these to specific behaviours/acts, via intermediary concepts such as 'impulsivity', 'aggression', 'personality traits', 'depression', 'disinhibition', etc. In the example chosen here (Träskman-Bendz and Mann, 2000), the behaviours discussed are murder, arson, infanticide and suicide, and these are constructed as in some way pathological by means of their connection to an underlying abnormal brain state. In connecting brain chemicals to behaviour a number of intervening concepts are described. So in addition to genes, brain chemicals, brain regions and acts there are also descriptions of brain functions (e.g. 'restraint system'), different personality characteristics (e.g. 'rebelliousness' or 'suspiciousness'), psychiatric disorders (e.g. 'personality disorders', 'melancholia'), groups of people (e.g. 'murderers', 'violent offenders', 'impulsive, alcoholic criminals', 'normals'), as well as a variety of feelings (e.g. 'anxiety', 'anger') and impulses (e.g. 'suicidal impulses' 'impulsive aggression'). The authority, or 'discursive currency', of this style of thought (broadly the linkage of biology and behaviour via types of people and their emotions) is enhanced by the use of some of the rhetorical strategies outlined in the previous section (the use of citations to achieve a sense of consensus and corroboration, and the construction of 'out-there-ness'). These are employed to give a sense that what are described are neutral descriptions of objects and relationships that exist in the world. The link between brain anatomical or chemical abnormalities and suicidal behaviours, via personality characteristics, associated behaviours, psychiatric diagnostic categories, and emotional states are rendered factual by means of those rhetorical strategies familiar to 'empiricist discourse' – that is statements are presented as objective, impartial and impersonal. By such means the authority of statements is enhanced, but equally, authority itself can come to be strengthened by producing demands for more knowledge that in turn requires an increase in knowledge-producing activities. Suicide comes to be constituted by reference to molecules and genes, diagnostic categories and personality types by means of knowledge produced through an 'assemblage' of researchers and research subjects, materials (samples of blood, tissue, etc.), practices of testing and inscribing using various forms of equipment, etc. (Colt, 2006, pp. 299–303 provides an insightful description of a trip to the neuro-anatomy laboratory of the New York State Psychiatric Institute's Mental Health Clinical Research Center for the Study of Suicidal Behavior).

In turn, the knowledge produced provides a rationale for further research, strengthens the position of psychiatry in general in relation to suicide (by confirming its pathological nature), and justifies psychiatric practices with regard to the suicidal (diagnosing and categorising, the prescription of pharmacological as well as 'talking' treatments, the monitoring of behaviour for signs of suicide risk, and maybe confinement and observation in hospital). Relations of power between researcher and those researched, as well as doctor and patient, are constituted within the terms offered by such knowledge, and enable the production of more truths in a circular process that is essentially productive in nature.

As with biological psychiatric accounts, writings that link mental illnesses to suicide also draw on a number of concepts, objects and subject 'types' to construct a picture of the real and true. Claims to truth are produced across a number of sites and by a variety of means, but the psychological autopsy report has here assumed a position of some importance. Thus, when Kay Redfield Jamison (1999) talks of 'study after study' showing the 'unequivocal presence of severe psychopathology in those who die by their own hand' (p. 100) it is, for the most part, psychological autopsy studies she cites in support of her claim (specifically; Robins et al., 1959/1996; Dorpat and Ripley, 1960; Barraclough et al., 1974; Hagnell and Rorsman, 1978; Beskow, 1979; Hagnell and Rorsman, 1979; Chynoweth et al., 1980; Fowler et al., 1986; Black, 1989; Tanney, 1992; Cheng, 1995; Foster et al., 1997; and Angst et al., 1999). Similarly, the statement by Jamison and Hawton (2005) asserting '[s]tudy after study of suicides worldwide have shown that the association between mental illness and suicide is extremely strong, with approximately 90% of those who commit suicide having a diagnosable mental illness' (p. 189) is backed up by citations of psychological autopsy studies, adding Vijayakumar and Rajkumar (1999) and Phillips et al. (2002) to the studies listed above. Bertolote et al. (2004) write that 'most psychological autopsy studies (from both developed and developing countries) have shown that over 90% of patients who committed suicide had a psychiatric illness at the time of death' (p. 147) and also cite Foster et al. (1997) and Vijayakumar and Rajkumar (1999), as well as Cavanagh et al. (1999) and Conwell et al. (1996). The truth of a link between mental illness and suicide is thus substantiated, for the most part, by reference to psychological autopsy studies.

A psychological autopsy usually involves the interviewing of surviving relatives and friends as well as consulting public and private documentation (such as medical notes) to seek to determine the 'state of mind' of the deceased prior to their death. Such studies are accepted, within 'suicidology' literature, as valid and reliable (Hawton et al., 1998) and a number of authors have also argued that they can move us closer to the truth of suicide. In a systematic review of autopsy studies, Cavanagh *et al.* (2003) write '[t]he fundamental question of what drives a person to take their own life remains unanswered despite numerous studies. The major obstacle to an understanding of suicide is that the victim cannot be interviewed and the reason directly ascertained. One solution has been the development of the psychological autopsy' (p. 395), the aims of which are 'to produce as full and accurate a picture of the deceased as possible with a view to understanding why they killed themselves' (p. 395). The authors go on to state that there are now 'in excess of 150 reports on psychological autopsy studies of suicide in the world literature' (p. 396). The review concludes that 'of the variables most often studied and regarded as clinically useful, mental disorders had the strongest associations with suicide' (p. 400). They then ask whether this 'strong and consistent' association is reliable, and conclude that '[f]irst, the psychological autopsy technique is regarded as valid in determining accurate diagnosis' and that '[s]econdly, our results are consistent with the strong positive evidence for the role of mental disorder throughout the suicide literature' (p. 401). An example of a psychological autopsy study is drawn upon here to illustrate the practices involved in the production of the truth of the presence of psychopathology in suicides.

Psychological autopsy: an example

As noted, psychological autopsy studies have become an important element in the claims to truth of the position that there exists a clear correlation between categories of mental illnesses and self-destructive behaviours. The claims made are often universal in nature; that is, the association between mental illness and suicide is held to be true not just for Western societies, but for all cultures (for example Jamison, 1999; Vijayakumar and Rajkumar, 1999; Bertolote *et al.*, 2004). An example of such claim-making will now be explored, as this will allow an examination not only of the practices involved in the production of authoritative knowledge, but also of how truths in relation to suicide can be constructed as acultural and ahistorical. By such means the 'discursive currency' of the claims can be enhanced, relations of power strengthened, and certain practices justified, which in turn can lead to the production of more knowledge in a circular relation.

The paper in question, 'Mental illness and suicide: A case-control study in East Taiwan' (Cheng, 1995), is of interest as the claims to truth of the relationship between mental disorders and suicide are taken to be applicable across cultures. The article concludes that findings 'strongly indicate that the psychiatric antecedents of suicide are the same in the East and the West. This work reveals a more universal nature of suicide than could previously have been assumed' (p. 603). The paper, as noted, is frequently cited as demonstrating the universality of the connection between mental illness and suicide. In a later article (Cheng, 2001), the author writes (in relation to suicide) that, 'the basic psychopathology is universal and that cross-cultural differences have derived from culture-specific illness behaviour' (p. 1).

The abstract states that the 'relationship between mental illness and suicide has not been well investigated in non-Western societies' (Cheng, 1995, p. 594), thus a 'case-control study of suicide among two aboriginal groups and the Han Chinese' in East Taiwan was undertaken. To generate data 'biographical reconstructive interviews were conducted for consecutive suicides from each of the three ethnic groups (a total of 116 suicides), 113 of whom were matched with two controls for age, sex, and areas of residence' (p. 594). As with the other psychological autopsy studies, interviews with 'key informants' ('close relatives and significant others') were conducted. 'The interview used a semi-structured biographical inventory, initially constructed as a considerably modified version of that used by Barraclough *et al.* (1974) in their suicide study in England, to fulfil the requirements for DSM III-R diagnosis' with changes including the insertion of 'psycholinguistic equivalents and native idioms for major emotional symptoms' (Cheng, 1995, p. 603).

It is possible to see how a number of assumptions (namely the universality and translatability of Western conceptions of mental illness) were present from the beginning of the study. The way in which the study was carried out was also consistent with these assumptions. The article states that; '[t]he validity of this study mainly depends on the accuracy of reporting from coroners and key informants and the reliability of the interview and psychiatric diagnosis' (p. 599). The paragraph continues:

In previous studies, relatives of suicides have been found to underestimate psychiatric symptoms and illness, owing partly to memory effects and their difficulty in recognizing nonobservable symptoms and abnormal behaviors and partly to reluctance to admit any mental problems of suicides. (p. 599)

Here we have an acknowledgement of an apparent methodological difficulty in psychological autopsy studies – namely, that the interviewees may not identify the psychopathology the investigators believe to be present. This potential challenge to the validity of the study is dealt with by suggesting that:

• mental illness was present but the relatives can't remember its being there;
• mental illness was present, but in 'non-observable' forms, and thus was missed by the interviewees;

- their relative was behaving in an abnormal way, but this was not recognised or noted by them;
- interviewees were reluctant to admit that their relative was mentally ill.

The author notes that '[s]uch biases might also exist in the study herein, particularly because mental illness bears a strong social stigma in Chinese society', and that '[r]elatives usually attributed the suicide act to life events or misfortunes, and rarely spontaneously mentioned suicides' abnormal behaviour' (p. 599). Further, evidence of mental illness was uncovered by the researchers, even though such illnesses were not discussed in the interviews, for '[e]xplicit mention of mental illness was avoided in this study's interview, which always started by inquiring about physical health and somatic symptoms' (p. 599). Certain relations of power-knowledge can be discerned to be at work here. Prior assumptions as to the universality and applicability of Western concepts of mental illness were present in the stated aims and methods of the study, as were assumptions about the relationship between psychopathology and suicide. As a consequence – despite explicit mention of mental illness being avoided, and surviving relatives 'rarely spontaneously mentioned suicides' abnormal behavior' and had 'difficulty in recognizing nonobservable symptoms', and that they tended to attribute the suicide to 'life events or misfortunes' – evidence was found of mental illness in 97–100 per cent of the sample. The author concludes that the 'high rate of mental illness in the suicides described herein implies that false negatives are few, if any. However, I do not think mental illness was overdiagnosed' (p. 599). Thus neither too many nor too few have been diagnosed. Nobody was missed (false negatives), but equally nobody was included who shouldn't have been.

The author continues, '[t]he possibility of a systematic bias from the interviewer seems unlikely, since interrater reliability among the three interviewers in the pretest was satisfactory, and the reliability between independent diagnoses by me and another psychiatrist in this study was very satisfactory' (p. 599). It is argued here not that there are biases, but that the study is to some extent circular and self-validating in its findings; the conclusions were to be expected given the premises and methods of the study. Such research, however, has a powerful effect in the formation of truths in relation to suicide – that is the association of suicide with Western notions of psychopathology. In Western societies this truth of suicide is reinforced through studies such as the one discussed, and through its frequent citing (Cheng's paper has been cited by, amongst others, Boothroyd *et al.*, 2001; Cornelius *et al.*, 2001; Koivumaa-Honkanen *et al.*, 2001; Wærn *et al.*, 2002; Hawton *et al.*, 2003; Castle *et al.*, 2004; Knox *et al.*, 2004; Khan, 2005; and Qin and Nordentoft, 2005). Such views also find their way into non-Western cultures. There may, of course, be benefits to the introduction of Western discourses and practices in relation to suicide. New possibilities are opened up with regard to the management of suicide in terms of prediction and control, diagnosis and treatment. The uncovering and treatment of previously undiagnosed mental illness, the argument runs, could help alleviate the misery of many people and thus reduce rates of suicide, but there are also potential pitfalls as well. One danger would be that traditional, culture-specific, explanations for suicide (in the study it is noted that '[r]elatives usually attributed the suicide act to life events or misfortunes' (Cheng, 1995, p. 599)) can come to be read as inaccurate, unscientific and thus less true than the Western notions imported by researchers. The utility of traditional 'folk' explanations could be hard to discern by those outside the cultures concerned, and the importation of beliefs of suicide as always caused by some form of internal pathology, and the necessity, therefore, of a medical response and medical expertise in relation to suicide may not be necessarily a benign process.

In Japan, for example, where for many centuries various forms of self-accomplished death have been taken to be honourable or noble acts, a more 'Western' approach to mental health issues, suicide and suicide prevention has more recently been embraced (Colt, 2006, p. 222). Pharmaceutical companies have strongly marketed anti-depressant medication alongside a Western 'medical model' of depression since the end of the 1990s, challenging traditional (mostly Buddhist) attitudes towards suffering. The annual number of suicides has also risen precipitously, '[t]he rising rate, perhaps not coincidently, comes at a time when the traditional Japanese conception of suicide has been changing':

The Japanese, it is said, now kill themselves for the same reasons as people kill themselves in the West. The military official who takes his life in shame over a security leak and the man who takes his life to protest a political action are now likely to be discussed as psychological misfits. (p. 224)

Even in Japan, with its history of *hara-kiri*, s*eppuku*, *kashitsu-shi* ('suicide to admit failure or to atone for a mistake' (p. 219)), *gisei-shi* (sacrificial suicide), *jyoshi shinju* (love-pact suicide) and *oyako shinju* (parent–child suicide), suicide has come to be read as essentially a pathological, and individual, phenomenon. It would be hard to establish a causal link between the shift in attitudes towards suicide in Japan and rising numbers of such deaths, but an uncritical acceptance of Western medical/psychiatric formulations and practices in relation to suicide may blind us to certain unintended, and possibly harmful, consequences.

The potentially problematic nature of Western constructions of suicide will be discussed in greater detail in the next chapter, but here the main objective has been to map how suicide is constituted in expert, author-itative accounts as in some way pathological in nature. It has been argued that suicide is taken to be primarily a matter of psychiatric concern. Two 'styles of thought' have been identified – a 'traditional' approach that asserts a relationship between mental illnesses and suicide (a causal relationship is often suggested) and biological psychiatric approaches that look to locate specific brain abnormalities or anomalies that could account for self-destructive behaviours. Each draw on rhetorical strategies com-mon to empiricist discourse to form accounts of suicide that could be read as accurate and true. Furthermore, such truths are also often presented as being universally applicable to other cultures and other times (for further examples of universal claims-making in relation to culture see Gangat *et al.*, 1987; Patel and Gaw, 1996; Cheng and Lee, 2000. With regard to claims that psychiatric 'truths' in relation to suicide are true for all times as well as all places see Thomas, 1980 and Pahor, 2006). As universal truths, such claims carry much force in determining how suicide comes to be thought of by mental health professionals, the suicidal, and relatives and friends of suicides. The authoritative knowledge produced by medical researchers and scientists, as well as practising clinicians could be said to constitute a certain 'regime of truth', and the relationships between patients, their friends and families, and mental health workers are in part determined by the production and circulation of such truths. The production of truths of suicide does not arise outside relations of power-knowledge. The production of authoritative knowledge is dependent on relations of power (doctor–patient; researcher–research subject; Western–'traditional'), and the truths formed can, in turn, strengthen and extend power. Such power or 'truth effects' of the production of a compulsory ontology of pathology in relation to suicide will be explored later, but some of the ways in which such truths come to be reproduced and circulated will now be examined.

Disseminating truths in relation to suicide: a compulsory ontology of pathology in media accounts of suicide

The previous section looked to explore how truths are constructed in relation to suicide. It was argued that certain rhetorical features were drawn upon to confer authority on accounts that linked suicide to pathol-ogy. The production of such truths tends to go hand-in-hand with their dissemination. Professional accounts are published in journals such as *Crisis: The Journal of Crisis Intervention and Suicide Prevention,* the *Journal of Suicide and Life-Threatening Behavior* and the *Archives of Suicide Research* and in books aimed at researchers and clinicians. Some, such as Kay

Redfield Jamison's *Night Falls Fast* (1999), a *New York Times* bestseller, aim to bridge the gap between 'expert' and 'non-expert'. Other means of dissemination include the everyday practices through which truths are enacted, which may include conversations between health professionals and patients, case reviews, professionals' meetings, and in particular the ways in which patients presenting as suicide risks are managed by mental health services. Here, risk assessment and risk management processes reproduce the formulations outlined earlier – suicidal patients are taken to be mentally ill and therefore irrational and not responsible for their actions. Responsibility passes to staff – mostly psychiatrists and mental health nurses – to ensure the patients' safety. The ways in which the 'responsible and accountable' clinician is constructed will be discussed when considering 'truth effects', but here it is worth noting that practices such as 'special observation' where patients are either under 'constant' or 'close' observation by a member of staff (Stevenson and Cutcliffe, 2006), the assessing and documenting of symptoms, diagnoses, treatments and level of risk, and compulsory assessment and/or treatment, all enable the collation of more knowledge on suicide and suicidal patients, but also act as means of reproducing the truth of suicide as arising as a consequence of pathology. Mental health practices in relation to suicide are based on assumptions of the presence of some form of psychopathology, and suicide prevention is taken to be achieved primarily through the detection and treatment of mental illness (Jamison, 1999; Hawton and van Heeringen, 2000; Department of Health, 2002; Duffy and Ryan, 2004; Jamison and Hawton, 2005). It is now difficult to imagine a response to a 'threat' of suicide not determined, to some extent at least, by the psychiatric formulations and practices outlined above as notions of pathology have come to saturate the field of knowledge with regard to self-accomplished death.

Also of interest are the ways in which professional truths come to be disseminated through non-professional channels. In this section a brief overview is provided of how media organisations are advised to present suicide. As examples, guidelines produced by the World Health Organization and the Samaritans (a suicide prevention charity) for the media are examined, in order to understand how suicide comes to be presented in newspapers, on television and radio, and in films. An example is later given as a means of illustrating how suicide comes to be associated with psychopathology in newspaper reports, even in cases where such pathology is not obviously present. The next section will then go on to address the possible effects of, and relations of power involved in, the continual reproduction of a compulsory ontology of pathology in relation to suicide.

Media guidelines on the reporting of suicide

In 2000, the World Health Organization published *Preventing Suicide, A Resource for Media Professionals*. This nine-page document talks of the impact of media reporting on suicide, and gives advice on how to report suicide, both in general terms and in specific cases. The WHO guide asserts a number of facts. The media are said to 'strongly influence attitudes, beliefs and behaviour, and play a vital role in politics, economics and social practice'. It is because of that influence, the report goes on, that the 'media also play an active role in the prevention of suicide'. How is suicide constituted in the text? 'Suicide is perhaps the most tragic way of ending one's life ... The majority of people who consider suicide are ambivalent. They are not sure they want to die' (WHO, 2000b, p. 5). Thus the media are asked to report such deaths in certain ways to prevent further suicides, and the following guidance is included:

- Reporting suicidal behaviour as an understandable response to social or cultural changes or degradation should be resisted.
- Sensational coverage of suicides should be assiduously avoided, particularly when a celebrity is involved. The coverage should be minimized to the extent possible. Any mental health problem the celebrity may have had should also be acknowledged.
- Suicide should not be reported as unexplainable or in a simplistic way. Suicide is never the result of a single factor or event. It is usually caused by a complex interaction of many factors such as mental and physical illness, substance abuse, family disturbances, interpersonal conflicts and life stressors. Acknowledging that a variety of factors contributes to suicide would be helpful.
- Suicide should not be depicted as a method of coping with personal problems such as bankruptcy, failure to pass an examination, or sexual abuse (WHO, 2000b, pp. 7–8).

Finally, the media are offered suggestions of appropriate information on help that can be provided to be passed on, and these include:

- Listing available mental health services and helplines with their up-to-date telephone numbers and addresses;
- publicizing the warning signs of suicidal behaviour;
- conveying the message that depression is often associated with suicidal behaviour and that depression is a treatable condition;
- offering a message of sympathy to the survivors in their hour of grief and providing telephone numbers of support groups for survivors, if available. This increases the likelihood of intervention by mental health professionals, friends and family in suicidal crises. (WHO, 2000b, p. 8)

The intention behind the advice is not to be faulted, for what is strived for is a way of reporting that lessens the suffering of those bereaved by suicide and reduces the risk of others harming or killing themselves. However, suicide is once again constructed as a tragic act of a mentally unwell individual. In the words of the guidelines such acts should not be represented as 'normal' or an 'understandable response to social or cultural changes or degradation' or a 'method of coping with personal problems'. Instead, it is suggested that any mental health problem should be acknowledged in reports, mental health services should be recommended, alongside the message that 'depression is often associated with suicidal behaviour and that depression is a treatable condition'. Little doubt is left that suicide is mostly an issue of individual mental health – and that 'appropriate, accurate and potentially helpful' reporting means restating and reinforcing this belief.

Following the publication of the WHO guidelines, the media in the UK were given further advice, both through the National Suicide Prevention Strategy for England (Department of Health, 2002) and by the Samaritans (2002). The NSPSE goal 4 was to 'improve the reporting of suicidal behaviour in the media', with the objective being to; '[p]romote the responsible representation of suicidal behaviour in the media' (NSPSE, 2002, p. 16). To this end action was planned to '[i]nfluence the training of journalists to ensure that they report issues about mental illness and suicidal behaviour in an informed and sensitive manner' (p. 27). What this may mean in practice is not detailed in the NSPSE, but some clues can be gleaned from the Samaritans' publication, *Media Guidelines: Portrayals of Suicide* (Samaritans, 2002). Among the recommendations contained in the Samaritan's text are:

- Encourage explanation of the risk factors of suicide.
- Encourage discussion by health experts on the possible contributory causes of suicide.
- Don't romanticise or glorify suicide. Reporting which highlights community expressions of grief may suggest that the local community is honouring the suicidal behaviour of the deceased person, rather than mourning their death.
- Don't overemphasise the 'positive' results of a person's suicide. A dangerous message from the media is that suicide achieves results; it makes people sorry or it makes people eulogise you. For instance, a soap opera storyline or newspaper coverage where a child's suicide or suicide attempt seems to result in separated parents reconciling or school bullies being publicly shamed may offer an appealing option to a despairing child in similar circumstances (Samaritans, 2002, pp. 10, 11).

Such guidance is obviously a genuine attempt to prevent suicides, and to lessen the distress experienced by survivors (families, friends, etc.) of those who have taken their own lives. There may be unintended consequences, however, in the reproduction of such a singular approach to the issue. The ways in which health professionals, the suicidal and survivors can think about the subject, and can act in relation to it, are much reduced by being presented with so narrow a picture of what suicide is and should be. Suicide is formulated as pathological and individual, as tragic, and not to be read as in any way 'positive'. To want to die is thus necessarily a sign of mental illness, an act of suicide is always read as a consequence of psychopathology and, further, to be mentally ill is to be at continual risk of suicide. Suicide therefore remains always something of an individual act, and can come to be dissociated from other cultural meanings that may render the act understandable or tolerable to survivors. Additionally, the resources available for the suicidal and their families, and for health professionals to draw upon to make sense of their thoughts, feelings and actions, are diminished. The next section looks to understand how the guidelines discussed above translate into practice by means of analysis of two newspaper reports concerning the death of a student in East Sussex in 2004. Here, the ways by which a compulsory ontology of pathology is produced and reproduced in the media are mapped.

An example

Given the advice handed down to newspaper and television editors, it is unsurprising that medical constructions of suicide predominate in the media, even in the absence of any obvious medical or psychiatric component to the story being covered. In August, 2005, the *Guardian* ran a news report entitled; 'Gifted student with place at Oxford decided "life is not for me"'. The article was in connection with a coroner's inquest that had the previous day returned a verdict of suicide after investigating the death of a young woman, Alice McGovern. At the inquest, three suicide notes, written on the day she went missing, were read out. One read:

For all those who loved me please don't feel in any way responsible for my death. Life is simply not for me. I am not filled with grief as I write these words. I simply have no will to carry on living and the idea of death does not scare me.

I would especially like to thank Alex [her boyfriend] for showing me a fantastic summer and making me truly happy. Good luck with everything in the future and don't let this event stop you from doing anything. Please don't mourn my death. (*Guardian*, 3 August 2005)

Other evidence given to the coroner pointed to an absence of mental illness as a factor in the young woman's death:

Her boyfriend ... told the inquest that he could never remember her being depressed. 'She was always very happy and extremely cheery and was the most upbeat character I had ever known' he said.

'She was always the sort of person to look on the bright side of life and I can't really recall her being upset or not happy.' (*Guardian*, 3 August 2005)

The day after the *Guardian* report, on 4 August, 2005, *The Times* Health Section ran a story 'Dying to succeed: fatal pressure on our children'. Again it is worth noting that it is the health section that the story appears in and that the article was authored by a GP. The article opens with a summary of what was known of Alice McGovern's life:

ALICE McGOVERN appeared to have everything to live for. She was an able student with 11 GCSEs at grade A. She had good prospects of excellent results in her A levels and had already been offered a place at the academically prestigious New College, Oxford.

Her parents were both successful school teachers and her home life appeared to have been happy. She was described as having an optimistic personality and as being someone who looked forward to life. She had a regular boyfriend with whom she had an excellent relationship.

There was no history of family discord, rows or unfortunate incidents that are better forgotten and might provide embarrassment later. In fact, none of the common portents of suicide in able young people was present and Alice was even planning her forthcoming 19th birthday party in Oxford. (*The Times*, August 4 2005)

That Alice could have been considered mentally unwell, given the above, seems unlikely. However, the article infers, in a number of places, that there probably was an underlying, if undetected, pathology at work.

In young adults, as in older people, there may be an underlying depressive or schizotypal personality that has remained undetected.

The contention of an 'underlying' but 'undetected' pathology is rhetorically powerful in that such a statement cannot be easily rebutted, at least by a non-expert. That the author attaches such pathologies to 'young adults, as in older people' seems initially puzzling, for no meaningful distinction is being made here – the statement, in effect, is saying all adults may have an 'underlying depressive or schizotypal personality that has remained undetected'. But by referring to 'young people' we think of the young woman Alice McGovern, and by association we could suspect she may have harboured an 'underlying', 'undetected' pathology. The article goes on to talk about other apparent personality oddities that by a process of association attach themselves to Alice McGovern:

Whereas less obsessional and driven people are prepared to admit to a fear of change, an inability to live up to expectations, uncertainty about examinations (however unfounded), those who have already been successful don't voice their anxieties.

There was no suggestion from any of the reports on Alice that she was in any way obsessional or driven, any more than she had a 'schizotypal' personality. As regards depression, the article continues:

The symptoms of depression in youth include all those found in older people such as loss of appetite, insomnia, feelings of hopelessness and an inability to look forward – none of these seems to have been present in Alice, or, if they were there, she kept them well hidden.

The use of the phrase 'if they were there, she kept them well hidden' in relation to a list of symptoms again suggests a refusal to countenance the absence of illness in Alice. Some form of pathology is again inferred by the following:

The super-conscientious with an obsessive streak in his or her nature is in greater peril of suicide than the pupil who trundles along a third of the way down the class, would be lucky to be in a team, let alone to captain it, and would never be considered a potential head of school. Later in life the youthful, eminent scholar or climber of Mount Everest may display vulnerability and an obsessive nature as well as determination and ability.

That Alice was deputy head girl at her private school, and that she captained the hockey team, was information revealed at the inquest, but not mentioned in *The Times* article. But the inference here is that Alice, as with other 'high achievers', was 'super-conscientious with an obsessive streak' in her nature, and thus vulnerable to suicide. The author, perhaps rather disingenuously given the aforementioned discussions, states that, '[w]ithout knowing the full history of Alice McGovern, it is impossible to speculate on the causes of her suicide', but the conjecture that some form of pathology is usually present in suicide continues: 'When suicidal feelings in young people are associated with a depressive illness, the treatment is usually medication combined with cognitive therapy. If there's any evidence of psychosis, a typical anti-psychotic will be essential'. And even following a denial of sorts that Alice was ill the author continues to suggest that some form of abnormality was present:

But in Alice's case there was apparently no evidence of any psychotic behaviour, bipolar disorder or previous impulsive patterns of behaviour in her medical history.

Even so, her extreme detachment when discussing her own death, and perhaps evidence in her notes of a lack of appreciation of its likely impact on her parents and boyfriend, were significant. A casualness about death, whether one's own or other people's, can be an important psychological symptom.

So Alice, according to the article, could not be judged sane or reasonable in her actions. Her 'extreme detachment' and her 'a lack of appreciation' of the impact on others of her actions, become symptoms. 'A casualness about death' could be constructed as a symptom of an 'underlying' and 'undetected' pathology but so could, presumably, a fear of death. The article concludes with the following:

Doctors are constantly confronted by the need to assess the seriousness of any expressed suicidal intent in a young person. When there is suggestion of this, however vaguely expressed, it has to be explored by an expert.

The long-term outlook will depend on any underlying psychiatric condition, for although medication used in conjunction with cognitive therapy may provide immediate help, it will have to be supported by family co-operation and reassessment of lifestyle.

Thus, suicide is medical. Certain relations of power are reaffirmed by the article; doctors are called upon to judge the seriousness of young people's talk of suicide and experts, presumably mental health ones, are needed to fully assess any suicidal intent. Finally, there is a return to the concept of 'underlying' psychiatric conditions that require treatment. All this in an article about a young woman who was, by the accounts of those who knew her, not considered to be in any way mentally unwell. The above case can serve as an illustration of the compulsory formation of suicide as pathological. Suicide, by such accounts, is always already pathological.

The article does of course provide information to those concerned about suicide in young people, particularly with regard to where help may be available. For young people experiencing thoughts of suicide, or their friends or family, such formulations of suicide risk in terms of psychiatric illness may provide an intelligible and useful framework through which to view any difficulties experienced, and further, the possibility of treatment and cure offers hope for the medical/psychiatric alleviation of suffering. To be positioned as ill rather than morally blameworthy can also act to reduce the sense of personal responsibility experienced. The advantages, as well as the necessity, of such a 'medicalised' response to suicide are frequently spelt out in journal articles, conference papers and books. By such accounts the suicidal are sick and in need of treatment and the only substantive discussion comes to be, as Battin (2005, p. 164) notes, over access to, and the efficacy of, differing forms of treatment. Such a 'monolithic' approach may have its dangers, however, for alternative readings of deaths such as Alice McGovern's may be foreclosed or marginalised by an insistence on a compulsory ontology of pathology. Intentions, constructed as they are as arising from within a private interiority with only the individual granted 'privileged access', mean that no definitive answer can be given as to why Alice acted as she did in ending her life. Similarly, mental illnesses and abnormalities are taken as internal aspects of the individual, and again as a consequence there can be no way to contest a reading based on 'unseen underlying' pathology by reference to what was 'really' on her mind, or happening in her brain, when she decided to die. What is apparent, though, in the reporting of her death, are the limited resources that can be drawn upon to make sense of self-accomplished deaths that are not obviously patho-logical. There would seem to be a certain resistance, evident in the media guidelines discussed above, to the idea that suicide could be in any way rational or freely chosen. The notion of a 'voluntary death', of one not determined to a greater or lesser extent by mental illness or abnormal-ities in the personality of the individual in question, cannot be counte-nanced. Similarly, each death by suicide is necessarily read as tragic, thus disallowing any sense of nobility or honour in acting in such a way. Finally, the insistence on individual pathology leaves us with an impov-erished set of tools by which to understand other elements that may have had a bearing on her actions – that is those cultural and historical forces that act to constitute suicide and the suicidal at any given time. These are discussed in more detail in later chapters. The next section addresses how certain subjects can come to be formed in relation to the dominant contemporary compulsory ontology of pathology set out here.

'Truth effects'

This section looks to trace the effects of the continual stating and restating of the truths of suicide outlined above. In chapter 2 the work of Michel Foucault with regard to processes of subject formation was outlined. For Foucault, processes of objectivation and subjectivation are connected (2000, p. 460), as the subject is constituted in relation to 'objective' knowledge as part of a particular 'game of truth' (p. 461). The formation of subjects in relation to the truths of suicide outlined above will now be explored. Initially some of the ways in which the 'suicidal patient' can be constituted (at what sites, by whom, in relation to which truths and by what practices) are considered, then the 'responsible, accountable and culpable clinician'.

The discursive formation of the 'suicidal patient'

As noted earlier, 'traditional' psychiatric accounts (e.g. those found in Hawton and van Heeringen, 2000) tend to discuss the suicidal patient in terms of discrete categories of illness. Thus, it is possible to have the depressed suicidal patient, the schizophrenic suicidal patient, the anxious, the bi-polar, the personality disordered, etc. Equally, within such accounts the mentally ill are taken to be at an increased risk of suicide. There is thus a two-way process at work – to be assessed as suicidal is likely to lead to some form of diagnosis, and to be diagnosed as mentally ill is to become considered a suicide risk. These forms of assessment and categorisation arise out of particular practices, conducted at specific sites, invoking certain knowledge(s) and involving various relations of power. As an example (here based on guidelines issued by the World Health Organization (2000a), and the University of Manchester's STORM training programme (undated)), if a person expressing suicidal wishes were to present at a general hospital's Accident and Emergency department (A&E), their first contact with staff (after the receptionist) would (most likely) be an assessment with the triage nurse. Here, if a wish to die were admitted, the individual (now identified as a patient or client) would be asked about their thoughts of suicide, any plans they may have formulated, and when (if at all) they were planning to act on their plans (see WHO, 2000a). If a suicide risk was suspected a referral would then be made to any liaison mental health staff who covered A&E (e.g. mental health nurse, crisis team, duty psychiatrist). Alongside an estimation of the degree of risk presented by the patient/client, a preliminary assessment would also be conducted of their 'mental state', initially by the triage nurse, more formally by the mental health staff. Such practices would be underwritten by knowledge of risk factors of suicide and symptoms and categories of mental illness (the practice of diagnosis generally only undertaken, however, by appropriately trained psychiatric doctors). If the person were to be considered to be at significant enough risk of harming themselves, and were taken to be suffering from a mental illness, they might be admitted to a more secure setting, most likely a psychiatric ward, either voluntarily or, following a further assessment, under a section of the Mental Health Act (1983). Either as an in-patient, or cared for outside hospital in the community, the patient would be monitored and, at intervals, their level of risk and mental state reassessed. If the patient was admitted to a psychiatric ward, practices such as 'special observation' might be deemed necessary, which could involve keeping the patient constantly in sight, and sometimes demand that an appropriate member of staff be within arms' reach of the patient at all times (Stevenson and Cutcliffe, 2006), in order, presumably, to restrain the person if they attempted to harm themselves.

Similar paths to patient status via assessment of mental state and suicide risk could begin in a GP's surgery, counsellor's office, community mental health team premises, police station, or even at school or workplace (WHO guidelines, 2000a; 2000c; 2000d; 2006a; 2006b). To confess a desire to die is to invoke practices and knowledge that act to constitute that person as at risk and in need of care and treatment. Once the individual is constituted as a patient at risk very many possibilities for further observations, examinations and assessments are opened up, and through such means new knowledge comes to be generated with regard to the patient. The information gathered – recorded in case notes, discussed at team meetings and ward rounds, confirmed or disconfirmed with friends and families – is formulated in medical/psychiatric terms that act to further reinforce that the situation at hand – the crisis facing the patient and significant others – is fundamentally a question of the patient's mental health and principally, therefore, a matter of psychiatric concern. The 'suicidal patient' is formed at the meeting-place of various practices, interactions with staff, and authoritative knowledge, within spaces mostly designated as medical/psychiatric in function. Such an 'assemblage' of sites, knowledge, practices and relations is immensely productive in terms of generating new knowledge as well as reinforcing the necessity of existing practices. By such means, psychiatric power in relation to suicide (in terms of assuming positions of authority and expertise, as well as the right to confine, observe and restrain patients deemed to be at risk) is strengthened. Relations of knowledge-to-power and power-to-knowledge are thus productive in maintaining suicide as pathological and medical in nature.

Knowledge drawn from biological accounts of suicide have also come to shape understandings of the nature of the suicidal patient, and also how such patients experience and interpret their lives. Through the dissemination of professional writings on the relationship between the brain and various normal and abnormal states, through journals, reports in the press and on television, on the Internet, etc., as well as through face-to-face encounters with health professionals, notions drawn from neurochemistry and neuro-anatomy can come to inform our understandings and experiences of moods, feelings and behaviours. Nikolas Rose, for instance, talks of us becoming 'neurochemical selves'. He asks:

How did we come to think about our sadness as a condition called 'depression' caused by a chemical imbalance in the brain and amenable to treatment by drugs that would 'rebalance' these chemicals? How did we come to experience our worries at home and at work as 'generalized anxiety disorder' also caused by a chemical imbalance which can be corrected by drugs? (Rose, 2003, p. 46)

How might we as 'neurochemical selves' conceive of suicide? The title of a book by Susan Rose Blauner (2002), *How I Stayed Alive When My Brain Was Trying To Kill Me*, perhaps gives us a clue. We, existing somewhere, somehow, outside our brains, can be persecuted by a malfunctioning brain, and have our lives threatened. Blauner writes that to 'shed her suicidal skin, I had to develop an understanding of how things work upstairs. Once I could see my mental landscape, it was easier to navigate' (p. 37). A metaphorical 'neuron superhighway' is described to illustrate how she sees the connections between brains, brain chemicals and thoughts and feelings, '[t]houghts and feelings are electrical impulses that travel along a complex web of specialized nerve cells in the brain called neurons, with the help of chemicals called neurotransmitters' (p. 37). Blauner asks us to 'pretend for a moment that you're flying above a busy highway at rush hour. Below you, cars and trucks on the road are streaming toward their various destinations. If you apply that image to how your brain works, the cars and trucks are your thoughts and feelings, and neurons are the highway they're traveling on' (p. 38). All is well as long as the system functions correctly. However, '[j]ust as faulty construction or improper maintenance can cause a highway to deteriorate, so brain function is compromised by severe trauma, stress, or chemical imbalance. My own mental landscape was full of accidents waiting to happen' (p. 38).

Blauner suggests she was born with a dysfunctional brain, and that her subsequent difficulties in functioning were primarily biochemical. Events in her life – the death of her mother and sexual abuse – are seen as relevant only in so far as they affected her brain:

I believe I was born predisposed to major depression, which is biochemical in nature. In other words I was brought into the world with creaky bridges. This chemical imbalance, combined with the death of my mom, sexual abuse, and the other factors I described earlier, weakened my bridge construction to the point where I had potholes the size of Rhode Island in my thought processes. (pp. 38–9)

Blauner continues, '[t]wo things happened: my body stopped making enough of the critical neurotransmitter serotonin, and what *did* get produced was used up too quickly. Instead of travelling safely over a waterway, my feelings and thoughts either crashed on the rocks or stalled at the tollbooth. And guess what, folks? I had no change' (p. 39).

Conceived within such a biomedical framework the solution to the problem would also need to be biological/biochemical. Pharmacology has come to play a significant role in the treatment of mental illnesses, and Blauner writes of her own experiences; 'Prozac is my "change". In addition to easing the symptoms of depression, Prozac is also thought to help with borderline personality disorder and post-traumatic stress disorder' (pp. 39–40). The effects of traumatic life events and even 'disorders' of personality become understandable, and treatable, by reference and recourse to brain chemistry; 'I have tried several different anti-depressants: for the past three years I've taken Prozac ... Prozac keeps my bridges intact, pays my tolls, and helps my brain get its work done more efficiently' (p. 40).

Blauner concludes her discussion on neurochemistry and suicide by stating, '[m]y brain wanted me to believe that my life was destined for pain, sorrow, and disappointment ... Suicide crept into my mind as a "solution" to the problem. A Grim Reaper took up residence under my skin and in my breath. He waited in the corners of my brain and became an angry tenant' (p. 40). The reasoning may be metaphorical, and Blauner herself admits her descriptions are 'far from scientific and drastically simplified' (p. 37), but the quotes above are included to illustrate how biomedical thinking can extend beyond academic and professional settings, and how individual experiences can come to be shaped by such accounts.

William Styron (1991) in *Darkness Visible*, talks of his depression and thoughts of suicide in a way similar to Blauner. Styron, Pulitzer Prize winner and author of *Sophie's Choice*, describes in *Darkness Visible: A Memoir of Madness*, how (to quote the book cover) in 'the Summer of 1985 [he] was overtaken by persistent insomnia and a troubling sense of malaise – the first signs of a deep depression that would engulf his life and leave him on the brink of suicide'. For Styron, what 'engulfed' him was a form of madness, and this 'madness' was primarily a medical issue:

The madness results from an aberrant biochemical process. It has been established with reasonable certainty (after strong resistance from many psychiatrists, and not all that long ago) that such madness is chemically induced amid the neuro-transmitters of the brain, probably as the result of systematic stress, which for unknown reasons causes a depletion of the chemical norepinephrine and seroto-nin, and the increase of a hormone, cortisol. (Styron, 1991, p. 46)

A link is made between mental illness, violence and suicide, '[s]ometimes, though not very often, such a disturbed mind will turn to violent thoughts regarding others. But with their minds turned agonizingly inward, people with depression are usually dangerous to themselves' (p. 46).

Styron's account again illustrates the ways by which expert discourses, vocabularies, images, stories and metaphors act to constitute, at least in part, first-person accounts of suicidal thoughts and actions. The truths of ourselves, and of our experiences, are formed in relation to those author-itative expert accounts given the status of truth – in Foucault's terms one can discern a connection between modes of subjectivation and those of objectivation (2000b, p. 460). Such a process can of course open up spaces of freedom as well as act to constrain. The first-person accounts given here do not present the formulation of suicide in terms of pathology as particularly problematic in any way. In Susan Rose Blauner's account, notions of brain chemical information superhighways offer a framework of understanding and the possibility, through psychotropic medication, of treatment and the alleviation of suffering. Similarly, for William Styron, medical advice and help was actively sought and in *Darkness Visible* he expresses regret that it took so long for him to be hospitalised. Again, such a position (the acceptance of medical truths and practices) also has an effect on the moral accountability of the subject in relation to their mental ill health, social functioning and suicidal thoughts and actions. Traditionally, differing constructions of madness have acted socially and in law to diminish the responsibility of those deemed to have transgressed social norms and codes of behaviour. With regard to suicide, up until the late nineteenth century in England a verdict of *non compos mentis* (not of sound mind) would spare the penalties that were liable if a person was found to be *felo de se* (felon of oneself) (MacDonald and Murphy, 1990). To be a victim of an illness offers different experiences from being constituted as a perpetrator of a crime or the willing transgressor of what is considered acceptable behaviour.

Although the constitution of subjects in relation to medical/psychiatric truths of suicide may enable or create certain domains of freedom it can also act to constrain the field of experience, and the situation with regard to suicide may be more problematic and ambiguous than is usually admitted. A study from New Zealand looking at young people's attitudes to depression and suicide gives us, perhaps, something of a clue as to what a few of the issues may be in this regard. Bennett *et al.* (2003) interviewed thirty young people who had attempted to end their own lives and found that for the majority of participants a medicalised discourse was drawn upon to make sense of their actions – one that constructed depression as a disease. They state that this 'discourse prioritised the voices of health professionals and suggested that depression was difficult to resist' (p. 289). Furthermore, 'a mechanistic cause-and-effect relationship between depression and suicidal behaviours' was noted in the participants' responses: 'attempting suicide was seen as an inevitable outcome of experiencing depression, and suicidal behaviours were inevitably undertaken by young people who were depressed' (p. 289). The authors conclude that this way of conceiving the relationship between depression and suicidal behaviours was difficult to resist, and argue that the agency of young people was consequently diminished for those who identified as depressed. This is illustrated by reference to 'Jack':

Positioning himself within a medicalised depression discourse has implications for Jack's sense of agency. In his account, Jack constructs himself as experiencing limited agency to disrupt this relationship. For example, depression is constructed as a disease which has to be passively endured 'it was just something you sort of go through', and is also out of his control 'it just becomes a habit'. Consequently, it is natural and inevitable therefore to believe 'nothing's worth living anymore' and 'everything's hopeless'. In this account, Jack articulates a mechanistic explanation of the contribution of depression to suicidal behaviours. He constructs his experience of depression as part of a linear, inevitable and natural pathway towards suicidal behaviours. According to Jack the 'depression track' begins with stress and worry, and progresses to be 'quite a heavy road'. Consistent with the medicalised depression discourse constituted by limited personal agency Jack suggests that departing from this pre-ordained pathway is difficult, unless one follows the appropriate medical treatment options. (Bennett *et al.* (2003, p. 293)

The authors suggest that within such medical settings the professional is seen as possessing the power to 'cure' mental illness, and the client or patient is positioned as the recipient of any intervention, required primarily to respond in an 'appropriate' way to treatment to optimise its benefits. Such positioning, it is argued, mediates further the young person's sense of agency.

What has been termed here the 'compulsory ontology of pathology' thus asserts itself in clinical practice. Bennett *et al.* conclude their paper by discussing some of the effects that follow from such a situation;

When discussing the contributions of depression to their suicidal behaviours, young people drew on a medicalised discourse which constructed depression as a disease. Within this discourse young people's agency (or their ability to behave and think a certain way) was restricted, as the voices of medical professionals were prioritised and depression was constructed as a disease which was difficult to resist.

The medicalised discourse prioritises the expert opinions of health professionals, and suggests that appropriate intervention and treatment for depression is only that which is provided within the medical paradigm. (Bennett *et al.* (2003)

Patients, within this dominant discourse, are positioned as passive victims of illness processes that may push them into self-destructive behaviours. Young people, in the study in question, report that such positioning is hard to resist, and that a medicalised discourse can act to form 'depressed' and 'suicidal' identities. It is argued by the authors that it follows that the agency of people so identified will necessarily be diminished. The other side of the coin is that clinicians, within such a discursive field that continually asserts a compulsory ontology of psychopathology in relation to distress and a desire to die, are positioned as responsible and accountable for the actions of their patients.

The accounts given by William Styron, Susan Rose Blauner and the subjects of Bennett *et al.*'s study all point to the way that certain subjectivities can come to be formed in relation to truths of suicide. In each, notions of biological processes and mental illnesses are used as a means to account for the presence of suicidal thoughts or feelings, but are also used as references for understanding their own identity. Styron, Blauner and 'Jack' in the New Zealand study are presented as standing in some way in relation to their illness. For 'Jack' depression is a hard road that must be gone down, for Styron and Blauner 'aberrant biochemical' processes lead to the experience of destructive suicidal impulses. Each describes themselves as 'depressed'. The assumption of pathological identities, the understanding of suicidal thoughts in terms of mental illness, even the metaphors used, are drawn from authoritative, scientific explanations of suicide. Expert accounts of suicide do not just reflect or represent reality in some way, but can also act to constitute the means by which the self and the world are experienced by those who come to see themselves as suicidal or mentally ill. Such processes of subject formation in relation to authoritative truths create or enable possibilities of experience, some of which could be said to be positive (a diminishing of moral responsibility, the provision of a framework of understanding and the possibility of treatment and cure), but they simultaneously constrain, most notably in terms of a sense of the inevitability of depression and suicide, a feeling of the 'illness' being out of one's control, and the exclusion of other, possibly more helpful, explanatory schemas (suicide determined more by social injustice than individual pathology, suicide as a form of resistance, an act of voluntary choice that could be read as noble, or a rational, responsible act). The next section explores similar issues with regard to the formation of clinical subjects in relation to suicide.

The discursive formation of the 'responsible, accountable and culpable clinician'

With almost all suicidal individuals taken to be in some way mentally ill (and often taking themselves to be ill) a number of consequences follow. Most obviously, once designated as mentally ill and as a 'danger to themselves', responsibility for their care and safety passes to others – most usually mental health services.

Cutcliffe and Stevenson (2007) discuss the issue in terms of 'body ownership', with mental health professionals read as taking temporary charge of suicidal patients' bodies while they remain a threat to themselves. As they note, 'the "power" to assume ownership of other people's bodies is enshrined in the mental health laws of numerous countries'

(p. 166). Obviously, such a situation is not necessarily problematic. As the authors state:

there are ample examples of when assuming the temporary ownership of another person's body resulted in a positive outcome and the thanks/appreciation of the person, e.g. when the basic rights of suicidal people are removed, forced hospitalization, restricted access to means and the person recovers to the extent that they thank the formal mental health carers. (Cutcliffe and Stevenson, 2007, p. 167)

Another issue alongside the benefits or otherwise to the patient, concerns the effects on staff of being repeatedly placed in 'possession' of another's body, one that is read as dangerous – intent on harm or destruction. The clinician is constituted as the responsible, reasonable agent in relation to the irresponsible, unreasonable (and probably irrational) patient. In terms of the relations of power immanent in such an arrangement, clinicians undertake a number of operations and procedures that position them in a dominant position in relation to the suicidal patient, certainly in hospital settings where there is an expectation that they will observe and control the patient's body in often the most detailed and exact way by means of confinement, surveillance (often continuous), containment and restraint. Even in less 'controlled' community environments clinicians are expected to be able to accurately assess the level of risk presented by the patient, to record and share this information and to document that they have done so, and to manage the risk of suicide in such a way as to prevent its occurrence (Appleby et al., 1999; World Health Organization, 2000a; Jobes, 2006). The reasonableness of such measures is certainly hard to fault if one accepts the assumptions upon which they are based – i.e. the diminution or absence of reason and responsibility in the mentally ill. Once individuals are constituted as dangerous and irresponsible, it is of course prudent to take steps to ensure that they are 'managed' appropriately. For the clinician, however, such responsibility can be physically and emotionally demanding. Cutcliffe and Stevenson (2007) highlight the emotional demands on clinicians, particularly mental health nurses, and state that 'even when there is a successful outcome, there is a good deal of stress experienced' (p. 152). A completed suicide can have a very strong negative impact on the worker (Kleespies et al., 1993), with one study suggesting that clinician survivors often experience stress levels equivalent to those of bereaved patients (Kleespies et al., 1990). Jobes et al. (2000) outline some of the effects such deaths may have: 'Often therapists have high levels of self-blame and guilt about their role in the patient's suicide, along with fears of losing standing with professional colleagues (Tanney, 1995). Many therapists lose confidence in their professional competence and may fear relatives' reactions and the possibility of malpractice suits (Valente, 1994)' (p. 548).

It is perhaps worth pausing and considering how the demands placed on mental health clinicians compare with those placed on general medical, nursing and other staff, who are also responsible for discharging their duties safely and effectively in relation to their sick patients, and can be held accountable if they fail to do so. There are some differences in how each are positioned, however. Oyebode (2005) uses the example of coronary heart disease as a contrast to suicide:

the subtle difference between suicide as a mortality measure in mental illness and death from coronary artery disease should not be ignored. The patient has a direct relationship with his own death in suicide, whereas the patient's own action is only distally related to his death from coronary artery disease. Thus, the degree to which clinicians or services are responsible for a suicide death is far less than for coronary artery disease death. Yet, in the current environment and sustained by documents such as the Confidential Inquiry reports and *An Organisation with a Memory* (Department of Health, 2000), the clinician's role and room to influence the outcome is quite often exaggerated. (p. 83)

In addition, deaths due to natural causes are often read as inevitable and unavoidable. They can usually be understood in terms of the natural processes at work, and it is often clear what procedures are effective in preventing or treating the condition. It is thus possible to say with a degree of precision whether 'correct' treatments were administered and consequently staff are able work within a more certain set of expectations and guidelines. With suicidal patients there is, as yet, no evidence base to fall back on so as to determine what works or doesn't (Oyebode, 2005), yet such deaths are usually read as both preventable and avoidable (Appleby et al., 1999; Appleby et al., 2001; Appleby et al., 2006). In addition, in general medical fields the tools of prevention and treatment are somewhat impersonal – drugs, surgeons' knives, medical dressings, etc. Within mental health it is often the 'self', or perhaps more accurately, the relationship between clinician and patient, that is the means of treatment. A suicide can thus represent, to the mental health professional, a rejection not only of the service they work in, or the treatment offered, but also of something more personal.

In addition to being held responsible for the safety of another, mental health staff are almost always held accountable for their actions following a death by suicide of a patient. This may be by means of informal discussion within teams or investigation by managers, or more formally in terms of an internal review or appearance as witness in a coroner's court. Such scrutiny of practice can again be justified in terms of ensuring the safety of those deemed to be a risk to themselves and reassuring patients, relatives and friends, managers and other staff that all is being done to prevent suicide.

Sometimes, staff are judged to be culpable in not adequately discharging their duties in relation to the suicidal patient, and can be charged with negligence. Oyebode (2006) discusses the possible grounds for a claim of negligence in relation to medical practitioners and suicide, but the grounds are also applicable to other clinicians:

Suicides are common causes of negligence claims. In a case of foreseeable but unforeseen suicide it is usually alleged that the doctor failed properly to assess the patient and thus did not recognise the risk. In the case of foreseeable but unprevented suicide the allegation is of failure properly to supervise or restrain a patient whose risk of suicide is already recognised. Premature discharge, negligent discharge or unjustified freedom of movement can also be alleged as the basis of a foreseeable but unforeseen suicide. (p. 225)

Clinicians can therefore be held accountable, and found culpable, within a court of law.

The view that suicide is preventable, and is therefore avoidable, has been reinforced by the reports of the UK National Confidential Inquiry into Suicide and Homicide by People with Mental Illness. This national research project was established at the University of Manchester in 1996, and has to date produced a number of rather tellingly titled publications:
      Safer Services (Appleby *et al.*, 1999),
      Safety First (Appleby *et al.*, 2001), and
      Avoidable Deaths (Appleby *et al.*, 2006).
These reports have had a tendency to infer that deficiencies in services could account for some suicides. *Safer Services* (Appleby *et al.*, 1999), for example, reported, '[t]he Inquiry's findings suggest the need for substantial changes to the way that mental health services currently operate. Some of these concern broad topics such as service priorities, training policy and information transfer; others concern specific aspects of clinical care' (p. 79). *Safety First* concluded that:

Inquiry recommendations are intended to achieve three kinds of change in service activity:
• General improvements in care that should improve safety
• Increased focus on the patient groups and treatment settings in whom most suicides/homicides occur
• Specific actions targeting particular features of suicides/homicides. (Appleby *et al.*, 2001, p. 149)

On occasion, there has been an inference that poorly trained and motivated staff could be an impediment to 'safer services', and the most recent report, *Avoidable Deaths*, sought to address the issue more directly:

It is time to change the widespread view that individual deaths are inevitable – such a view is bound to discourage staff from taking steps to improve safety. It may be a reaction to the criticism of services and individuals that can happen when serious incidents occur. Therefore, if mental health staff are to give up the culture of inevitability, it is up to commentators outside clinical practice to give up the culture of blame, to which it is in part a self-protective reaction. (Appleby *et al.*, 2006, p. 17).

It is perhaps not so much that there exists a 'culture of blame' that leads clinicians to conclude that not all suicides are avoidable and that some come to be seen as inevitable. The difficulties in predicting such deaths are well known (Pokorny, 1983, 1993; Shergill and Szmukler, 1998; Geddes, 1999; Eagles *et al.*, 2001; Simon, 2006) and the apparent fatalism of clinicians may have more to do with an understanding of the limitations of their ability to prevent suicide. Clinicians, however, continue to be constituted as responsible for another's life, and such a position is inevitable given the formation of the suicidal patient as irresponsible and unreasonable. Although invested with many powers to ensure the patients' safety within such a relationship their power is far from total, for the patient has always the option of removing at a stroke any authority the worker may have had (cf. Foucault, in Bernauer and Rasmussen, 1987, p. 12). Then, in the wake of suicide, the clinicians' conduct can become the focus of inquiry, and censure may follow.

Suicide prevention

If suicide is a consequence of mental illness, it follows that the prevention of suicide should rest on the detection and treatment of these conditions. This is the argument most commonly made within 'suicidology' by psychiatrists, psychologists, psychotherapists, etc. Kay Redfield Jamison, for example, writes; '[t]he causes of suicide lie, for the most part, in an individual's predisposing temperament and genetic vulnerabilities; in severe psychiatric illness; and in acute psychological stress. Addressing only one of these causes at the expense of others is unlikely to be enough to keep suicide at bay' (1999, p. 236). Thus suicide prevention is diagrammed by reference to the mentally ill individual. It is the biologically vulnerable, psychiatrically ill individual that is the focus of prevention, rather than a relationally defined person situated within the context of culturally meaningful 'life events':

Suicide usually requires multiple 'hits' – a biological predisposition, a major psychiatric illness, and an acute life stress – but only some of these 'hits' are amenable to change. There is, for example, relatively little a doctor can do to control many of the major stresses in a patient's life: they occur too randomly, and thus are difficult to predict and even more difficult to govern. But there *are* things that can be done to influence or treat the underlying biological vulnerabilities to suicide, as well as the mental illnesses closely linked to suicidal behaviour. (Jamison, 1999, p. 239)

The suicidal patient is advised to become 'well informed about mental illness', to be 'actively involved in their own clinical care', and to seek out 'books, lectures, and support groups that provide information about suicide prevention, depressive and psychotic illnesses, and alcoholism and drug abuse. They should question their clinicians about their diagnosis, treatment, and prognosis and, if concerned about a lack of collaborative effort or progress in their clinical condition, seek a second opinion' (p. 258). The suicidal individual is read almost entirely as a patient – biologically vulnerable and mentally ill – and is asked to further immerse themselves in this 'role'. As has been acknowledged, the compulsory ontology of pathology in relation to suicide opens up the possibility for diagnosing and treating suicidal patients. As such it can offer hope, and reposition the individual as a victim of illness rather than a perpetrator of some form of transgression. But such subjection, it is argued, also acts to restrict the resources that can be brought to bear in terms of alternative readings of a desire to die (as an act of a subjected individual who believes their life 'unlivable', for example, or a strategy of resistance to being so pathologised), and thus closes off the possibility that the 'role' of psychiatric patient can feel unbearable for many.

Preventing suicide by means of identifying and treating mental illness possesses a strategic logic that enables its diffusion. As mental illness is said to be found in all areas of life, present in a wide range of ages and ethnic groupings, then it follows that there is a role for mental health education to prevent suicide by means of screening and 'psy' intervention across a range of populations and sites as exemplified by the National Suicide Prevention Strategy for England (NSPSE) launched in September, 2002 by the UK Department of Health. The language of the NSPSE suggests, at times, the planning of a military action – with talk of strategic actions, targets, objectives, implementation plans, identifying 'hotspots', and combating discrimination. There are high risk 'target groups': 'people who are currently or have recently been in contact with mental health services', people who self-harm, young men, prisoners, and 'high risk occupational groups' – such as farmers, doctors and nurses (p. 12). Further, a number of other populations are targeted for the promotion of their 'mental well-being'. There is set up something akin to a war on suicide, conducted via an attack on mental ill health and the targeting of populations deemed to be vulnerable to such illnesses, or at the least the absence of mental well-being. There is, of course, a certain logic or rationale behind all such activities. Suicide is habitually read as a kind of abnormal or pathological act, the result of an internal, destructive 'drive', one liable to manifest itself within specific populations constituted as risky. Such groups – the mentally ill, drug users, criminals, even teen-agers – are taken to be prone to dangerous behaviours due to their poor mental health, and thus in need of treatment, part of which may involve containing their dangerous propensities. Mental health professionals, in turn, are charged with identifying, assessing and managing such tenden-cies, and are held accountable and possibly culpable if found wanting in the execution of their duties, despite the many uncertainties that exist over the utility of their practices.

Conclusions

An attempt has been made in this chapter to map what are taken to be contemporary truths of suicide. The texts analysed are by no means marginal pieces, selected somehow to illustrate a prior ideological argu-ment. The UK government suicide prevention strategy and policy docu-ments, a bestselling book by a professor of psychiatry at Johns Hopkins University, textbooks written by experts in the field, newspaper reports from two national UK publications, a report from the Samaritans, and guidelines produced by the World Health Organization are not peripheral pieces, but rather, it is argued, represent mainstream thinking on the subject. It is, of course, not difficult to locate writings that interpret suicide in terms of some form of illness or abnormality and that is, to an extent, the point of this chapter: suicide is, almost always, taken to be an act of pathology. The ways in which such closed readings of acts of self-accomplished death may be considered problematic are considered next.

4   Problematising a contemporary 'regime of truth' in relation to suicide

Problematising contemporary discursive formations of suicide

Within the field that has come to be known as 'suicidology', suicide itself is constituted as an object of scientific study, as are suicidal patients. Epidemiological studies seek to establish the truth of suicide in terms of quantifiable factors such as age, sex, and means while psychological autopsy studies have sought to correlate acts of self-destruction with categories of mental illness. More recently, studies into the biology and genetics of suicide risk have looked to find evidence of neuro-chemical, neuro-anatomical or genetic abnormalities that could explain why people kill themselves. It is this meeting of science and medicine that dominates the field of suicide studies. In practice too, for the most part those considered expert on suicide and the management of suicidal people are doctors, particularly psychiatrists. Other professions – psychology, social work, nursing, occupational therapy – tend to work within a medically delineated, and to a large extent controlled, space. Through this meeting of scientific study and medical/psychiatric practice the truths of suicide have come to be (and continue to be) formed. Such ways of thinking and acting come together to produce and reproduce a form of suicide that could be characterised as individual, pathological and medical. Suicide is taken as arising as a consequence of mental illness, a form of pathology or abnormality situated within the individual, and it is thus a matter of medical/psychiatric concern. It is now difficult to talk of suicide without recourse to some notion of mental illness, usually depression, or reference to the 'mental state' of the person involved. Margaret Pabst Battin notes that suicide has become 'primarily a matter of mental illness' and a 'tragedy to be prevented'. Battin also draws attention to the paucity of debate and critical thinking on the subject, with the 'only substantive discussions about suicide in current Western culture' concerning 'access to psychotherapy, or improved suicide-prevention programs, or more effective antidepressant medications' (2005, p. 164).

That the dominant view on suicide tends towards the 'normatively monolithic' need not be a problem in itself. What can be construed as problematic are some of the consequences that follow – the 'truth effects' – in terms of (1) practices and the formation of certain objects, subjects and subjectivities, and (2) in the foreclosure or marginalisation of possibilities for other readings of acts of self-accomplished death. If the truths of suicide are formed along medical/psychiatric lines, and if these are then carefully disseminated through a regulated media, then what could be said to be the effects?

Contemporary formations of suicide as problematic

As has been argued, suicide is constructed within dominant discourses as a unitary act with a singular meaning – pathology. The statement in *Night Falls Fast* (Jamison, 1999) that to ignore 'the biological and psychopathological causes and treatments of suicidal behavior' is 'clinically and ethically indefensible' (p. 255) is indicative of how strongly such a position has come to be maintained and defended. What such a stance makes difficult is the development of other ways of constituting suicide and the formation of alternative objects, concepts and subjectivities in relation to self-accomplished death. Instead there is a continual reproduction of suicide as the tragic act of a mentally unwell individual. As this is taken to be necessary, real and true – described here in terms of a compulsory ontology – it becomes difficult to critique, and shortcomings and negative (even if unintended) consequences that follow from so constituting suicide are for the most part unexplored.

In looking to understand how contemporary formations of suicide may be problematic the starting point should probably be that suicide itself is taken to be a problem, at a social level, at an institutional level for psychiatry and the other 'psy' disciplines, and at the level of suicidal individuals and suicide survivors (that is, the family and friends of those who have died by suicide). It is an event that engenders suffering – and this is in many ways the central issue. In terms of a practice of critique, certain questions follow from this; in what ways does the production and reproduction of the truths of suicide outlined above act to contribute to the maintenance of such problematic events? How might such truths also lead to either an exacerbation or a diminution of suffering in relation to self-accomplished death? These are not easily answered. However, as this book has set out to be a critical enquiry into the formation of suicide as pathological and medical, it is necessary to address the ways in which contemporary approaches to suicide could be said to relate to the prevention of suicide, and suffering in relation to suicide, in less than straightforward ways.

The problematic nature of the object and subjects most often (re)produced   As outlined, attempts to explain suicide by reference to notions of abnormality and pathology often fall back on ideas and images of unseen, unhealthy forces, impulses and desires. An analogy with physical conditions that lead to death is often implied, particularly when seeking to establish a connection between mental illness and death by suicide, but as yet it remains unclear how it is that mental illness leads to self-destructive acts. There is something of a theoretical and methodological paradox at the heart of medical research in relation to suicide; objective knowledge is sought and often claimed yet the objects of enquiries are seemingly nebulous and somewhat elusive – mental states, 'private' thoughts and feelings of research subjects, unlocated drives and impulses, destructive desires, connecting pathways from the molecular to the molar, from the chemical to the level of behaviour.

Part of the difficulty for medical science in relation to suicide would seem to be that a behaviour or action, or even potential action, is framed in terms of illness or disease. Aetiological links have yet to be made between death by suicide and mental illnesses in the same way as between heart disease and death by heart failure. Is suicide a disease? This is no longer claimed. Is it a symptom? In the latest edition of the *Diagnostic and Statistical Manual* of the American Psychiatric Association (DSM-IV-TR, 2000) the category 'Major Depressive Episode' includes as symptoms 'recurrent suicidal ideation without a specific plan, or a suicide attempt or a specific plan for committing suicide'. So thinking of suicide or making plans can be said to be symptomatic of major depression. Again, the desire to establish an objective medical science of suicide that has as the object of enquiry an individual's thoughts and plans in relation to a possible future event would seem to be somewhat problematic. What would seem to be required is some form of introspective examination on the part of the patient and a confession to the doctor for such symptoms to become known, with all the epistemological difficulties entailed in such practices. It may well be that researchers overcome such problems and establish a science of suicide in line with other medical specialties. It would of course be no bad thing if accurate diagnosis and effective treatments became available for suicidal patients. It has been a long-term hope of many researchers and clinicians that a test for suicidality could be developed – perhaps a simple blood test that when analysed would reveal a susceptibility to self-destructive behaviour, or perhaps genetic tests that would enable researchers to pin-point those predisposed to such actions (e.g. Asberg *et al.*, 1976; Stanley and Mann, 1983; Pandey *et al.*, 1995). Yet, it seems hard to imagine that the complexities involved in human behaviours such as suicide could be predicted by means of identifying biological markers. The apparent heterogeneity of motives for acts of self-accomplished death would seem to make the development of a 'one test catches all' unlikely – for would the biological markers of an act that could be characterised as primarily driven by anger be the same as for one undertaken in despair, or one made after long contemplation and reflection that life was no longer worth living? The consequences of a high number of false positives, or indeed false negatives, would also make such a test difficult to administer without creating further problems.

Once established as a medical concern, suicidal patients are obviously offered treatment – these days most usually some form of pharmacological intervention. Here, too, problems have arisen. It would be expected, given the degree of certainty that has been expressed within psychiatry that suicide occurs as a consequence of mental illness and equally that effective pharmacological treatments of these illnesses are available, that suicide rates would have fallen in line with the increased use of such drugs. Herman van Praag (2005) summarises; '[s]ince depression and suicide are postulated to be causally related, and antidepressants are considered to be an effective treatment in depression, one may rightly expect suicide rates to have gone down in proportion to prescription increases. However, this has not happened' (p. 240). After considering possible explanations, Van Praag concludes:

Over the last decades the rate of completed suicide has remained quite stable, and that of suicide attempts seems to have even increased. These are puzzling observations, since depression is the major precursor of suicide and antidepressants have been increasingly used in the treatment of depression. These observations have not attracted sufficient attention, possibly because they do not accord with consensus opinions about depression treatment in psychiatry today. (van Praag, 2005, p. 254)

The possibilities excluded by van Praag include the ineffectiveness of antidepressants, that such drugs increase the risk of suicide in some patients (as asserted by Healy, 1994, 2000), or the poor 'fit' between formulations of suicide as a medical problem to be tackled in the same way as heart disease or pneumonia, and an event or form of death such as suicide.

Despite the difficulties apparent in medical formulations and treatment of the suicidal, medicine, and most usually psychiatry, remain at the forefront of research and practice in relation to suicide prevention. Interestingly, what is often absent from psychiatric accounts are descriptions of the most commonly used form of treatment, namely, the confinement, observation, containment and restraint of the suicidal patient. Whilst many books, chapters and journal articles discuss at length issues of diagnosis, pharmacological interventions, risk factors and prevention strategies at population and individual levels, comparatively little is said in relation to the most common practices implemented in the name of medical treatment. Brian Mishira, Director of the Centre for Research and Intervention on Suicide and Euthanasia, Quebec, writes (in Cutcliffe and Stevenson, 2007): '[o]ne would think that there must be a vast amount of scientific literature about how to treat inpatients in order to reduce their suicide risk. However, this is simply not the case. There is a paucity of writings that specifically examine what must occur during a hospital stay in order to reduce the risk of suicidal behaviours' (p. xiii).

Even those professions whose job it is to implement such procedures, most usually nursing staff, have not explored the issues that arise with regard to such practices in any detail. Cutcliffe and Stevenson (2007) in the *Care of the Suicidal Person*, talk of a 'dearth of evidence and theory to inform nurses' of how to safeguard people at risk of suicide (p. 24). Why this absence? One possibility could be that such practices, although medically prescribed and most usually implemented under the supervision of medical staff, are just not *medical* enough to attract the interest of researchers. Constructed within a medico-scientific framework, practices such as forced confinement and physical treatment in hospital, constant watching, restrictions on movement and physical restraint when deemed necessary do not sit easily. Hardly anywhere else in medicine are such ways of working to be found. A science of confinement, of restraint, or other daily practices in the treatment of suicidal patients is unlikely to be forthcoming.

What is more certain is that suicidal individuals will continue to be constituted as patients. Here certain difficulties could be said to arise in terms of the subjectivities constituted in relation to those truths that take suicide to be an act of pathology, and the experiences of patients subjected to those practices seen as essential to their treatment. Suicidal patients, as has been noted, are taken to be objects of knowledge within medical/psychiatric approaches to the problem of suicide. A desire to die is not merely treated, but is usually first identified and assessed and then managed (e.g. Jobes, 2006). So the suicidal person can be subjected to certain procedures in order to ascertain the risk they present to themselves. Now, such measures could be experienced as helpful by the client – they may feel relief that someone cares enough about them to enquire as to whether they wish to end their life, and the reasons why this may be so. However, there is also the possibility that such questioning may be experienced as objectifying and perhaps dehumanising; that is they may feel that the central concern is less with their experiences and reasons for feeling suicidal, or with the forging of supportive human ties, and more with the accurate evaluation of their risk, and prevention by any means necessary, of their acting on their 'impulses' or destructive propensities.

Equally, clinicians, even those who wish to prioritise some form of 'engagement' over assessment and management (not that the two are necessarily separate activities, just they can become so), in being positioned as responsible and accountable in relation to the dangerous and irresponsible patient, would themselves be at risk of censure if they were not seen to be acting in accordance with 'good practice' – usually taken to mean the accurate assessment, observation, containment and treatment of the risk of suicide. Such practices may well be experienced as dehumanising by the client, but are required by the organisation. Cutcliffe and Stevenson (2007) talk of observation of suicidal patients by mental health nursing staff as 'a system that was designed originally to inform (absent) psychiatrists and now, at least in part, is concerned with meeting the needs of the healthcare organization; it is primarily a "defensive" practice', and that, further, it is 'a crude, "custodial" orientated form of intervention to meet the highly complex, convoluted and sophisticated care needs of this client group' (p. 29). They also conclude not only that observation does not address the needs of the client group, but that it is also highly stressful for the nursing staff. In having constituted the patient as an object of knowledge, in having conceptualised suicide as arising due to an internal, physiologically based form of pathology, the 'management' of such a force would involve assessing its strength, observing the patient for signs of its eruption, and containing or restraining the patient if they show signs of acting on such urges or impulses. For both patient and clinician, then, such practices may be experienced negatively.

Another aspect to the continual linking of mental pathology or abnormalities to risk of suicide is that those diagnosed as mentally ill are confronted with the issue of their own danger to themselves. To be designated as mentally ill is to be constituted as a potential risk – sometimes to others, more often to oneself. What is more, an adequate explanation of why this may be so is not available. As noted, the exact means by which mental illnesses could be said to lead to death by suicide are not generally known, so patients do not have the same understanding they might have if confronted by a potentially lethal physical disease or illness. Instead, 'chemical imbalances' may be invoked by the clinician to explain the desire to die. Again, such an explanation may not be experienced negatively, and may in fact help the individual feel that there is a 'natural', physiological or biological explanation for their experiences. Such a position could act as a protector against any charges (from others or from the person themselves) of moral weakness or failure. The absolving of blame or responsibility can be a relief. Alternatively, to believe that a malign, destructive force could overwhelm one's reason and lead to self-destruction is surely not a comfortable experience.

Further, to the wider public, mental illness is reproduced as dangerous and unpredictable, with all the attendant difficulties that arise with regard to stigmatisation and marginalisation of those designated mentally ill.

The necessity of expert knowledge at the expense of other ways of understanding The positing of an internal, destructive force, either as an element of a mental illness or biological abnormality or in some way secondary to them, as a cause of suicide can be problematical for a number of reasons. For a start, the question of the presence or absence of such a force within an individual, and the likelihood of it being acted upon if present, becomes something necessitating expert judgement. An understanding of suicide is now taken to involve the acquisition of a range of specialist knowledge – of mental illness, of the signs and symptoms associated with self-destructive acts, of different treatments, possibly even of specialist imaging equipment, biological processes, neuro-anatomy and -chemistry, and of laboratory procedures and equipment (see Colt, 2006, pp. 299–303). Yet, despite such specialisation and the accumulation of ever more knowledge, suicide seems to remain a mysterious act, and indeed it could be argued is becoming more so. Such a view is not intended to imply that suicide is in fact less complex than it is presented, or that the endeavour to locate a cause of suicide will not at some stage bear fruit. Rather, it is to suggest that the continual reproduction of suicide as primarily a question of individual, internal, unseen pathology is to create a form of suicide that moves increasingly beyond the comprehension of non-specialists. It is to create an inexplicable act for most people, one not readily grounded in everyday understandings. As a consequence there is a constant deferral to authority and expertise in relation to self-destructive acts – a knowing that, in the last analysis, suicide can best be explained by others more knowledgeable.

Again, this is not to suggest that the possibilities for the production of useful knowledge do not increase alongside the application of ever more specialist investigations, but rather that such an approach can lead to the exclusion, or at least the devaluing, of other forms of knowledge. Foucault talked on occasion of 'subjugated' knowledge (e.g. 1980, pp. 81–2), that is, those forms of knowing that have been hidden by more dominant accounts or those considered 'insufficiently elaborated knowledges: naive knowledges, hierarchically inferior knowledges, knowledges that are below the required level of erudition or scientificity' (2003, p. 7) and thus are disqualified or marginalised. With regard to suicide, it could be said that the dominance of certain ways of thinking and acting – the compulsory ontology of pathology that leads to suicide being understood almost solely in relation to notions of illness, diagnosis, treatment, prevention, etc. – has disqualified other ways of approaching the subject. However, the uncovering of subjugated knowledge with regards to suicide is difficult, not least because those who have killed themselves are not around to tell of their experiences. Suicide notes, it is generally held, do not cast much light on the subject as they tend, more often than not, to be brief and pragmatic (giving specific instructions regarding finances, etc.) (Shneidman, 1973; Maris *et al.*, 2000), and those few books or journal papers that have set out the stories of survivors of suicide attempts have tended to frame and interpret these for the most part in terms of causal relationships between pathologies or abnormalities of the individual and self-destructive behaviours (e.g. Shneidman, 1996, 2004; Heckler, 1996; O'Connor *et al.*, 2000).

What is perhaps then absent, or at least in short supply, is a way of discussing suicide outside the terms offered by psychiatry and medicine. A return to simple moral injunction would perhaps not be much of a step forward, so it is necessary to consider what other, possibly useful, ways of knowing in relation to suicide are excluded or marginalised by the insistence on reading suicide almost solely in terms of pathology.

The foreclosing or marginalisation of alternative readings of suicide

What alternative readings of suicide are foreclosed or marginalised, and in what ways may they be of use to service users, the suicidal, relatives and friends of those who have ended their own lives?

Self-accomplished death as a voluntary act   Accounts that take suicide to be pathological in nature have often been opposed by 'voluntarist' ones that foreground, in the place of the victim of mental illness, the 'free-choosing', autonomous individual. There are, of course, many nuances to such a position, but as examples one could think of the Romantics in the nineteenth century, for whom suicide was glorified as the ultimate expression of individual liberty (Lieberman, 2003; Battin, 2005). More recently Jean Améry (1999) and Thomas Szasz (1999) have argued that it is a right of each individual to kill themselves. However, it is the belief that an individual has chosen to end their own life that is often the most troubling for survivors of suicide, that is those bereaved by the suicide of somebody close to them (Department of Health, 2006). Here, understanding death as caused by mental illness can act to lessen feelings of guilt, anger or rejection. Contemporary accounts that take suicide to be caused by mental illness or abnormal brain chemistry thus could be read as helpful in this regard.

The reading of suicide as a voluntary act, however, may lessen the sense that such deaths are necessarily tragic. The idea that such an 'exit' has been freely chosen can open the door to descriptions of suicide as brave, noble, dignified, fearless, perhaps even heroic. Such formulations are no longer available when the act is taken as determined by illness. One can be brave in the face of illness, maybe heroic in fighting the disease, but suicide here is rather of the nature of a succumbing or a defeat to a superior force.

For mental health staff, the idea that suicide could be considered a voluntary act would have implications for how they are positioned in relation to the suicidal. As has been discussed, a belief in suicide as the tragic outcome of untreated or under-treated mental illness lends itself fairly clearly to clinicians being constituted as the responsible and accountable party, and to the main priority in any interaction with suicidal patients being the prevention of suicide by almost any means available. When suicide is understood as a voluntary act, or as a form of dying that a person had a *right* to choose, clinicians have no such role. Indeed, suicide prevention on the grounds of a paternalistic acting in the best interests of the incapable or irresponsible 'other' would no longer be justifiable. The finer points of such ethical issues have been discussed at length elsewhere (Battin, 1982; Fairburn, 1995; Burgess and Hawton, 1998; Cutcliffe and Stevenson, 2007) and do not need to be rehearsed in detail here. It is worth noting, however, that psychiatric formulations of suicide do not generally give space to considerations of agency or autonomy, but rather take suicide to be determined by illness.

If suicide can be conceived as voluntary, at least to some degree, then the door is also opened to consideration of the act in political terms – if politics is taken to arise where choices are possible in a contested cultural field (Butler, 1997). Such a position then opens up the possibility of interpreting suicide in terms of resistance, refutation or protest. Power relations and questions of social justice and inequalities could come more to the fore in discussions of suicide.

Suicide as a cultural product, formed in relation to authoritative accounts The works of Foucault would suggest that an easy adoption of a 'voluntarist' position is itself problematic (cf. Osborne, 2005, pp. 284–7, 292). As outlined in chapter 2, Foucault's writings sought to cast doubt on the notion of the sovereign subject. In Foucault's account, certainly when addressing processes of subjection (e.g. 1977), we are formed and re-formed always in relation to cultural norms and truths, and the belief in there being a separate 'space' within us that we could retreat into in order to avoid such cultural forces, that we can ever act with complete freedom, is taken to be no more than another effect of relations of power. With regard to suicide, such a reading would allow focus to shift to those cultural forces that act to constitute suicidal subjects and not retreat into either a simple 'voluntarist' position whereby suicides are understood solely in terms of individual choice, or one where suicide is read as primarily caused by 'naturally arising' kinds of pathology. In both forms of analysis what could be considered cultural and historical 'lines of force' that come together to form suicide and the suicidal tend to be dismissed as an irrelevance, or do not even enter into the equation. In 'voluntarist' accounts, historical and cultural forces are seen as very much of secondary importance as the individual is read as separate, beyond the reach, for the most part, of culture and history, and thus free-choosing. In accounts that foreground pathology, the illnesses taken to cause suicide are also read as largely outside the influence of time and place, with the expression of the illness, rather than its underlying essence, being subject to cultural variation.

Thought of in this way – that is suicide and the suicidal as cultural products – self-accomplished deaths can come to be read less as statements concerning the internal, mental state of isolated individuals, but rather as outcomes of a play of culturally situated, relationally unequal forces. Issues of social justice, of fairness, the means by which certain groups come to be marginalised and vilified within a culture can come to the fore in discussions of the reasons why a person may have ended their life. Rather than suicide being interpreted either as an unreasonable, irrational act, determined by illness, or a rational course of action freely chosen, it could perhaps be understood as a product of cultural forces situated outside the individual. Such forces could be understood as constituting the suicidal individual, and even of forming, over time, the act itself. So conceived, psychiatric discourse and practices (and those of related disciplines) no longer stand 'outside' suicide and the suicidal, battling to contain and neutralise a naturally arising destructive force, but rather can be understood as operating within a culture that itself acts to form all aspects of suicide. Here, truths of suicide can be read not merely as objective, 'external' reports of events seen from outside and judged only in terms of their perceived veracity, but rather as productive or formative elements in a complex play of forces. To state that mental illnesses can kill, that suicide is caused by abnormal or pathological processes located within the individual, is to produce an effect and not just to report on what is thought to be true.

What is suggested here is not in any way an alternative theory of suicide, or even that such a thing would be desirable, but rather that through a sort of realignment, a change in our line of sight, it may be possible to 'make visible' that which has, over time, slipped from view. That is to say that the production and circulation of truths in relation to suicide may not be free of effects and that it may be possible to isolate and examine what these may be. Or put differently, the relationship between scientific medicine/psychiatry and suicide may be more tangled and complex than merely being a relationship between a pathological, 'naturally arising' force of destruction, and the identification, containment and treatment of that force and the ongoing accurate, truthful reporting of its nature in professional journals and books, at conferences and in the wider media. In order to understand more fully the complex workings of such a relationship it may be necessary to first disavow ourselves of the notion that present-day formulations represent expressions of universal truths in relation to suicide. Some attempt was made in the last chapter to demonstrate the processes by which such an effect is achieved within authoritative texts. It may also be necessary to find examples of self-accomplished deaths so different from our own that the contingency, that is the historical and cultural specificity, of present-day understandings is brought into view. Then, the means by which contemporary truths have come to be formed over time could be traced, and their effects mapped, in order to show that medical science (and later psychiatry), rather than standing 'outside' suicide looking in, has, in fact, acted to constitute the object of its investigations and practices in a somewhat problematic way.

Conclusions

In an interview in 1980 Foucault spoke of his work in the following terms: '[m]y problem is to know how men govern (themselves and others) by means of the production of truth' (in Castel, 1994, p. 238). Foucault clarifies that here he does not mean 'the production of true statements but the administering of realms in which the practice of the true and the false can be both regulated and relevant' (p. 238). The analysis presented in this and the previous chapter has sought to cast light on the means by which truths of suicide are produced, administered and regulated, and their effects in terms of the objects, concepts and subjectivities that are formed. An attempt has been made to show how such truths may be read as problematic, and it is argued that the truths and 'truth effects' discussed are not inevitable or necessary, but contingent and thus open to change. One means by which the universality or inevitability of 'taken-for-granted' truths can be thrown into question is by undertaking a 'history of the present'. By examining the past, Foucault argued, we may better understand the problems of the present. In so doing, the past can be made to be no longer present and new ways of thinking and acting may emerge (O'Farrell, 2005). The next part of the book thus explores the contingency of our truths of suicide, the means by which such truths have come to be formed over time, and looks to understand what was formed in relation to these truths, in terms of objects, concepts and subjects, as well as what they foreclosed.

Part III

A history of the present

It is one of my targets to show people that a lot of things that are a part of their landscape – that people think are universal – are the result of some very precise historical changes. All my analyses are against the idea of universal necessities in human existence. They show the arbitrariness of institutions and show which space of freedom we still enjoy, and how many changes can still be made.   (Michel Foucault, 1988b)

The hypothesis I would like to put forward is that there are two histories of truth. The first is a kind of internal history of truth, the history of a truth that rectifies itself in terms of its own principles of regulation: it's the history of truth as it is constructed in or on the basis of the history of the sciences. On the other hand, it seems to me that there are in society (or at least in our societies) other places where truth is formed, where a certain number of games are defined – games through which one sees certain forms of subjectivity, certain object domains, certain types of knowledge come into being – and that, consequently, one can on that basis construct an external, exterior history of truth.   (Michel Foucault, 2002a)

Introduction to Part III

In Part II of the book an attempt was made to map a contemporary 'regime of truth' in relation to suicide. It was argued that certain truths of suicide – as pathological, caused by illnesses or abnormalities located within the individual, and thus primarily a medical/psychiatric concern – arise out of particular relations of power-knowledge.

Such a 'regime of truth' can be difficult to contest – to do so within the terms established by such a power-knowledge configuration is to risk being positioned as both immoral and irrational, as Butler (2004, p. 313) suggests. Equally, to seek to prove that psychopathology is not a causative factor in suicide by the same means that it has been proved to be so is to invite defeat. Instead, the contingencies of such truths need to be highlighted, and attention drawn to relations of power-knowledge involved in their production and circulation – a 'politics of truth'. So an effective critique of the dominant, governing position involves not so much saying it is *wrong*, as showing that things need not necessarily be that way, pointing to the fragility of the dominant view, and highlighting that it may be possible, and useful, to consider other ways of thinking and acting in relation to suicide. Foucault pointed to the need to 'speak about that which is while making it appear as capable of not existing or capable of not being as it is' (in Davidson, 2001, p. 189). One tool in this venture is the 'recourse to history' to show that, 'that which exists didn't always exist, that is to say, that it is always at the confluence of encounters, of accidents, through the course of a fragile, precarious history that things are formed that give us the impression of being the most obvious' (p. 189). By looking to history it may be possible to locate other 'regimes of truth' in relation to suicide, and to map the means by which contemporary realities have come to be formed. In so doing the contingencies of our present truths, experiences and practices may be highlighted. Such a move may act to free us a little from the apparent necessities of the present, the compulsory ontology of pathology discussed in chapters 3 and 4, by showing that other possibilities exist, and have existed, with regard to self-accomplished deaths. At the least it is hoped that by setting out an account of how we came to be as we are in relation to suicide, of how the objects, ideas and subjects that seem so unchanging and unavoidable were formed from contingent historical and cultural events and forces, involving particular relations of power, we may prompt reflection on whether what is taken to be self-evident is as necessary or useful as tends to be argued or assumed. Part III thus draws on accounts from history to call into question the presumed naturalness or inevitability of contemporary truths of suicide.

5 Self-accomplished deaths at other times and in other places: the contingency of contemporary truths in relation to suicide

Descriptions of self-accomplished deaths in ancient Greece and Rome

Both linguist David Daube (1977) and historian Anton van Hooff (1990) have noted that neither classical Greek nor Latin has a single word synonymous with our word 'suicide'. Indeed, van Hooff (1990) lists more than 300 ancient Greek and Latin words and expressions that can be said to describe forms of self-accomplished death, and Daube's (1977) analysis of the linguistics of suicide provides many more.

Examples of Roman phrases include:
- 'voluntary death' (*mors voluntaria*);
- 'destroying oneself' (*conficere se, eximere se, finire se, finem vitae facere, interficere se, occidere se*);
- 'to take the last measure' (*consulere extremis rebus/vitae (durius)*);
- 'to strive after death' (*appetere/oppetere mortem*).

These terms were not euphemistic – that is they were not alternative expressions for an act that was in some way too terrible to name. Rather, 'suicide' did not exist as a concept in either ancient Greece or Rome, and thus the idea of one word or expression did not arise. As van Hooff notes, 'the idea behind these terms obviously is much broader and more diffuse than just "suicide"' (1990, p. 138). Descriptive variety becomes possible when a number of terms are available within a language, and these terms can allow for apparently similar acts to be given different meanings. By contrast, the ubiquitous 'suicide' rather tends to flatten out any such nuances, and we are left with a somewhat impoverished set of resources for constructing meaning around acts of self-accomplished death. As argued, for us suicide has come to mean a tragic death caused by some form of individual mental pathology, and although such ways of thinking have proved productive in terms of the accumulation of knowledge and in the systematic application of preventative practices, in other ways our thought is perhaps too much constrained, as illustrated by the limited responses available to us to make sense of the death of Alice McGovern (see pp. 47–51).

Descriptions of Roman self-accomplished deaths are of interest in that they can highlight, by means of contrast, the contingencies and constraints (as well as freedoms) inherent in our own discourse and practices.

Romana mors: self-accomplished death as relational, philosophical and political

Scholars have long expressed puzzlement over 'suicides' from other cultures and historical periods that seem to deviate from our own understanding of the subject. Timothy Hill (2004), by reference to the forms of self-accomplished death practised by the Roman aristocracy throughout the late Republic and Julio-Claudian Principate, gives reasons as to why this may be. Hill begins his analysis by noting that, as was outlined in the preceding chapters, suicide today is considered primarily an individual act. His comments are worth quoting at length:

> In the modern world, suicide is a grim business. It is understood primarily as an act arising out of intense, morbid, and pathological states of mind, representative of the furthest extreme of human misery. It is above all an isolated act, isolated not only in the sense that suicides of the modern era tend to seclude themselves from others before attempting their final act, but in the sense that suicide is held by modern writers to express a sense of personal alienation so complete that others cannot conceptualize this psychological nadir even in imagination. Suicide is, in this view, a supremely individual act, utterly inscrutable to all outside observers.
> (Hill, 2004, pp. 1–2)

Hill continues, '[h]opeless, despairing, and mentally ill, the suicide is seen in modern literary, psychological, and sociological discourse as driven to death by the intolerable pressure of some peculiarly internalized torment' (p. 2).

It is Hill's argument that Roman 'suicide' is not like this at all. 'To begin with, the *Romana mors* is only very rarely associated with anything even broadly recognizable as "depression", or with any form of pathological state at all' (p. 2). Many scholars, however, convinced of the necessarily pathological nature of self-killing, have been unwilling to move too far from such an understanding in their analyses of Roman self-accomplished deaths (Hill cites Alvarez, 1971, p. 68; Griffin, 1986, pp. 197–8; and Plass, 1995, pp. 133–4 as examples). This process of interpreting other cultures' forms of self-accomplished death according to our own concepts and beliefs touches on an argument of this book – namely that 'suicide' is perhaps too broad an umbrella term for a variety of actions that could more productively be understood by reference to the cultural and historical contexts in which they arose. In contrast, much present-day research would seem to be based on an assumption of an acultural and ahistorical object of study, with true knowledge of the nature of suicide, arrived at by means of psychiatric, psychological and medical research into genetics, biology, neuro-anatomy and -chemistry, held out as a possibility. From such a position – involvement in the accumulation of the truths of an unchanging, universal essence of suicide – Roman descriptions of their ways of death that we would classify as suicide are perplexing, for they do not exhibit what we expect to be there in terms of individual psychopathology. Thus, scholars are forced to explain away the seemingly unemotional, rational, deliberate and resolutely public 'suicides' either as unrepresentative as to what really went on, or as positioning the Roman aristocracy as somehow aberrant in their views and practices with regard to killing themselves, in contrast to every other period in history and to those of ordinary, non-aristocratic, members of Roman society. Alvarez (1971), for example, sees as 'admirable, even enviable' the 'icy heroism' found in descriptions of Roman aristocratic 'suicides', but concludes that 'it also seems, at least from our perspective, curiously unreal. It seems impossible that life and behaviour could ever be so rational, and the will, at the moment of crisis, quite so dependable' (p. 83). 'The overall picture presented by modern writers on the *Romana mors*,' Hill contends, 'is clear: through-out the Late Republic and the Early Empire the Roman aristocracy labored under an artificial and fundamentally wrong-headed conception of suicide' (2004, p. 8). They were either inaccurate in their reporting, or they deviated from a transhistorical norm. Such views preserve present-day truths and belief in an ahistorical essence of suicide, but at the expense of a realisation of the fluidity, the cultural and historical specificity, of any description or act of self-accomplished death.

   In order to understand *Romana mors*, as well as to cast light on the contingency of our own truths of suicide, it may be necessary to question our assumptions regarding agency and the nature of the self, and ask whether what we take to be an individual is applicable to other times and cultures. Whereas modern Western discourse draws upon terms and concepts such as 'identity', 'self', 'character' and 'personality' when discussing the individual in an abstract way, Latin writers, by contrast, tended to make use of 'broad terms such as *nos* ("we/ourselves") and *homines* ("people")', and thus made very little distinction between 'individualized and generic conceptions of the person' (Hill, 2004, p. 16). Hill concludes that 'the Roman self that emerges from Latin writings on suicide is in the final analysis purely socially defined' (p. 17). It is on this point – the very different conceptualisations of the individual – Hill argues, that precludes an easy understanding of *Romana mors*. For despite the acknowledgment of scholars that Roman forms of self-accomplished death were in many ways quite different from suicide today (all note, for example, the highly social character of Roman self-killing in contrast to modern conceptions of an essentially private act), they still work from modern, Western foundationalist presuppositions concerning the autonomy and individuality of the agent, and this serves to effectively render Roman discourse on self-killing incoherent or paradoxical – for Roman perspectives on suicide are only explicable if understood as 'operating entirely without reference to any notion of the self-constituting subjectivity as the sole final reference point of thought and action' (Hill, 2004, p. 15). It is thus perhaps inevitable that 'presentist' value judgements will creep in if acts of Roman self-accomplished death are read by reference to notions of an autonomous, separate, individual agent as the basis for understanding human behaviour. Van Hooff (1990), for example, characterises Roman 'suicides' involving questions of honour as symptomatic of a general malady that affected Roman society as a whole – namely that Romans were 'excessively involved in their social role' (p. 113). By this account suicide remains a symptom of individual pathology, but it is a view that would hold little meaning within a Roman discourse on deaths related to *pudor* or 'sense of honour'.

If the 'self' in Roman self-accomplished death is markedly different from our own conception, and 'psychopathology' something of an alien concept – van Hooff (1990, p. 76), for example, notes that there 'was no interest in the psychic forces which accounted for a suicidal disposition' (here again assuming 'psychic forces' to be an ahistorical fact) – the role of medicine also differed. Rebecca Flemming (2005) writes, in relation to the notion of a 'good death' in Imperial Rome, 'value was everything: questions of agency were definitely subordinated to more important matters, and medicine also played a more minor role, contributed little to either the management or meaning of mortality' (p. 301). The nature of the doctor's role is expanded upon later in Flemming's paper. The doctor is characterised as 'an efficient technician of death' (p. 315), and largely uninvolved in the establishment or elaboration of the central cultural values – honour, status and ethics – that were bound up with the notion of a 'good death' (see p. 316).

Self-accomplished death, then, was not primarily a medical concern, nor an act that was understood to arise due to some form of 'psychopathology'. How can it be more generally characterised? As hinted at above, notions of honour and status were important concepts. Hill (2004) argues that to understand 'Roman "suicide" one has to understand the "highly status conscious and socially orientated"' (p. 10) nature of Roman culture as a whole. Roman assessments of self-accomplished deaths are governed entirely, he argues, 'by the degree of correlation perceived to obtain between the manner of an individual's death and the social standing he or she possessed in life' (p. 10). Hill continues:

Within this framework Roman discourse on 'suicide' is highly coherent. Good deaths are deaths that serve either to confirm an individual's social standing or to elevate this. Bad deaths are inappropriate to an individual's social status, and that therefore act to lower or denigrate it. The central dynamic governing the practice of the *Romana mors*, is, in short, honor rather than agency. (Hill, 2004, pp. 10–11)

Contemporary judgements on the pathology of Roman 'suicides' thus represent a poor 'fit' in that concepts of the self so central to Western psychiatric formulations (a self governed by 'internal beliefs, desires, commitments, thoughts, and feelings', Sadler, 2005, p. 271) are not easily or unproblematically translatable into Roman contexts.

Rome, AD 66

Acts of Roman self-accomplished death were thus largely socially orientated rather than individual in nature. Hill emphasises the necessity of understanding 'honour' not as an individual attribute (as other historians have tended to) but rather as a 'social and systemic' concept that acted as an 'incentive to political action, a check upon political ambition, and as both the indication and reward of political legitimacy' (Hill, 2004, p. 204). 'Suicide' was consequently something contemplated and 'performed' not in private but more often in the presence of an audience of family and friends, and politically rather than personally motivated. Hill gives many examples of such deaths from the Julio-Claudian era, the time when, he argues, 'suicide appears to have become slowly endemic amongst the upper classes' (p. 183). Here is Tacitus's description of the death of Thrasea Paetus in AD 66:

Then, as evening approached, the consul's quaestor was sent to Thrasea, who was waiting in his garden. He had brought together numerous groups of distinguished men and women, and paid special attention to Demetrius, a teacher of the Cynic philosophy. With him, as could be gathered from his earnest expression of face and from words heard when they raised their voices, he was discussing the nature of the soul, and the separation of the spirit from the body. Then Domitius Caecilianus, one of his closest friends, came to him and told him in detail what the Senate had decided. When everybody around him began to weep and lament, Thrasea encouraged them to depart quickly and not to mingle their own perils with the fate of a condemned man. His wife Arria, who aspired to follow her husband's end and the suicidal example of her mother, he counselled to preserve her life, and not to rob their daughter of her only support. Then he went out into a colonnade,

where he was found by the quaestor, joyful rather than otherwise – as he had learnt
that Helvidius, his son-in-law, was only exiled from Italy rather than sentenced to
death. Once he had heard this decision of the Senate he led Helvidius and
Demetrius into a private room, and having laid bare the veins of each arm, he let
the blood flow freely. As he sprinkled it on the ground, he called the quaestor to his
side and said, 'We offer this as a libation to Jupiter the Liberator. Look upon this,
young man, and may the gods avert this omen – but you have been born into times
in which it is useful to fortify the spirit with examples of courage.' Then, the
slowness of his death bringing with it grievous torment, he turned his eyes on
Demetrius. (*Annals*, 16.34–5 in Hill, 2004, p. 186)

Here, then, self-accomplished death is considered philosophically, decided upon with little expression of strong personal feeling, and enacted in
the presence of others. An interesting figure here in Tacitus's description
is that of Demetrius the Cynic, or rather it is Demetrius's relationship with
Thrasea that is of interest. What role does he perform in relation to
Thrasea at this event? Foucault (2004), in a lecture as part of a series
addressing the 'hermeneutics of the subject', characterises Demetrius as a
'suicide counselor' giving 'support in his final moments with a discourse
on immortality' (p. 497). Foucault talks of the existence in Roman aristocratic families of private counsellors – Philodemus and Athenodorus are
named as examples alongside Demetrius. Here, the head of family 'takes
in and houses a philosopher who serves him as counselor' (p. 142) for the
important events of life:

Demetrius, for example, accompanied Thrasea Paetus for an entire period of his
life, and when Thrasea Paetus had to kill himself, like many people of this epoch he
naturally staged his suicide in a very solemn manner. He called his entourage
around him, his family, etcetera. Then, bit by bit, he dismissed everyone. The last
to remain with him, when he was closest to death, the only one who kept watch
beside him, was precisely Demetrius. When the poison took effect and he began to
lose consciousness, he turned his eyes towards Demetrius, who was therefore the
last person he saw. Of course, the final words exchanged between Thrasea Paetus
and Demetrius concerned death, immortality, the survival of the soul, etcetera.
(p. 142)

For Foucault, the role of private counsellor 'is not that of private tutor any
more than it is entirely that of friendly confidante. He is, rather, what could
be called a counselor of existence who gives his views on specific occasions.
He is the person who guides and initiates someone who is both his patron,
almost his employer, and his friend, but his superior friend' (p. 143).
Demetrius, present at the self-accomplished (though mandated) death of
Thrasea Paetus, offers spiritual guidance, a discourse on the immortality of
the soul, the separation of the soul from the body, etc. In the context of the
necessity of staging an honourable death, Thrasea Paetus looks to Demetrius

for support, guidance, instruction and comfort – a role that would be hard to imagine as sanctioned now within a 'regime of truth' centring on the compulsory ontology of pathology and demands for prevention.

The *Romana mors*, exemplified by the death of Thrasea Paetus, could also be considered political in nature, for, as Hill writes, a 'well-executed suicide' had the 'very real potential … to stir up *invidia* ('unpopularity') against the Emperor' (2004, p. 192). Most obviously, Thrasea Paetus's actions were 'readily traceable to the suicide of Cato Uticensis' (p. 186). Cato's death in 46 BC, Catherine Edwards (2005) notes, 'rapidly acquired a huge symbolic value among Romans' (p. 201). Faced with the prospect of living under Caesar's tyranny, Cato resolved to die instead. 'The night before his death,' Edwards writes, 'Cato is calm and discusses Stoic philosophy over dinner with his companions'. He offers his friends 'reasoned arguments for his suicide' (p. 202) and later that night tries to kill himself, unsuccessfully. The next day he completes his plan in the presence of his companions. Thrasea Paetus thus 'cites' Cato's death – and enacts a form of suicide that could be characterised as social or relational, philosophical and political, rather than one arising out of 'intense, morbid, and pathological states of mind' (Hill, 2004, p. 1), or resulting from personal isolation and alienation.

Deaths such as those of Cato and Thrasea Paetus are, of course, open to retrospective redescription. In the early eighteenth century Joseph Addison's *Cato a Tragedy* reinterpreted the main protagonists' actions in the light of contemporary political concerns and attitudes, and here Cato is represented as a virtuous figure – a beacon of liberty (Edwards, 2005). Later, alienist Forbes Winslow (1840), in his *Anatomy of Suicide*, pronounces Cato's suicide the result of 'pride and timidity' (p. 4), and 'an act of insanity' that 'appears more the effect of private pique and despondency than a demonstration of public virtue or courage' (p. 5). Thus Cato's death could, when reconstructed from a medical/'psychiatric' discourse, become individual, internal, pathological and medical. But to claim it as such, to position oneself, as Winslow does, as able to judge the 'condition of Cato's mind' (p. 6), is to historically decontextualise his death. Hill's account, by contrast, rigorously contextualises the accounts of the *Romana mors* that are available to us, and offers a compelling argument that such deaths can be read as challenging the universality of modern medical, scientific positions on suicide outlined in the previous chapters. The historical records drawn upon by Timothy Hill serve to cast doubts on the belief in suicide as an unchanging, ahistorical concept.

The description of the final moments in the life of Thrasea Paetus offers a glimpse of a form of self-accomplished death that can be read as motivated primarily by questions of politics and honour rather than determined by mental pathology. As noted previously, however, historians of suicide often wish to posit psychopathology at work even if the apparent existence of such forces went unnoticed or unremarked by contemporaries. Rosen (1975), for example, writes, under a heading of 'psychopathology, philosophy, and suicide', of Seneca's notion of *displicentia sui* – a 'self-dissatisfaction' – that may lead to suicide 'especially amongst individuals with mental or emotional disorders' (p. 8). Rosen talks of suicide being 'tolerated, even extolled, in the Imperial period until it became almost a social disease' (p. 10).

Such a situation did not change, argues Rosen, until 'Christian views began to influence social and legal attitudes' (1975, p. 10). Rosen comments on the deaths of Christian martyrs in the first centuries of the millennium, and notes pathological elements in the 'craving for martyrdom' (p. 9). But again, as with the retrospective redescriptions of *Romana mors* in terms of individual pathology, such terms gloss important differences in thought and practices between then and now. The next section highlights some of these differences, and looks to understand how self-accomplished death came to be read as a sin and a crime – a transgression against the absolute authority of God and sovereign.

Self-accomplished death as a sin and a crime

It was perhaps less individual pathology, more an ambivalence about the worth of earthly existence, which led so many Christians to seek martyrdom in the first few centuries after the death of Christ. It is generally held (see, for instance, Minois, 1999) that alarm at the numbers of such deaths, and their promotion by such groups as the Donatists, led the early Church to seek to foster 'a moral climate favourable to the prohibition of suicide' (p. 26). The best-known example of such an attempt at prohibition can be found in Augustine of Hippo's *City of God* (c. 412–16). For Augustine, self-accomplished death should be read as a form of killing that violated the sixth commandment, 'Thou shalt not kill'. Augustine's redescription of self-accomplished death as a form of murder repositioned the deceased as the perpetrator of a mortal sin. Later, a series of Canon Laws sought to criminalise self-killing: the Church synod at Arles in 452 prohibited self-killing based on the idea that 'whoever kills himself, kills an innocent person and commits murder'; the Church synod at Braga in 563 determined that no church rites would be dispensed after a self-killing; the Church synod at Toledo in 693 decided to implement sanctions by excommunicating anyone who killed him/herself; and the Church synod at Nîmes in 1096 decreed that those who commit the act of self-murder would be denied the right to be buried in consecrated soil. Self-accomplished death came to be, through processes of redescription and the acts of law, a form of killing and murder, a sin and a crime. It thus became commonplace during the Middle Ages in Europe under canon and common law to punish those found guilty of deliberately ending their lives (MacDonald and Murphy, 1990, chapter 1). An example can help illustrate such practices and their underlying rationality, here drawn from an account of a coroner's inquest in Elizabethan London.

Aldgate, 1590

In 1590 a 'crowner's quest' or coroner's inquest was held in the Parish of St Botolph within Aldgate, in London, to investigate a suicide. The coroner, Master Thomas Wilbraham, wished to

examen howe Amye Stokes the wyfe of Henrie Stokes a sawyer Dwellinge in Jhon Ansell his yeard ... Did com by her death who hanged her selfe in her chamber beinge over a sawpitt in the forenamed Mr Ansell his yeard the seventh day of september ano 1590 abowte the ower of ix of the clock in the forenoon in manner and forme followinge. That is to saye she had cast a cord abowte a beame in her sayd chamber Fastning it to the sayd beame and puttinge the same with slydinge knott abowte her neck as it appeared standing upon a three Footed stool weh with one of her feete she had thrust from her and so hanged her selfe her feete standing Bent upon the flower or borde of the sayd chamber and being fownde by the Jurie or Crowners quest that she Fallinge from god had hanged or murthered her selfe, Where upon judgement was given ... by the sayd crowner that she should be carried from her sayd house to some cross way neare the townes end and theare that should ha[ve a] stake dreven thorowgh her brest and so be buried with the stake to be seene for memoryall that others goinge by seeyinge the same might take heede for comittinge the lyke faite. And the sayd Amy Stokes was so buried in the crossway Beyond sparrows corner neare to the place wheare the owld cross ded stand the sayd vij[th] Day of September ano 1590 abowte the owere of viij or ix of the clocke at nyght she was abowte three skore yeares owld. (Forbes, 1971, pp. 164–5)

This account is of interest for a number of reasons. One can gauge the concerns of the coroner and jury, and through their account understand a little of the ways by which self-accomplished deaths were constituted and the practices that had arisen for dealing with self-murder by the end of the sixteenth century.

As with other coroner's records, the manner by which Amy Stokes met her death is recorded in detail in order to demonstrate, by reference to the circumstantial evidence, that she had instigated and accomplished her own death, rather than that she had been murdered by another, or had died accidentally or of natural causes (MacDonald, 1986). The body would have been examined by the coroner and jury where it was found and witnesses would have been summoned to provide testimony as to the circumstances of the death. A judgment would then be made as to whether the deceased was considered a *felo de se* (literally felon of themselves) and thus guilty of self-murder, or *non compos mentis* (not of sound mind) and consequently innocent of a crime. The term 'suicide' was not coined until the middle of the seventeenth century and not taken up into popular discourse until the eighteenth, so one was either a criminal and a sinner, or mad. The guilty self-murderer had to be capable of premeditating his crime, thus 'idiots and lunatics' were spared the penalties associated with a verdict of *felo de se* (MacDonald and Murphy, 1990, pp. 15–16). And as can be seen from the record of the punishment of Amy Stokes, these were often severe, for self-murder was 'a felony in criminal law and a desperate sin in the eyes of the church' (p. 15). 'For the heinousnesse thereof', observed Michael Dalton [in 1626], 'it is an offence against God, against the king, and against Nature'. As a *felo de se*

their moveable goods, including tools, household items, money, debts owed to them, and even leases on the land that they had worked were forfeited to the crown or to the holder of a royal patent who possessed the right to such windfalls in a particular place. The suicide of an adult male could reduce his survivors to pauperism. Self-murderers were denied Christian burials; their bodies were interred profanely, with a macabre ceremony prescribed by popular custom. The night following an inquest, officials of the parish, the churchwardens and their helpers, carried the corpse to a crossroads and threw it naked into a pit. A wooden stake was hammered through the body, pinioning it in the grave, and the hole was filled in. No prayers for the dead were repeated; the minister did not attend. (MacDonald and Murphy, 1990, p. 15)

Self-killing represented above all a form of transgression – a challenge to the authority of God and sovereign – one that required punishment that at the same time was visible (so that others would see that such deaths were punished and would not be tempted to imitate such an act), had material consequences (as a form of redress), and was also in some ways symbolically excluding (profane burial in unconsecrated ground). By such means the authority of the Church and the sovereign and their respective laws were publicly re-established in the face of an act considered a challenge to public order, to the rule of law, and to the expected relations between God, the king and their subjects. The manner of Amy Stokes's burial, then, was by no means exceptional for this time in England. MacDonald and Murphy characterise the period as 'the age of severity', with the laws against self-murder 'rigorously enforced in the sixteenth and early seventeenth centuries' (p. 16). Prior to about 1500, they explain, 'suicide' was punished less frequently, and after about 1660 processes of secularisation and decriminalisation can be detected. The move from condemnation and punishment of self-killing read as a form of transgression, to the constitution of 'suicide' as an act that could come to be thought of as worthy of pity, and later medical treatment, will be considered in the next chapter.

Conclusions

This chapter has mostly focused on questions of the contingency of modern truths of suicide discussed in the preceding chapters. There it was argued that suicide is most often read as a singular act to be investigated in terms of its association with various forms of pathology. This chapter has sought to cast doubt on such a formulation by drawing attention to:

- the multiplicity of terms formerly used to describe the variety of acts now 'collapsed' into one term – suicide;
- the fact that at other times and other places different forms of self-accomplished death were not considered to arise due to internal pathology. Many practices arose in relation to such acts, but rarely involved physicians except as peripheral figures;
- that constituted according to different coordinates, in relation to other forms of authoritative knowledge and practices, acts of self-accomplished death do not much resemble our own. Certain examples of *Romana mors* can be understood as enacted according to notions of honour and the self far removed from contemporary ways of thinking. Similarly, when formed in relation to the authority of the Church and state, self-killing comes to be read as a kind of transgression, one that required immediate and public redress, and involved practices somewhat alien to present-day sensibilities.

What has been challenged is the belief that suicide somehow possesses some unchanging essence that we are now uncovering through the application of the techniques of scientific medical research. It is of course possible to retrospectively redescribe the deaths of Thrasea Paetus, Cato or Amy Stokes in terms of modern conceptions of psychopathology, and to maintain that the act itself, and the reasons why people are driven to such acts, have remained essentially the same throughout history. Such an approach, though, tends to underplay the extent to which notions of the nature of the individual, ideas as to why people act to end their own life and the practices that arose in relation to such acts have varied according to time and place. Different cultures, at different times, produce different forms of self-accomplished death, often in relation to contemporary authoritative knowledge (be it clerical, judicial, medical or scientific), and the next chapters trace the formation of our own ideas, practices and experiences in relation to such a way of dying.

6   Conditions of possibility for the formation of medical truths of suicide: 1641–1821

Introduction

This chapter explores the conditions of possibility for the medical refor-mulation of suicide in the early nineteenth century, and identifies those elements and forces that came together to enable such an event. It is not claimed that the formation of suicide as primarily a medical concern was in some way inevitable, more that certain related changes in the period prior to the nineteenth century – the use of the term 'suicide' as a unitary descriptor, an increasingly secular society, the establishment of a scientific medicine, changing rationalities of power, and the creation and use of asylums for the confinement, observation and treatment of the insane under medical management – could be said to have enabled such an occurrence.

Inventing suicide

The word 'suicide' is first found in Sir Thomas Browne's *Religio Medici*, written in about 1634 and published in 1642. The increasingly wide-spread use of the word, at the expense of phrases such as 'self-slaying', 'self-killing' and 'self-murder', in the following centuries reflects, in many ways, changing conceptions of the individual subject. Edwin Shneidman writes:

The difference between self-killing or self-slaughter (and all the circumlocutions and phrases) on the one hand, and 'suicide', on the other, may seem to be a small one, but it is not a trivial distinction. It is a significant, albeit a subtle difference, reflecting a major shift in man's relationship to himself and to his God – and to his disavowal of gods – and of his role in his own ultimate fate. It is as old as history that a man could destroy himself by ruining his reputation and his career, or take his own life; but it was a seventeenth century insight and invention that a man could forever terminate his not-so-immortal existence and do more than inimical things to himself. He could – dispensing with the notion of soul and hereafter – for the first time, 'commit suicide'. (Shneidman, 1985, p. 14)

The term 'suicide' was not taken up overnight. For a time after a number of other phrases were employed that were suggestive of a self-inflicted death. John Donne, in his posthumously published *Biathanatos* (probably written in 1607–8 and published in 1644–7), coined the phrase 'self-homicide' as a more neutral, less damning, alternative to 'self-murder' (Daube, 1977). Robert Burton's *Anatomy of Melancholy* (1652) avoids talk of people committing self-murder, and instead makes use of a number of phrases, including (much in the manner of ancient Rome): to procure their own death; to free themselves from grievances; to offer violence unto themselves; to fall by one's own hand; to let himself free with his own hands; to execute themselves; to dispatch themselves; to take death into their own hands; to die voluntarily (in Shneidman, 1985). These phrases are again suggestive of subtle differences in the meanings and intentions of such acts – to say a person executed themselves implies an act undertaken in circumstances and in a context different from one where the person has sought to free themselves from grievances. But the word suicide gradually came to replace such phrasings.

Sir Thomas Browne's use of 'suicide' is as follows; '[h]eirin are they not extreme that can allow a man to be his own assassin and so highly extol the end by suicide of Cato' (in Shneidman, 1985, pp. 10–11). As Alexander Murray (1998) notes, it is perhaps surprising that the word, that has a Latin basis, '*suicidium* putatively meaning "killing of oneself" on analogy with genuinely Latin words like *homicidium* and *matricidium*' (p. 38), was not coined earlier. Murray, as Shneidman, points to changing conceptions of the self as a reason for this. He writes that suicide today is defined 'as a deliberate act of self-homicide. Put another way, it is the result – one's own death – combined with an intention – in one's own mind – to secure it. But this moral syntax is relatively modern' (p. 39). Murray argues that 'men's [*sic*] underlying moral conceptions were not at the stage of needing a word for so specific a definition, a definition founded, that is, on a particular compound of intention and act' (pp. 39–40). Suicide, as a description of an intentional, knowing act of the self against itself, required the formation of a reflexive subject.

The emergence of such a subject has been traced by many writers to the seventeenth century (Taylor, 1989; Mansfield, 2000; Strozier, 2002; Seigel, 2005; Martin and Barresi, 2006). From this time, it is argued, notions of a human 'interiority' separate from the 'exteriority' of the world come to be formed, and increasingly such an interiority became the point of reference for individual identity; 'from Descartes on', Robert Strozier (2002) writes, 'interiority is increasingly recognized as constituting human identity, universal at first and then increasingly individual' (p. 211). It was from this historically formed interiority that were later said to arise suicidal thoughts and desires that only the subject, through processes of introspection, was seen as having 'privileged access' to. Alongside the emergence of notions of a separate 'interior' space within the individual there also came to be formed a belief in an 'external' reality that such a subject could obtain objective knowledge of. There thus arises the possibility of 'objective' descriptions of acts of self-accomplished death (increasingly subsumed under the singular term 'suicide'). The subject/object split, characteristic of thinking from the seventeenth century on, enables the formation of a suicide that comes to be read as both an individual 'internal' phenomenon (arising from within the subject) and one that can be objectively studied. A science of suicide thus becomes possible, but one faced with the difficulty of gathering objective knowledge of such acts taken to arise from within an individual interiority not directly observable from 'outside' (these themes will be further explored in the next chapter when certain problems associated with the emergence of a medical science of suicide are discussed).

The secularisation of suicide in early modern England

As discussed, Edwin Shneidman (1985) links the take-up of the concept of 'suicide' with a 'major shift in man's relationship to himself and to his God' (p. 14), traceable to the seventeenth century. It is generally held that between the middle of the seventeenth century and the end of the eighteenth a 'secularisation' of suicide, in England at least, takes hold. Historians such as Rosen (1971), MacDonald (1986, 1995, 1997), MacDonald and Murphy (1990), Watt (2004), Brown (2001) and Healy (2006) all note the gradual diminishing of supernatural explanations for suicide during this period, and an increasing influence of 'rational' approaches.

As MacDonald (1995) notes, changing attitudes to suicide are 'as complex and variable as the very complicated social and cultural systems in which they existed' (p. 631). MacDonald here, and in *Sleepless Souls* (with Murphy, 1990), draws attention to the political, social and cultural forces at work behind the change from the 'age of severity' in the sixteenth and early seventeenth centuries (illustrated by the coroner's report on Amy Stokes quoted in the previous chapter) to the more tolerant approaches that characterised the period from the mid-seventeenth to the early nineteenth centuries. Popular disquiet regarding the fairness of the laws of forfeiture, the gradual diffusion of Enlightenment explanations of suicide as a rational choice, and the increasing use of *non compos mentis* verdicts ('insanity') all contributed to (or reflected) a weakening of desire to punish suicides (MacDonald, 1995).

Of interest here is the increase in 'insanity' verdicts referred to by MacDonald. Historians noting this increase tend to talk of the medicalisation of suicide as a gradual phenomenon, the origins of which can be traced to the seventeenth and eighteenth centuries, continuing on into the nineteenth. Medical involvement in suicide is thus characterised as constituent of wider processes of enlightenment – a rational, secular progression away from the irrational, superstitious beliefs and barbaric practices of the previous, unenlightened age. Such a reading somewhat overstates the continuities in the meaning of both 'suicide' and 'insanity' between the seventeenth and eighteenth centuries and the nineteenth. As Foucault argues in *History of Madness* (2005), if this period is read for discontinuities rather than continuities it is possible to describe what can be characterised as an 'epistemic shift' at the end of the eighteenth and beginning of the nineteenth centuries, with the emergence of modern notions of mental illness. Such a shift, it is argued here, occurs with regard to conceptions of 'suicide' and 'insanity'. Whereas madness in relation to suicide prior to the end of the eighteenth century tended to involve the ancient concepts of either *furor* or *dementia*, after this time ideas of madness changed, and a wider range of behaviours began to be considered evidence of the suicide being *non compos mentis*. As will be discussed in a later chapter, by the early decades of the nineteenth century it was possible to argue that all suicides should be considered *non compos mentis* unless there was clear evidence to the contrary (e.g. Chevalier, 1824), and that suicide itself should be taken to be a sure sign of insanity, even in the absence of any other symptoms (e.g. Winslow, 1840). A clear shift, from a narrow definition of what constituted *non compos mentis* in relation to suicide to a situation where an act of suicide itself was considered sufficient evidence of insanity, can be discerned.

Non compos mentis: suicide and insanity

In discussing the 'medicalization of suicide', Michael MacDonald (1997) writes that the 'meaning of suicide transformed utterly between about 1660 and 1800. The ruling classes lost faith in the devil's power to drive people to kill themselves; coroner's juries gradually ceased punishing suicides' (p. 89). Juries did this by passing more *non compos mentis* verdicts than *felo de se*. MacDonald's research suggests that the proportion of *non compos mentis* judgments stood at 8.4 per cent in the 1660s, 15.8 per cent in the 1680s, rising to 42.5 per cent in the first decade of the seventeenth century. Such verdicts continuing to increase 'more or less steadily until they comprised almost 80 per cent of suicide verdicts in the 1750s, over 90 per cent in the 1760s, and so on up to over 97 per cent by the end of the century' (MacDonald, 1997, p. 90). It would be tempting to attribute increases in 'insanity' verdicts to a growing influence of medical men, but MacDonald argues that physicians and medical writers remained peripheral to the cultural changes characterised by historians as the 'secularisation' of suicide between the mid seventeenth and the late eighteenth centuries: '[p]hysicians made no notable contributions to the understanding of suicide in the late seventeenth and eighteenth centuries. When they mentioned the subject at all, they were content to repeat the Renaissance commonplace that melancholy (sometimes rechristened the vapors or the spleen) often led to self-destruction' (MacDonald, 1997, p. 95).

Suicide in this period was, for the most part, constituted in relation to the distinctions licit/illicit, or sinful/innocent. Within such schemes, verdicts of *non compos mentis* reflected more a communal desire to spare surviving families the tribulations that followed verdicts of *felo de se*; that is, a way of indicating innocence in the face of a serious legal and theological accusation (of a heinous crime and mortal sin), rather than a 'taking-up' of new ideas or theories of insanity in relation to suicide. As MacDonald (1997) notes, the 'eighteenth-century loss of confidence in diabolical powers did not ... require the invention of a new psychology of suicide' (p. 98). Such new ways of thinking arose later, in the early nineteenth century, and the next chapters trace the emergence, and subsequent diffusion and dominance, of medical theories and practices in relation to suicide. First, however, it is necessary to locate the sites from which such ways of thinking and acting with regard to the suicidal could emerge.

Alienism, and the asylum as laboratory for the production of medical truths

Foucault traces the emergence of the asylum in his *History of Madness* (2005; first published in France in 1961 under the title *Folie et déraison: Histoire de la folie à l'âge classique*). Other historians have subsequently covered similar ground, most notably Andrew Scull (1993) and Roy Porter (1987), with many, including both Porter and Scull, contesting many of Foucault's central arguments, in particular his claims of the scale of the confinement of the insane in the seventeenth century. The accuracy, or otherwise, of the *History of Madness* is not at issue here. Rather, it is how the asylums, regardless of the numbers incarcerated, could act as the site both for the emergence of a professional group of physicians specialising in the management of the insane and for the production of truths in relation to madness and suicide.

Foucault (2005) famously argued that the lazar houses of the Middle Ages, left empty after the decline in leprosy, provided a solution to the problem of what to do with those considered mad in the early modern period. Later, beginning in about the middle of the seventeenth century, Foucault talks of a 'great confinement' when nearly 1 per cent of the population of Paris came to be confined in institutions. Within such 'houses of confinement' could be found the destitute and criminals, as well as those deemed insane. Towards the end of the eighteenth century and the beginning of the nineteenth, there was a move to rehouse the insane in special institutions, not so much, Foucault argues, due to concern with the conditions of the insane but more because the previous arrangement was considered to be unfair to the criminals. The lunatic asylum, such a feature of the nineteenth and twentieth centuries, was thus born.

Within the space of the asylum it became possible to observe, classify and control large groups of people, to subject individuals to disciplinary measures aimed at managing the 'unruly' but also to 'reform' those deemed to have become alienated from their true, rational and calm, natures. Such measures were not wholly repressive, but rather can be read as constituent elements of a power-knowledge network essentially productive in its effects. Through techniques of hierarchical surveillance, normalising judgement and the examination (Foucault, 1977), extensive, detailed knowledge could be produced of the suicidal subject that in turn, in a circular relation, acted to justify disciplinary practices.

The asylums came to be constituted as medical spaces, managed by doctors specialising in mental medicine known as alienists. Positioned as medical scientists, alienists sought to objectively study insanity; Philippe Pinel, physician at the Asylum de Bicêtre from 1793, for instance, wrote of the 'spirit of minute and accurate observation' (1806/1962, p. 1) necessary in the study of mental diseases. Within the enclosed, ordered space of the asylum, patients could be closely observed, notes kept detailing symptoms, various classifications made, diagnoses and treatments recorded, and through such means the possibilities for the objectification of the insane – those methods that formed patients as objects of scientific knowledge – increased. Others followed Pinel's lead, most notably his student Jean-Etienne Esquirol who, in the early decades of the nineteenth century, wrote at length on various forms of 'mental maladies' based on his observations of the insane under his management at the Salpêtrière asylum. By means of such practices asylums became something akin to laboratories for the production of medical truths, initially of insanity in general, and later of suicide. Such truths – of the dangerousness of insanity, of the existence of internal, pathological lesions and impulses that led to acts of harm against the self or others – acted as a rationale for the very procedures that had established such knowledge. Thus, confinement, constant watching, and the control of the patient's body through its positioning in the asylum space and the ordering of its movement in time through the imposition of rigid routines all enabled the accumulation of individualised knowledge. Such knowledge allowed for the theorisation of the nature and causes of propensities to suicide, and the necessity of confinement, containment, constant watching and restraint followed from the truths thus formulated – a circular power-knowledge relationship that was productive in that increasing amounts of information were accumulated throughout the next two centuries, and also enabled the consolidation and extension of psychiatric power.

The asylums, designed as they often were to mirror a general hospital, enabled alienists to establish their claims to be considered doctors in possession of specialist medical knowledge. Lunatic asylums gradually came under medical control (codified in French law in 1838, and in England in 1845), and through such means a distinct 'psychiatric' profession gradually emerged. Within the asylums, in relation to the practices of the mental medics, the 'mad' could come to be formed as patients. Here the doctor, seeking to confirm the medical nature of his work, would examine the individual brought before him, question him, uncover the truth of his illness, formulate a diagnosis, prescribe treatment and keep a permanent file recording what the patient had done and what the doctor knew (Foucault, 2006, p. 185). Medical knowledge and practices thus functioned to constitute different types of patient and, once assigned an illness and allocated an appropriate place, they could be closely observed and 'objectively' described in medical treatises such as those of Pinel (1806) and Esquirol (1805). It was thus within the space of the asylum that the truth of the suicidal patient could be uncovered and confronted (and such a process is explored in more detail in chapters that follow).

Accounting for the shift from punishment to confinement and treatment: a new 'economy' of power?

The previous sections of this chapter have considered certain 'conditions of possibility' for the 'medicalisation' of suicide in the early nineteenth century; namely, the 'coinage' and uptake of suicide as a unitary descriptor; changing conceptions of knowledge and the subject from the seventeenth century on; the 'secularisation' of suicide; and the creation of asylums where practices of confinement, observation, examination and classification could enable the production of medical truths of insanity and, later, suicide.

Certainly from the seventeenth century on it is possible to discern a shift from punishment to confinement and treatment in relation to suicide and the suicidal. The processes identified above can be understood as constituent, as well as constituting, elements in such a move, but a question remains as to how such changes could be accounted for. Here, Foucault's (1981) concept of differing 'economies' of power may prove a helpful tool of analysis.

The last section of volume I of Foucault's *The History of Sexuality* (1981), 'Right of death and power over life', contains an analysis of two contrasting 'economies' of power. The section begins with a description of what Foucault characterises as 'sovereign' power. For a long time, he argues, one of the privileges of sovereign power was the right to decide life and death. Such a form of power, he suggests, could be traced to the practices of the father of the Roman family – the right to 'dispose' of the life of his children and slaves (p. 135). By the Classical Age (the seventeenth and eighteenth centuries) the exercise of such rights had come to be limited to those occasions when the sovereign himself was threatened – 'the power of life and death was not an absolute privilege: it was conditioned by the defence of the sovereign, and his own survival' (p. 135). Under such a formation, the sovereign was said to have 'exercised his right of life only by exercising his right to kill, or by refraining from killing; he evidenced his power over life only through the death he was capable of requiring' (p. 136). He could thus, in Foucault's formulation, either '*take* life or *let* live', and sovereign power was essentially a 'right of seizure: of things, time, bodies, and ultimately life itself' (p. 136). The punishment of suicides deemed *felo de se* by means of the confiscation of goods and the denial of a Christian burial thus could be read as an expression of such a form of power – the sovereign, in response to having had removed the power of death that was his alone, seeks redress.

Foucault argues that such a right to take life or let live has been replaced 'by a power to *foster* life or *disallow* it to the point of death' (Foucault, 1981, p. 136) since the Classical Age. Such a power comes to work by means of inciting, reinforcing, controlling, monitoring, optimising and organising the forces under it; it is now 'a power bent on generating forces, making them grow, and ordering them, rather than one dedicated to impeding them, making them submit, or destroying them' (p. 136). It is a form of power, Foucault argues, that comes to be 'situated and exercised at the level of life' (Rabinow and Rose, 2003): 'Now it is over life, through its unfolding, that power establishes its domination: death is power's limit, the moment that escapes it; death becomes the most secret aspect of existence, the most 'private' (Foucault, 1998, p. 138).

Foucault draws on suicide as an example of the shift from sovereign to what he calls 'bio-power'. There was, Foucault argues, a turning away from death towards the fostering of life, and thus:

It is not surprising that suicide – once a crime, since it was a way to usurp the power of death which the sovereign alone, whether the one here below or the Lord above, had the right to exercise – became, in the course of the nineteenth century, one of the first conducts to enter into the sphere of sociological analysis; it testified to the individual and private right to die, at the borders and in the interstices of power that was exercised over life. This determination to die, strange and yet so persistent and constant in its manifestations, and consequently so difficult to explain as being due to particular circumstances or individual accidents, was one of the first astonishments of a society in which political power had assigned itself the task of administering life. (Foucault, 1998, p. 138)

The new responses to suicide in the nineteenth century also illustrate the two poles of this administration of life according to Foucault's analysis. The first centred on 'the body as a machine' (p. 139), and involved a disciplining and optimising of its capacities and capabilities, the second on 'the species body' (p. 139), the regulation of the population through a concern with 'propagation, births and mortality, the level of health, life expectancy and longevity, with all the conditions that can cause these to vary' (p. 139).

Bio-power, its concern with maximising the potentialities of both the individual body and the body of the population, its contestations and strategies constituting a bio-political sphere – an 'anatomo-politics of the human body' alongside a 'bio-politics of the population' (p. 139) – is more or less productive in its effects. Whereas sovereign power was exercised mainly through 'deduction, a subtraction mechanism, a right to appropriate' (p. 136), bio-power is deployed through the application of numerous techniques that sought 'no longer to kill, but to invest life through and through' (p. 139). Suicide, within such a bio-political field, was thus no longer something to be reacted to after the event by means of a taking away (of goods, of the rights of Christian burial, etc.) but rather could come to be a target of management at both the population and the individual level. Confining the suicidal in asylums, as well as the system-atic counting of suicides undertaken in England and France in the early nineteenth century (Hacking, 1990), could be considered early expres-sions of a bio-political rationality. Within such an economy of power suicide presents a new kind of problem. Whereas in relation to sovereign power suicide could be considered a problem of transgression that demanded the enactment of appropriate punishments (confiscation of goods, desecration of the corpse, excommunication, burial in uncon-secrated ground), within a bio-political economy of power suicide represents something of a challenge to those techniques and strategies that aim to foster health and vitality (in short, life itself) in the face of disease and decay (and ultimately death). Such deaths are not read as inevitable, and the problem of suicide now is that it is an unnecessary death – it is, and should be, avoidable and preventable. Suicide therefore represents a failure of power to preserve life, and further, it is a waste of life – the loss of an asset to power, and in the final analysis, a tragedy. Within such a biopolitical rationality certain strategies emerged to deal with the problem of suicide as it came to be conceived, and these were different solutions from those developed to punish the transgression of sovereign laws. At the level of the individual, problems could be addressed in terms of *what will be* (by means of practices that seek to make visible the potential to suicide) or *what is* (those practices that seek to manage the suicidal in the present) rather than *what was* (the punishment of an already committed sin or crime), and a proliferation of discourses and associated technologies concerned with identifying, examining, confining, watching, restraining, diagnosing, and treating the suicidal – in short, a set of practices centred on the prevention of suicide that also enabled the production of knowledge – have come to be formed. It is the emergence of solutions to a form of death newly problematised that are considered in the chapters that follow.

Conclusions

This chapter has argued that changes in conceptions of suicide and the subject from the mid seventeenth century on, processes of secularisation, and the creation of asylums and asylum practices each acted as conditions of possibility for the formation of new medical truths in relation to suicide in the early nineteenth century. During this time suicide became less a transgression to be punished, rather a problem to be managed, and such a move can be accounted for by reference to the emergence of a new 'economy' of power that sought to foster life and disallow death. The next chapters analyse the relationship between the production and circulation of new medical truths of suicide, beginning with Esquirol's 1821 dictionary entry on suicide for the *Dictionnaire des sciences médicales*, and the emergence of techniques of prediction, control, diagnosis and treatment with regard to suicide and the suicidal.

7　Suicide as internal, pathological and medical: Esquirol 1821

Introduction

This chapter offers a detailed analysis of a key text in the formation of suicide as pathological and medical. Jean-Etienne Esquirol's 1821 entry on suicide for the *Dictionnaire des sciences médicales* redescribes suicide as a disease, or as a symptom of a disease, and as Ian Hacking (1990) notes, his text effectively claims the right of doctors to 'guard, treat, control, and judge suicides' (p. 65). Whereas previously suicide had been condemned as a sin and a crime, and judicial and canonical laws acted as a deterrent through fear of eternal damnation and earthly punishment for surviving relatives, now the 'discovery' of premonitory medical signs of a disposition to suicide opened up the possibility of intervention before a suicidal act could be committed. Medicine not only claimed expertise and authority, but also promised a more effective, rational solution to the problem of suicide. The lengthy dictionary entry is analysed (along with Esquirol's slightly revised version published in 1838 as part of his *Des maladies mentales*) in order to understand more fully the medicalised form of suicide that begins to emerge in the early decades of the nineteenth century.

As was suggested in the previous chapter, new relations of power were also formed in the asylums, and analysis of Esquirol's text offers the possibility of understanding by what means medicine claimed expertise and authority in relation to the truths of suicide, how such knowledge was produced through practices of observation and examination in the asylum, and how the knowledge thus gained acted to justify the confinement and restraint of those constituted as suicidal patients. In short, Esquirol's text may allow light to be cast on relations of power-knowledge as they involved asylum practices in the early nineteenth century, particularly with regard to the formation of objects and subjects of knowledge.

'Pathologie interne'

Jean-Etienne Esquirol, pupil of Philippe Pinel, *médecin ordinaire* (later physician in chief) at the Salpêtrière Hospital in Paris, and initiator of the first formal education in France for *des maladies mentales*, wrote in 1821 the entry on suicide for the *Dictionnaire des sciences médicales*. It begins; 'SUICIDE *(pathologie interne)*' (p. 213), and here, by constituting suicide in relation to the distinctions 'internal/external', 'normal/pathological', a new object of study is formed. Esquirol locates the causes of suicide within the individual and declares the 'internal space' where it resides to be pathological. As a *pathologie interne* suicide was thus an issue of medical concern, as Esquirol makes clear from the beginning of his article:

It does not belong to my subject to treat of suicide in its legal relations, nor, consequently, of its criminality. I must limit myself to showing it to be one of the most important subjects of clinical medicine. (Esquirol, 1845, p. 254. trans. E. K. Hunt[*])

[Il n'est point de mon objet de traiter du suicide sous le rapport legal, par conséquens de sa criminalité; je dois me borner à faire connaître le suicide comme un des objets les plus importans de la médicine clinique.] (Esquirol, 1821, p. 213)

In his dictionary entry Esquirol largely sets aside any consideration of suicide as a sin or a crime and instead frames acts of self-destruction in medical terms. Over the seventy-five pages of the article Esquirol draws on a general medical vocabulary of 'organic functions' *(fonctions organiques)*, 'symptoms' *(symptômes)*, 'causes' *(causes)* 'acute' *(aigu)*, 'chronic' *(chronique)*, 'treatment' *(traitement)*, 'epidemic' *(épidémie)*, 'hereditary' *(héréditaire)* 'lesions' *(lésions)*, 'pathology' *(pathologie)*, 'medicines' *(médicines)*, 'diseases' *(maladies)* and 'to cure' *(guérir)*. The use of such a vocabulary lent the statements on suicide a degree of credibility and authority – Esquirol's treatise is constituted as a discourse of truth underwritten by practices of objective observation, diagnostic specificity and therapeutic processes (Foucault, 2006, p. 12). However, as well as drawing upon established medical language and practices, alienists also sought to create a separate medical speciality concerned with all aspects of *les maladies mentales*, and one feature of this endeavour was the integration into traditional medical discourse of contemporaneous terms relating to insanity but given distinct medical/scientific meanings as well as the

---

[*] Hunt's translation is from Esquirol's 1838 *Des maladies mentales*. This book collected Esquirol's various essays and papers and included a slightly revised version of his dictionary article on suicide of 1821. The revisions were few, and relatively unimportant – for instance, '*Il n'est point de mon objet*' of 1821 becomes '*Il n'est point de mon sujet*' in 1838. These minor alterations are not drawn attention to unless they are considered to be of substance.

formation of a number of new terms and phrases. As Jan Goldstein (1987) notes:

> Like Pinel before him, but again more insistently, Esquirol looked to linguistic change as an additional vehicle of medicalization, as a way to demarcate a specifically medical domain and to indicate the placement of insanity within it. Pinel had spoken of the desirability of purging medicine of everyday language, of the 'jargon circulating in the commerce of civil life'; he had urged the substitution of the word *aliénation* for the vulgar *folie*. (p. 133)

So Esquirol's 1821 suicide text also talks of 'delirium' (*délire*), 'mental disease' (*maladies mentales*) 'melancholy' (*mélancolie*), 'temperament' (*tempérament*), 'mania' (*manie*), 'hypochondria' (*hypochondrie*), 'lypemania' (*lypemanie*), and Esquirol's own creation, 'monomania' (*monomanie*). These words were to be given a medical meaning by their contextual use alongside a general medical vocabulary, and as such allowed the alienist to be constituted as doctor (with the authority and expertise such a designation conferred) and the suicidal as patient (with the abrogation of rights such a position most often entailed).

The structure within which these terms were employed Esquirol later sets out in *Des maladies mentales*, in the section 'Insanity', and again it is analogous with the practices and discourse of medicine:

> For our guidance, in this chaos of human miseries, we will reduce to four principal divisions, what we have to say concerning insanity: 1st, we will analyze the symptoms which characterize this malady; 2d seek, for its causes; 3d, trace its progress, and mark its different terminations; 4th, and finally, we will lay down the general principles of its treatment (Esquirol, 1845, p. 21).

So 'monomania', for instance, was classified as a form of 'mental disease', and was seen to have causes (moral and physiological), was characterised by certain sets of symptoms, and could be contrasted with other 'mental diseases' (e.g. 'lypemania'); the 'progress' and termination of the 'disease' were traced and specific treatments suggested. The chapter on suicide similarly looks to classify different types ('acute' or 'chronic'), causes ('passions', 'pathological lesions', 'climates, seasons, age and sex') and treatments. Discussion of what could be classed as 'progress' or 'course' is mostly absent, but in other respects, on the surface at least, suicide comes to be successfully inserted into a medical domain, albeit one that is in the process of being changed and extended by the practices of alienism itself.

Such a redescription in medical terms, both with regard to the vocabulary drawn upon and the structure within which it is understood, proceeds hand-in-hand with the development of new practices and the formation of new truths in relation to suicide. Within the asylum, those who, having being constituted as patients, are read as suicidal can be confined and their movements can be ordered so that they can be meticulously observed at all times and at particular points (on admission, during the visit of the doctor, for example) medically examined. These processes allowed for the gathering of information and led to theorisation as to the organic/physical causes of a propensity for suicide, the relationship of suicide to insanity and insanity to suicide and the nature of alienism as a medical speciality. Through the formation of suicide as a kind of madness, and of insanity as dangerous, asylum practices could be justified and the necessity of the alienist confirmed. This re-forming of suicide as a concern of medicine did not just allow for the introduction of repressive techniques of containment and restraint, but was also productive in that it enabled the accumulation of knowledge and the development of theories as to causation, treatment and cure of suicidal states. The workings of a certain formation of power-knowledge can be discerned – for the establishment of medical power in the asylums allowed for the production of knowledge which in turn acted to consolidate and extend such power. Esquirol's text of 1821 is illustrative of such a power-knowledge configuration; here various forms of *pathologie interne* are said to lead to acts of suicide, and the production of knowledge of such pathologies is dependent on certain relations of power within the asylum (the constitution and subjugation of the patient in order that they may be observed and examined by the concurrently constituted medical authority), and the truths that emerge from these encounters serve to justify and strengthen such imbalances of power. The production and use of 'the passions' in relation to the causation of suicide in Esquirol's text may cast some light on these workings – for in centring his theory of the causation of suicide on the passions, and by understanding the importance of the passions as lying in their pathologising effects on the body, it became possible to constitute suicide as an individual, somatic and thus medical issue, the uncovering of its truth and its treatment requiring confinement and isolation away from friends and family. Such a move opened up many possibilities for thought and action in relation to the threat of suicide, but also at the same time acted to restrict others, and these are discussed.

The passions

A key element to Esquirol's formulation of suicide as a medical issue, indeed a central element of his and Pinel's construction of mental maladies per se, was his use of 'the passions'. In 1805, aged 33, Esquirol published his doctoral dissertation, 'The passions viewed as causes, symptoms and treatments of mental alienation' (*Des passions considérées comme causes, symptômes et moyens curatifs de l'aliénation mentale*). It was in many ways a continuation of the work of Pinel. As Gauchet and Swain (1999) note, 'Esquirol, like Pinel, believed that the origin of mental illness lies in the passions of the soul and was convinced that madness does not fully and irremediably affect a patient's reason' (p. 19). It was thus a break from earlier notions of madness as 'false judgement', as articulated, for instance, in John Locke's influential *An Essay on Human Understanding* (1690/1959). For Locke, 'madness was a disease of ideas rather than a disease of men' (Gauchet and Swain, 1999, p. 47). Madness, in Pinel's and Esquirol's conceptualisation, could leave reason and judgement partially intact, and there thus arose, conceptually at least, the possibility of treatment and cure, for something 'healthy' remained in the mad person:

According to Esquirol, madness does not affect the intellectual faculties alone; it is a total phenomenon that touches on all aspects of human personality. Yet madness does not completely abolish the self; it allows the mentally ill to preserve part of their personality and presence to the world. For Esquirol, madness is neither simply a brain lesion nor a failure of the intellect, but a divisive force that affects the entire human being by turning the sick half against the healthy one. (Gauchet and Swain, 1999, p. 149)

The 'intellectual faculties' are not central to Pinel and Esquirol's scheme, although they are not altogether expelled either. They remain part of the 'animal economy' (Huneman, 2003), subject to 'influence' and in turn influencing, but they are not the primary site of madness, or principal effect. As Esquirol's thesis title makes clear, it was the passions that were to be viewed as 'causes, symptoms and treatments of mental alienation'. The body, as with the intellect, was part of this balanced whole – the system of the 'animal economy' emphasised 'an exchange between parts' (Huneman, 2003), and was both a medical and a psychological concept, dealing with a psychic as well as an organic life. Thus Pinel and Esquirol scorned the idea of there being specific local lesions responsible for particular forms of mental alienation. Instead they talked of a generalised 'epigastric' area, where the passions were to be located. This 'place of the passions', was

a place from which all the physical and moral dimensions of a human being can be simultaneously mobilized, seized, and overturned, without the slightest harm being done to the integrity of the brain or any other organ … a place of immediate reciprocity between what belongs to the body and what belongs to the mind, a place where no modification in one register, however minimal, ever takes place without repercussions and instantaneous translation in the other register. (Gauchet and Swain, 1999, p. 152)

Recovery was possible within this scheme because all aspects of the system remained potentially intact, and equally, those elements that remained untouched could be mobilised to balance the whole. Importantly, then, alienation as conceived by Pinel and Esquirol did not amount 'to annihilation, to obliteration, or destruction of the subject' (p. 153). Alienation was, by definition, always partial – there remained a self that was aware and unblemished. As a consequence, the mad were not lost to treatment, did not need to be permanently restrained but could be studied in terms of the relationship between sick and healthy aspects, and cures could be formulated that would lead to the restoration of sanity and productive functioning. Alienism as a medical speciality therefore emerges in relation to the possibility of the development of cures for such alienation, and it was to be through the accumulation of specialist knowledge within a medically delineated and controlled space that would allow for such cures to be effected.

For Pinel the passions 'arose from internal rather than external sensations, were "sensed" by bodily organs other than the senses'. Their centre, home (*foyer*), or 'congregating place' was considered to be the epigastric region. From here 'passional impressions' affected, according to their particular nature, 'digestion, respiration, circulation, excretion'. Eventually, these 'impressions' found their way to the brain, transmitted along neural pathways, where, if they were violent enough, they would disrupt its functioning (Goldstein, 1987, p. 94). Passions were constituted as intimately tied to the organic functioning of the body, and thus were taken to be of medical concern. Such a step was significant in that from here any observed 'disturbance' in an individual could be interpreted in terms of its organic effects, so passions now came to be read less in terms of their cultural meaning – the ways in which they arose in relation to social situations or pressures (debt, divorce, shame, political discontent, etc.) – and more by reference to the (pathologised) body of the individual patient. Constituted as a form of *pathologie interne* certain expressions of feeling now took on a distinctly organic, and thus medical, interpretation. So, for instance, discontent could be read as both symptomatic and cause of organic pathology – a form of madness that could lead to the commission of dangerous acts. It may then become necessary for a person so afflicted to be confined and restrained for their own and others' safety. Once confined they could be observed, examined and tested, and the truth of their illness uncovered – the new knowledge produced through such means strengthening the claim that pathology was at work in certain acts of transgression. Through the deployment of the notion of the passions as symptom and cause of insanity, medical/'psychiatric' power-knowledge came to be extended into new areas and to reach a new constituency of individuals who could be formed as patients, i.e. anyone who could be said to be exhibiting an excess of passion.

Another related step was the removal of notions of agency and responsibility from those deemed alienated from their true nature. Although the law had long recognised that the deranged and distracted could be excused their actions to a degree, alienists began to argue that those suffering from a wide variety of conditions were also unable to control their actions. The postulation of an essential core self, alienated from itself but aware of its actions, directly challenged traditional moral beliefs about the degree of agency and responsibility the individual possessed. One of the consequences of Pinel's, and later Esquirol's, distinctive use of the concept of 'the passions', was to effectively reshape or redefine the notion of the individual's power over themselves, their 'moral strength'. Specifically, Pinel, and later Esquirol, redescribed the relationship between autonomy, morality and awareness by proposing that an individual could be aware of the harm he is doing, yet is nevertheless 'irresistibly led in spite of himself to do harm and is thus irresponsible' (Gauchet and Swain, 1999, p. 159). As Gauchet and Swain note, 'to acknowledge that presence to oneself does not procure power over the self *ipso facto* is, in fact, to destroy the bases of the moral conception of the human being as it has been traditionally understood' (p. 159). Such a reconception of agency and responsibility had consequences in terms of relations of power between alienists and patients, as well as helping to define the function of the alienists themselves. For if the patient, due to their alienation, is not responsible for their actions then it becomes the duty of the asylum doctor to ensure they do not act in an irresponsible way and the domination of the patient becomes a medical necessity, one undertaken in the best interests of both the patient and society. The alienist assumes a role of protector of both individuals and society against the threat of the irresponsible madman.

By the linking of insanity to the passions, in the reformulation of ideas around agency, autonomy and responsibility, and the interpretation of certain actions as arising as a consequence of some form of pathology within the interior space of the individual, new truths in relation to suicide (and new forms of suicides and suicidal subjects in relation to these truths) could come to be formed. The old moral vocabulary, by which suicide could be constructed in terms of guilt, sin, self-killing, evil, perpetrator, righteous, impropriety, wickedness, self-murder, vice, soul, temperance, temptation, idleness and horror (these terms are taken from a two-volume treatise on suicide by the Reverend Charles Moore, 1790), gave way in authority to medico-scientific descriptions within which suicide could be constituted in terms of treatments, prevention and cures. Suicide could now be understood less by reference to a licit/illicit distinction, and more as arising as a consequence of internal pathological processes that could impel a person to act in ways that were destructive to themselves. A direct linking of the passions, organic pathology, insanity and suicide is to be found in the texts of Esquirol, and the means by which the truth of suicide in relation to the passions was produced, and the consequences in terms of 'truth effects', will now be addressed.

'Suicide provoked by the passions'

Returning to Esquirol's 1821 medical dictionary entry 'Suicide', there are fifteen pages devoted to 'Suicide provoked by the passions'. The section begins with a formulation of the role of the passions in relation to the overall 'animal economy': '[t]he passions, when strongly excited, ever produce disturbance, either in the organism or understanding of man' (1845, p. 256) ['les passions, violemment excités portent le trouble dans l'homme, soit dans son organisme, soit dans son intelligence' (1821, p. 216)]. Thus, the passions can 'overthrow reason' ['en bouleversant la sensibilité' (1821, p. 217)], but equally can affect the bodily constitution; they are both moral and physiological in their effects. A causal chain is proposed that links the soul, the affections, organic functions, reason, consciousness, delirium and behaviour:

When the soul is strongly moved, by a violent and unexpected affection, organic functions are perverted, the reason is disturbed, the individual loses his self-consciousness, is in a true delirium, and commits acts the most thoughtless; those most opposed to his instinct, to his affections and interests. (1845, p. 256)

[Lorsque l'âme est fortement ébranlée par une affection violente et imprévue, les fonctions organiques sont bouleversées, la raison est troublée, l'homme perd la conscience du moi, il est dans un vrai délire, il commet les actions les plus irréfléchies, les plus contraires à ses affections, à ses intérêts.](1821, p. 216)

The discourse is obviously one of pathology rather than morality. Esquirol argues in this section that 'violent affection' could impel a man to act against his reason and interests, and that our response should not be one of censure. Even the law, he argues, does not condemn such actions that arise from strong affections: '[d]o not all laws acquit him who has committed, during the first transports of a violent passion, an act, which would have been criminal had it not been for this circumstance?' (1845, p. 257) ['Toutes les lois n'acquittent-elles pas celui qui a commis, dans le premier emportement d'une passion véhémente et desordonnée, une action qui eut été criminelle sans cette circonstance?' (1821, p. 217)]. Absent from the 1821 dictionary entry, but included in the 1838 *Des maladies mentale,* is an even clearer statement relating to the individual's responsibility and agency. Here, Esquirol concludes that '[t]he actions of a man, transported by a sudden passion, are regarded as performed without free agency; and are judged of, as the effect of a temporary delerium' (1845, p. 257) ['les actions d'un homme, emporté par une passion vive sont regardées comme faites sans liberté morale, et sont jugées comme l'effet d'un délire passager' (1838, p. 533)]. Esquirol positions his patients as unable to prevent themselves acting against their own interests and reasoning, driven ('transported') as they are by irresistible forces. The effect of these may be short lived, '[b]ut the acute delirium provoked by the passions, is temporary, and the suicide which it provokes is promptly executed. If not consummated, the impulse is not, ordinarily, renewed' (1845, p. 257) ['Mais le délire aigu, provoqué par des passions est passager. Le suicide qu'il provoque s'exécuté promptement; s'il n'est pas consommé' (1838, p. 533); 'Mais le délire des passions est passager. Le suicide qu'il provoque est instantané; s'il n'est pas consommé' (1821, p. 217).

Such formulations were set out not as speculations but as authoritative medical truths. Esquirol, as had Pinel, sought to ground his theoretical reasoning in clinical observation. E. K. Hunt, in the translator's preface to 1845 English edition of Esquirol's *Mental Maladies,* wrote, '[n]o one at all conversant with the subject on which he treats, will fail to observe, that he speaks from the abundant stores of practical knowledge; every thought which he expresses, and every suggestion that he makes, carrying with it the force of truth, and the evidence of profound investigation' (Hunt, Translator's Preface in Esquirol, 1845, p. v).

The constituting of medical formulations of suicide as empirical and scientific truths acted to strengthen the position of alienists in relation to competing claims from the law and the Church. The law obviously relied on a distinction between legal/illegal in cases of suicide but was challenged by the emergence of a body of knowledge that appeared to cast doubt on the accuracy of such a simple binary division. It was a similar situation for those who sought to act in relation to suicide based on theological/moral distinctions between sinfulness and innocence. As discussed in the previous chapter, clerical and judicial power tended to be sovereign in nature, and thus could be characterised as more repressive than productive in its effects. Church and state reacted to deaths by suicide post-mortem in a punitive manner consistent with the act read as a form of transgression, and when called upon to justify their own often unpopular actions (of excommunication, burial in non-consecrated ground, seizure of goods from surviving family members, etc.) could do so only by appealing to an absolute authority (the Law of the king or God). Medicine, by contrast, could claim not only to be able to identify those with a propensity to suicide before the commission of such an act, but also to be able to produce true knowledge of such propensities that could lead to treatments and cures for those so afflicted.

The production of truths of suicide, based around notions of excessive passions, organic lesions and classifiable forms of insanity, strengthened the position of medicine in relation to competing legal and moral/theo-logical claims, but this should not lead us to conclude that somehow the problem of suicide then became merely a matter of pathology without social or political effects. It may well be the case that suicide came to be talked of and addressed less and less as a moral and legal problem (the laws against suicides were repealed in stages in both France and Great Britain throughout the nineteenth century) but this in itself had political and social consequences. By claiming the truth of suicide to be an act of insanity evidenced by the presence of excessive passions it became possi-ble to position alternative explanations as less scientific and therefore of less value. So (in Esquirol's examples) the shoemaker who kills himself due to debts; the young wife who quarrels with her mother over her new husband and then ends her life; the suicide of a sixteen-year-old girl nearly 'violated' by her father; or the forty-three-year-old who kills himself after falling 'victim to an act of injustice', can all be understood primarily by reference to an individual's insanity (now a rather broad category if its existence was to be established by the presence of 'excessive' passion) rather than any potentially readable social and political context from which such actions arose.

The constituting of suicide as fundamentally a question of individual passions, organic pathology and insanity was not without its problems for alienists, however. In Esquirol's 'Suicide' article there is an attempt to demonstrate how the passions can overwhelm or overpower a man's reason, albeit temporarily, and that such acts of 'involuntary and acute form of suicide' ('le suicide involontaire aigu') can best be explained by reference to the strength of the internal reaction to the external event. This internalised reaction, however, gives no visible, outward sign that can be observed, the act (suicide) is the only sign. It has no *positivity* by which it can be grasped or empirically demonstrated. And here, in positing suicide as caused by an internal, invisible force, a certain tension arises between theoretical claims and means of investigation. As an idea it possessed considerable flexibility and potential for adaptation; however, as Castel (1988) notes, the lack of positivity meant the key to understanding acts such as suicide and (Castel's example) homicide lay in the investigation of a reactive, internalised 'force' that could not be observed. Thus intervention and treatment would always be, at best, somewhat speculative, and in the case of the 'moral management' expounded by Pinel, Esquirol and their respective circles, theoretically inconsistent. For how, asks Castel (1988), could, 'such a drive, represented as irresistible, indefinable and mysterious, yield to the technology of moral treatment, which postulated that madness is malleable when faced with the deployment of an armoury of rational means?' (p. 156). The legacy would be the formation of suicide as an object of medical, scientific investigation, based on the principle of 'minute and accurate observation' (Pinel, 1806/1962, p. 1), yet at the same time the primary cause of self-destructive acts, it was asserted, arose within the unobservable interiority of the suicidal subject, was somewhat mysterious in nature, and could be known only through its effects.

The positing of an internal, unseen, destructive force was, however, a useful explanatory device – flexible enough to account for a variety of otherwise 'inexplicable' acts, and hard to disprove. Equally, it was also hard to prove, and given the positioning of alienist truths of suicide as forms of medical science there was something of a necessity to locate the exact physiological 'seat' of such a force. In a conclusion added to the 1821 text for inclusion in 1838's *Des maladies mentales*, after recounting a number of his own post-mortem findings, Esquirol sets out his position with regard to the anatomy of suicide:

From the cases related by authors, and from those which precede, what consequences can we deduce, so as to determine those organic lesions which will enable us to fix upon the seat of suicide? In this respect, we experience the same difficulty as in assigning the seat and organic lesions, of those whose existence the delirium of mental maladies informs us. (1845, p. 307)

Specific lesions that might point to a 'seat' of suicide prove to be elusive to Esquirol and his colleagues. For alienists, suicide has by theoretical necessity a physiological basis but one that cannot be located with any certainty. It is an act of an individual, but not one acting of his own volition as reason has most commonly been overthrown by the passions; questions of agency and responsibility thus become less clear. It is an object of scientific study – by the careful observation of those visible aspects of the suicidal patient (age, sex, gestures and expressions, physical and 'moral' symptoms), as well as investigations of the corpses of suicides by means of autopsies to search for organic causes – but includes as well unobservable aspects, for suicide is now considered to be caused by some form of internal pathology not directly visible to the medical gaze. These ambiguities and tensions are present from the first and remain the focus of medical attention in relation to suicide.

Conclusions

The production of medical truths in relation to suicide emerged out of certain practices of the asylum. Patients there were confined, observed and examined in order to establish the nature of their particular form of insanity. Those marked as suicidal were constantly watched, not only to ensure their safety (although this was undoubtedly one rationale) but also as a means of gathering information, of accumulating knowledge that would, it was hoped, lead to a more complete understanding of their propensity to harm themselves. Such knowledge was recorded in individual case notes, and many found their way into the writings of Esquirol and his colleagues (Esquirol's *Dictionnaire* entry makes reference to over 100 cases). If patients did come to effect their own deaths their corpses would be dissected in a search for organic lesions – the 'seat' of suicide. From their positions in the asylum, alienists such as Esquirol theorised as to the cause and possible treatments of suicide. The need to formulate such theories in a manner consistent with the principles of the medical science of the time led to the production of knowledge that was individualistic and organic in nature – the truths of suicide were to be found in the pathologised body of individual patients. The production of such truths enabled the consolidation and extension of medical power in relation to competing legal and moral/theological claims to expertise, and acted as a rationale for those asylum practices that facilitated the accumulation of more knowledge.

Power-knowledge thus functioned in a circular relationship, one that was productive but not without its problematic aspects, both for the alienists themselves and for those with whom they came into contact. Within Esquirol's 1821 text there are a number of tensions that arise concerning the nature of suicide itself, and how its truth can come to be known. These primarily concern the definition of the object of study, problems of direct and indirect observation in relation to claims of 'objective' knowledge, and the role of value judgements and prior assumptions in the construction of suicide by means of a medical/scientific vocabulary. The effects of the production of medical truths in terms of the formation of related subjects (doctor and patient) are also touched upon here.

Defining the object of study

The object of enquiry is presented in different ways. Suicide is initially described as an act – 'that act, by which man terminates his existence' ['l'action par laquelle l'homme met fin à sa propre existence' (Esquirol, 1821, p. 213)]. Later it is asserted that 'undoubtedly suicide is idiopathic, but it is more often secondary' ['sans doute le suicide est idiopathique, mais il est plus souvent secondaire', p. 269]. Thus the suicide that emerges in Esquirol's 1821 text is an act, sometimes a disease but more often a symptom. Such differences in how suicide is conceived are never wholly disentangled, but for the most part Esquirol takes suicide to be an act caused by disease.

Direct and indirect observation in relation to claims of 'objective' knowledge

Esquirol takes his formulation of suicide as an act caused by some form of internal pathology as objective knowledge arrived at by direct, unmediated observation. Such assertions, however, gloss over the extent to which unobservable phenomena were invoked to explain how disease led to death by suicide. As noted before, Esquirol and his colleagues primarily considered themselves to be medical scientists. Esquirol opens the preface to the 1838 *Des maladies mentales* with these words:

The work now offered to the public, is the result of forty years' study and observation. I have noticed the symptoms of insanity, and have studied the manners, habits, and wants of the insane, in the midst of whom I have passed my life. I have also tried the best modes of treatment. Confining myself to facts, I have arranged them according to their relations. I have stated them as they have been observed, without, in general, attempting to explain them; and have avoided systems which always appeared to me more seductive by their splendour, than useful in their application. (Esquirol, 1845, p. 3).

Here the alienist is represented as neutral and objective, seeking and describing only the facts. With regard to suicide it is claimed that the facts speak for themselves, that the doctor merely transcribes what he has seen without explanation or interpretation. But the object of observation is not entirely clear. Except in rare circumstances, suicide is not witnessed, so a direct observation of suicide as an act is not considered. Instead, as Esquirol's text makes clear, he is more interested in the events surrounding the act, what causes can be ascribed to it, and the symptoms and illnesses of the person who acts. Some of these elements were open to direct observation, but many were not, but the existence of one was implied by the other. Thus, the gestures and expressions of the patient were interpreted as manifestations, or symptoms, of internal diseases – a *pathologie interne*. By Esquirol's own reasoning, suicide is caused, first and foremost, by the internal effect of the passions. The passions, again by Esquirol's own definition, are not directly observable, but they are talked of throughout his work on suicide. How does Esquirol know of the passions? At best they are assumed by their effects, so we move further away from any notion of direct, unmediated access to the facts in Esquirol's descriptions. Signs of the effects of the passions are sought within the corpses of suicides, and the brains and other internal organs are examined in an attempt to locate traces of their action, but nothing is found. The passions exist as an explanatory concept, they are inferred but not observed, and there arises within Esquirol's text a certain circularity of argument – suicide is taken to be caused by the passions, but the passions are only revealed in acts such as suicide.

Value judgements and prior assumptions

Direct, unmediated observation of 'the facts' is claimed, but prior assumptions, values and judgements pre-existed Esquirol's formulation of suicide. Much of the interpretative framework within which suicide was conceived as a symptom of mental disease was a product of Esquirol and his alienist colleagues. Again, there was a degree of circularity involved. This is not necessarily problematic in itself, but in the writings of Esquirol, and others who followed, this is glossed over by assertions of the facts speaking for themselves, of discoveries and findings appearing fully formed before the eye of the attentive but disinterested observer. The initial value judgements – that suicide arises as the result of an internal pathology, and that suicides are insane – are not reflected upon. For these judgements arose not from the facts – for the 'internal pathology' did not suddenly reveal itself to an observer watchful and perceptive enough to notice that it was there, and always had been there, awaiting discovery. Esquirol, armed with the vocabulary of the doctor and alienist (in part created by him and his circle of colleagues and students), redescribed, in medical terms, a behaviour previously described in terms of a vocabulary of sin and of crime. One interpretation (newer, more certain, and full of possibility) replaced another (older, less plausible, and unpopular with the public), but such a move was not provoked or initiated by an act of unmediated observation of phenomena that had always already existed but had escaped notice before then.

The necessity of the subjugation and domination of the suicidal patient

The suicidal patient is constituted within Esquirol's text as led to act against their will due to the presence of a destructive internal force that arises secondarily to some form of pathology. The patient is insane, dangerous and irresponsible, and thus a number of practices would seem necessarily to follow. The patient is to be constantly observed by the doctor and his staff, confined under the orders of the doctor and restrained by his attendants if required. The identification of the destructive propensities of the patient is a primary aim, as well as the prediction of when such a force may erupt, but given the difficulties of observation outlined above, practically useful knowledge of this 'hard to find' force is in somewhat short supply, so the patient must be carefully watched at all times and have their movements ordered and monitored and their possessions checked. Meticulously detailed measures for the management of the suicidal in the asylum at Salpêtrière are set out in Esquirol's texts. A 'ceaseless watch' at night together with a 'classification which will permit a constant oversight during the day of all those who are supposed to be inclined to suicide' (Esquirol, 1845, p. 310) are recommended. The suicidal 'should not be placed in isolated cells, but in public halls, where they may be better watched, both by their fellow patients, and the attendants' (p. 310). At all times the patient is to be in sight, and total restrictions on movement, possessions, and actions of the patient are needed in order to ensure their safety. Suicidal patients were thus not sorted in the asylums according to their particular diagnosis (melancholic, monomaniac, etc.), but rather placed in areas of maximum visibility and minutely monitored and controlled – not according to a rationality that proceeded from diagnosis to treatment to cure, but to one of confinement, containment and restraint of the body. That such measures made suicide less likely for individual patients at any one point is very probable, but the effects of the continual restating of the inherent irresponsibility and dangerousness of madness, and of the enactment of such practices over a period of time, are harder to quantify. These themes will be pursued in more detail in the next chapter, where the dissemination and diffusion of medical discourse and practices in relation to suicide in the nineteenth century will be mapped.

This chapter has looked to map and problematise the relationship between asylum practices, the production of truths and the formation of objects and subjects of knowledge with regard to suicide as found in Esquirol's 1821 text. The insertion of the problem of suicide into a medically delineated space created the possibility of the establishment of a productive configuration of power-knowledge, one that led to an increase in the knowledge accumulated as well as acted as a rationale for the early alienists' practices of confinement, control and restraint under the guise of medical treatment. The next chapter follows the development of this power-knowledge nexus, and traces the emergence, over the course of the nineteenth century, of certain effects of power in the shape of the changing objects and subjects of study formed in relation to alienist (later psychiatric) truths of suicide.

The production, dissemination and
      circulation of medical truths in relation
      to suicide: 1821–1900

Introduction

Esquirol's 1821 text argued that as suicide was madness and madness was
medical, it followed that suicide was medical (Hacking, 1990). But if
suicide was madness, what kind of madness was it? Was it always madness
to kill oneself? And what sort of treatment did a propensity to suicide
require? These questions were repeated throughout the nineteenth century by those specialising in the medical management of insanity, and the
answers functioned to define more clearly the changing boundaries of the
emerging psychiatric profession.

As previously noted, the redescription of suicide as a form of insanity
was contemporaneous with the emergence of a medical discourse on
madness. Suicide was re-created/reconstructed by recourse to a medical
discourse on insanity, and, reciprocally, the nature of insanity – its con-
tours, boundaries and meaning – became shaped by the medical discourse
on suicide. From Esquirol on, madness is in part defined by reference to
suicide, and suicide by reference to madness.

Esquirol's 1821 text acted as something of a catalyst for further descriptions. In both France and England medical constructions of suicide were
formulated and discussed at length. The 'Esquirol circle' (Goldstein,
1987) of Falret (1822), Cazauvieilh (1840) and Brierre de Boismont
(1856), all wrote treatises on suicide largely in agreement with their
teacher's thesis. Ideas were also exchanged, after the Napoleonic Wars,
across the Channel. Chevalier (1824), Morison (1828, 1840, 1848),
Burrows (1828), Seymour (1832), Prichard (1835, 1840), Mayo (1838),
Ellis (1838), Millingen (1839), Tweedie (1840), Forbes Winslow (1840,
1860), Steward (1845), Noble (1853), Copland (1858), Bucknill and
Tuke (1858), Robinson (1859), Radcliffe (1862), Fielding Blandford
(1871/1976), Wynter (1875), Davey (1878), Knighton (1881), Savage
(1884, 1893), Wynn Westcott (1885), Maudsley (1892a and b, 1895),
Bevan Lewis (1889), Mercier (1890), Tuke (1892) and Strahan (1894)
had all written on the subject from a medical perspective before the end of

the century. The views of the medical men on suicide spread beyond the pages of medical textbooks and found their way into journals such as *The Lancet*, the *Monthly Gazette of Health*, *Medico Chirurgical Review*, *London Medical Gazette*, *London Journal of Psychological Medicine*, *Medical Magazine of London*, *Journal of Psychological Medicine* and the *Journal of Mental Science*. Beyond this, medical aspects of suicide were discussed in publications with a more general readership, for example the *Monthly Review*, *Quarterly Review*, *Annual Register*, *Once a Week*, *Contemporary Review* or more local publications such as the *Illustrated London News*. Newspaper reports and stories also acted as conduits for the dissemination of medical ideas on suicide, particularly when reports were carried of the evidence given in coroners' inquests (Anderson, 1987, p. 214–15).

These writings will now be explored in order to understand how, after Esquirol, suicide was constituted in relation to insanity, and how the medical discourse on suicide came to define the boundaries of both insanity and the psychiatric profession itself until the end of the nineteenth century. The effects of the production and circulation of authoritative truths in relation to suicide are traced in terms of the formation of new objects and subjects of study.

Defining suicide by reference to insanity: what sort of madness was suicide?

Nineteenth-century medical readings of suicide can be divided, broadly, into three main styles of thought:

1 Suicide is initially conceived of as a morbid action of the body, the result of pathological anatomy. The signs of underlying disease are said to be written on the surface of the body.

2 Around mid-century, as the search for the 'seat' of suicide in diseased organs continues to yield few positive results, suicide comes to be represented as arising from an internal impulse. This impulse 'possesses' the individual, 'overwhelms' his reason and will, 'perverts' his natural instincts and 'impels' him to suicide.

3 Finally, towards the end of the century, suicide comes to be read as a symptom of degeneracy – the outcome of a constitutional weakness.

These ways of thinking about the causes of suicide came to co-exist with the search for pathological anatomy continuing alongside talk of impulses and diseased instincts; these approaches were later supplemented by a discourse of degeneracy.

Throughout the century suicide is constituted as an object of scientific knowledge. The emerging psychiatric profession, in representing itself as a form of medicine and as a science, came to possess sufficient authority to make claims to truth with regard to the nature and causation of suicide, despite the considerable difficulties encountered in generating empirical findings to support their theoretical claims. Although wishing to deal primarily with observable material objects in a similar fashion to general medicine and the natural sciences, alienism and psychiatry often fell back on notions of dangerous hidden forces to account for self-destructive acts. Initially these were taken to arise as a consequence of pathological anatomy, later of perverted or diseased instincts. By recourse to such notions, a propensity to suicide came to be constituted as pathological, as a kind of dangerous madness to be confined, contained and restrained. Such a formulation acted to consolidate psychiatric power by justifying asylum practices – and such practices in turn provided the emerging psychiatric profession with the opportunity to observe, examine, classify and treat suicidal patients, and therefore to produce new truths. Truth and power thus existed in a circular relationship often more productive in its effects than repressive.

Suicide as a morbid action of the body, the result of pathological anatomy

Medical discourse required, as Esquirol (1838/1845) noted, reference to 'symptoms', 'causes', 'progress and terminations', and 'treatments' (p. 21). Since it aspired to be seen as a form of natural science, allusion to anything immaterial had to be avoided. As a consequence medical discourse on suicide was almost bound to be constituted by reference to solid, observable objects. For the nineteenth-century doctor interested in mental maladies, the body was the obvious site of exploration.

How Esquirol located the propensity to suicide in the internal actions of the body – how too strong passions could lead to morbid processes that occasioned the development of pathological lesions of various bodily organs (most notably the viscera and brain) – was outlined in the previous chapter. The intellectual and moral faculties were undermined and weakened by this morbidity, and could no longer act, as they usually did when healthy, to restrain the unhealthy propensities that arose within the individual. This formulation, of morbid actions, pathological anatomy and unrestrained propensities that could lead to suicide, found its way into many of the medical writings of the time.

One can compare, for instance, Thomas Chevalier's *Remarks on Suicide* (1824), to Esquirol's formulation. He writes:

The first view to be taken of the subject, in order to understand its nature, is that which Medicine, or rather Human Pathology, affords; and which is to be sought not in theory, or in conjecture, but in facts. It is material that the public should

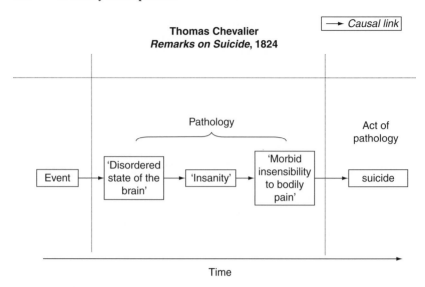

Figure 8.1 Style of thought in Thomas Chevalier's *Remarks on Suicide* (1824).

know, and that coroners and jurors especially should know, that *the attempt at self-destruction is OFTEN the FIRST distinct overt act of insanity.* (Chevalier, 1824, pp. 367–8, emphasis in original)

Suicide is madness and medical, and should be studied by reference only to the 'facts': '[t]hat severe affliction and mental distress will sometimes so overwhelm the mortal fabric, as to produce madness is true. But when it does thus, it is probably, in all instances, by inducing a physically disordered state of the brain' (Chevalier, 1824, pp. 369–70).

As with Esquirol, insanity, as a consequence of pathological anatomy, is at the heart of suicide: '[I]t is difficult to believe they [suicides] would have courage and endurance enough to go through their attempt, were not that *morbid insensibility to bodily suffering, which is almost peculiar to insanity, first produced by a disordered state of the brain*' (Chevalier, 1824, p. 371, italics added).

This can be illustrated as shown in Figure 8.1.

A similar style of thought can be detected in Esquirol's 1821 text (see Figure 8.2): '[w]hen the soul is strongly moved, by a violent and unexpected affection, organic functions are perverted, the reason is disturbed, the individual loses his self-consciousness, is in a true delirium, and commits acts the most thoughtless; those most opposed to his instinct, to his affections and interests' (1845, p. 256).

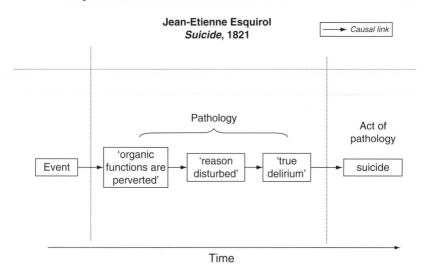

Figure 8.2 Style of thought in Jean-Etienne Esquirol's 'Suicide' (1821).

As with Esquirol, Chevalier speaks of 'the facts', and of the medical man as embodiment and bearer of the truth. Thus, '[t]he general experience of mankind, and especially of practitioners in Medicine and in Surgery, presents facts which ought not to be overlooked, and which indeed speak loudly on this subject' (Chevalier, 1824, p. 368).

Empirical findings in support of the claims made proved, however, hard to come by. Whereas the medicine that concerned itself with physical ailments could, more often than not (and increasingly so as the century wore on) locate lesions through autopsies and the mapping of the signs of disease on the body, mental physicians could assert the presence of pathology within the body, or signs on the body, that it was claimed accounted for the various forms of insanity, but they could find little consistent evidence to support them. Esquirol (1821) wrote that 'the opening of the dead bodies of suicides, has shed little light on this subject' (p. 269), and this continued to be the case. Similarly, Falret noted that dissections of the brain had not illustrated the causes of suicide, but continued to assert that the brain is always primarily affected (*Monthly Gazette of Health*, 1822). For although the elusiveness of locatable pathology was sometimes acknowledged, the belief in its presence was continually asserted throughout the century. George Mann Burrows, a general physician from London who, after travelling to Paris in 1817 to study the work of the French *aliénistes* (and later argued with Esquirol over the relative propensities to suicide of the English and French), came to specialise in mental medicine, writes in his chapter on suicide in his *Commentaries on the Causes, Forms, Symptoms, and Treatment, Moral and Medical, of Insanity* (1828) that '[t]he apparent absence of lesion or disease in any organ of the body, I repeat, does not disprove the existence of a morbid condition' (p. 416). For the most part Burrows follows Esquirol – it is the viscera and, to a lesser extent, the brain, that are the seats of the moral and intellectual faculties, and it is here where we should expect to find disease and decay. The exact locations and actions of the diseased organs were speculated upon but a tension remained between confident assertions of the presence of pathology and the lack of positive results from attempts to locate it throughout the century.

That different forms of pathological anatomy could lead to suicide was not doubted, and here a variety of elements were brought together to construct a plausible account of the relationship between the two. Burrows (1828) writes of the body in terms of viscera, bile, blood and the encephalon. These elements, he notes, may possess inherited traits. There are also the mental and moral faculties to be considered, linked to emotions, the mind, volition, the spirit and reason. These may become diseased, and different kinds of insanity may arise, such as melancholia, mania or derangement, and from here a suicidal disposition may manifest itself, which, if untreated, could lead to suicide itself. The elements were taken to interact with each other, so that, as in Esquirol's (1821) formulations, too strong emotions could make an impression upon the brain that could lead to a suicidal propensity. Suicide is thus constituted as arising as a result of pathology, with the site of pathology either acting to cause disturbance in the organism as a whole (faulty reasoning, immoral behaviour, lowness of spirits, etc., consequent upon a brain lesion), or with disturbance in the organism causing pathological lesions (too strong passions, vice, etc., leading to an injury to the brain). As such suicide, medically constituted, could be studied scientifically through the search for lesions by means of autopsy or through those signs of lesion said to be evident on the surface of the body. Such formulations consolidated medical power in relation to the suicidal through reducing explanations of the causes of suicide to the level of anatomy and physiology: it was the body that held the truths of suicide, and these could be uncovered through processes of observation and examination undertaken only by those deemed to possess medical expertise. New relations of power were formed: the suicidal individual is constituted as a patient to be watched and examined when alive, and as a corpse to be dissected when dead; and the doctor is taken to possess authoritative knowledge and capability in reading the premonitory signs of a propensity to suicide or the lesions in those who succumbed to such a death. In such a formation the patient's body is the site of exploration and it was therefore necessary to contain and make docile the patient in order that the body could be better observed and examined. Practices of confinement and restraint could thus be justified and medical expertise increased through the production and circulation of knowledge gained through the application of medical procedures.

The speculations as to what organs were involved in suicide, and in what ways, continued. James Cowles Prichard (1835) wrote that 'in a great proportion of cases suicide is certainly the result of physical disease' (p. 400), but admitted that 'we must confess that the same obscurity yet involves the physical causes of suicidal as of other forms of insanity' (p. 401). Prichard asserts that it has been established that disease can account for many suicides, yet also confesses that some 'obscurity' remains as to the exact processes involved. Others were less doubting: Sir William Ellis (1838) argued that it was 'the brain sympathizing with the liver' (p. 117) that could account for suicide, thus agreeing with Burrows (1828, p. 415). Mayo (1838) also implicates the brain, but also adds that a 'bilious indigestion' can increase the risk of suicide (p. 71). The brain/viscera explanation proved popular until towards the middle of the century. Forbes Winslow, in the tellingly titled *The Anatomy of Suicide* (1840), wrote, 'the disposition to commit self-destruction is, to a great extent, amenable to those principles which regulate our treatment of ordinary disease; and that, to a degree more than is generally supposed, it originates in derangement of the brain and abdominal viscera' (1840, p. v).

Winslow, like Burrows before him, draws on a number of other concepts and objects in linking pathology to suicide. Winslow is fonder than Burrows of moral causes as explanations for suicide, but for the most part he draws on similar concepts. However, despite the strength of claims to a physical basis for suicide, findings of anatomical abnormalities or pathology remained elusive. As Davidson (2001) notes, '[p]athological anatomy could not serve psychiatry either as an explanatory theory for so-called mental diseases or disorders or as the foundation for the classification and description of these diseases' (p. 2). Examining the corpses of suicides yielded little that was of theoretical use and proved to be a rather unfruitful endeavour in terms of uncovering evidence to support the belief in a physical basis of self-destructive acts. Yet the possibility of finding a 'seat' of suicide, of locating pathological lesions within the body of suicides, held much allure. The obvious rationale for the continuing search to find a physical cause of suicide was that if specific lesions or abnormalities could be identified then treatment and cure of the propensity to suicide could be effected. The production of medical knowledge in relation to suicide in the first half of the nineteenth century offered much promise but little of practical use and as a result of the paucity of findings pathological anatomy begins to fade from view. Instead alternative concepts and theories based on notions of diseased instincts and unrestrained impulses – 'functional' disorders – come to the fore, traceable to James Cowles Prichard's influential *Treatise on Insanity and Other Disorders Affecting the Mind* of 1835. One still finds assertions that in the case of suicide the brain was diseased (e.g. Winslow, 1860, pp. 248–9; Davey, 1878, p. 255) but only occasionally are the liver and other viscera implicated (e.g. Copland, 1858, p. 559).

The lack of findings of pathological anatomy through autopsy thwarted the development of authoritative 'organic' theories of suicide to an extent, but alongside the 'opening up of corpses', the mental doctor also focused his gaze on what were taken to be the visible, external manifestations of internal abnormalities.

Reading the signs written on the body

The body, it was assumed, displayed the signs of underlying pathology on its surface, and it was here, if one was in possession of the necessary expertise and experience, that the evidence of interior abnormalities (moral, physical) could be observed and correctly understood (see Rimke, 2003, for a detailed analysis of the ways in which nineteenth-century psychiatry read the body as an interpretable text). These signs were often described in detail. Burrows (1828) noted that in the individual contemplating suicide 'sorrow, despair, or horror, is portrayed in deep traits on his countenance' and the 'eye becomes injected, hollow, and sunk, but glistening, roving, and wild' (p. 422). Here it is the medical gaze that settles on the patient, and a 'hermeneutics of the body' (Rimke, 2003, p. 247) brought to bear to decipher the precise meaning and significance of what is observed. The heat of the patient, for instance, could act as a clue to the nature of the unobserved mental state; an 'embarrassment all over the body' can be discerned, and the patient is 'subject to great flushings, partial heats, and sweats about the body' (Burrows, 1828, p. 422). Such signs are seen to be open to categorisation according to the dominant feeling that is acting upon the patient. Hence, revenge is observable; '[t]here is a transient animation, a hurried and vacillating manner, doing and undoing all day; the face has a hectic flush, the pulse is quicker, respiration is increased, and the patient is sleepless. There appears strong marks of cerebral excitation' (p. 432).

In Ellis (1838) the drawing of the 'muscles of the face into particular forms' or a 'singular expression of countenance, especially in the eye' could be read as 'an unvarying attendant on a disposition to suicide' (p. 119). Similarly, in Forbes Winslow (1840) as in Ellis and Burrows, the eyes signalled intent, and the 'experienced physician and accurate observer will be able to detect, before the mental alienation becomes apparent to others, the early dawnings of derangement' (p. 162). Later, he writes, '[s]uicidal mania is easily recognised by the experienced physician. The surgeon of a large establishment in the environs of the metropolis informed me, that in six cases out of ten he could detect, by the appearance of the eye, the existence of the desire to commit self-destruction' (p. 204).

It was these signs that required expert reading, and in postulating the necessity of medical expertise in the decipherment of such premonitory clues of impending self-destruction, medical authority and power in relation to competing knowledge claims and practices (the Church and judiciary as obvious examples) were consolidated. For while the Church could pass judgement on the soul of the suicide and refuse to bury the body in consecrated ground, and the law could punish the surviving family, such (sovereign) power was essentially repressive in its functioning, acting (in some cases perhaps) as a deterrent but unable to produce knowledge that would aid in the prevention of the commission of such terrible acts. Medicine, despite the apparently limited utility of much of its knowledge, offered the possibility of identifying treatable causes of suicidal states. The confinement of those suspected of harbouring suicidal propensities was thus justified not only in terms of preventing deaths but also by reference to the accumulation of knowledge that arose as a result of patients being subjected to medical practices of observation and examination while confined – a productive rather than repressive relation of power-knowledge.

It came to be held that there were 'common physiognomical principles' (Ellis, 1838) that underlay the correct reading of the countenances of the insane and suicidal. It was this notion that saw physicians interested in mental maladies seeking to complement written descriptions with portraits (drawings, later photographs) that could provide guides to aid physicians in their interpretations. Such an approach also sought to strengthen the view that mental medicine was involved in a form of natural history, systematically classifying and cataloguing the various species and sub-species of diseased humanity, much as botanists of the age produced books of illustrations organised according to categories that were held to be a mirror of nature's own schema (see also Rimke, 2005, for a description of how nineteenth-century psychiatry used 'visual documentation' as a means of mapping (and constituting) 'immoral interiorities'). Esquirol himself had commissioned nearly 200 plaster casts of the faces of the insane, and his collection also contained a series of drawings and paintings produced by the renowned French painter, Theodore Géricault. Alexander Morison, a physician who instituted the first formal lectures on mental disease in Britain in 1823, visited Esquirol in Paris and viewed his collection. Inspired, Morison set about creating his own material, and in 1840 he published his *Physiognomy of Mental Disease* with illustrations of patients representing the various categories of insanity. Morison divided insanity into the standard 'Mania, Monomania, Dementia, and Idiotism or Idiocy' (p. 2), and illustrations of patients exhibiting the 'suicidal propensity' are to be found mostly in the section on monomania. An example is shown in Figure 8.3.

Morison's collection was widely known and commented upon, and often published alongside commentaries on insanity. The *Medical Times and Gazette* of 1858 published, for instance, 'Suicidal Melancholy' (Figure 8.4).

Later, with the increased availability of the necessary equipment, it became more common to photograph asylum patients (Gale and Howard, 2003). These images were often used for teaching purposes, and a few found their way into medical books (Bucknill and Tuke's (1858) *Manual of Psychological Medicine,* for instance, contained seven photographs, including one titled *'Acute Suicidal Melancholia'*).

The reading of the body, however, like the search for pathological anatomy, even aided by illustrations and photographs, seemed to promise more than it could deliver. The hope, or expectation, that the expression or gestures of the patient would reveal the presence of an underlying 'suicidal propensity' was not fulfilled. By positing, however, that the manifestations of such a propensity were visible on the surface of the body it was possible to assert that such signs were only readable by those possessing sufficient expertise, and that their interpretation required specialist knowledge. The pathologised body became, from Esquirol on, the primary site for investigations into the truth of suicide, and medicine declared its rights, authority and expertise over this domain.

Suicide arising from an internal, irresistible impulse: possession, perversion and impulsion

With the search for diseased internal organs that could account for suicide bearing little fruit, and the limited usefulness of closely observing the bodies of the insane for manifest signs of underlying pathology becoming apparent, new ways to construct suicide as a medical and scientific concern arose. As with the attempt to find evidence of the 'seat' of suicide in pathological anatomy, it was within the individual that mental medicine located the primary cause of suicide. The idea of diseased and disordered

MELANCHOLIA WITH FEAR.

Figure 8.3 'Portrait of a female, in whom delusive fear of every object and person *Panaphobia* keeps her in a state of perpetual distress. It is necessary to watch her closely to prevent her committing suicide' (Morison, 1840, p. 99, plate 36). (Wellcome Library, London)

instincts, consequent upon an 'overwhelming' internal impulse, overtook those of diseased and disordered organs. No longer a kind of madness centred on notions of pathological anatomy, suicide rather is constructed as arising due to an involuntary impulsion, a form of madness that was also

Figure 8.4 'Suicidal Melancholy', *The Medical Times and Gazette*, 37 (January–June) 1858: plate 2 opposite p. 64 (Wellcome Library, London)

associated with, so it was argued, a perversion of the natural instinct of self-preservation.

The idea of innate instincts was not new, of course. It was long believed that God and nature had placed within man two fundamental instincts, those of procreation and of self-preservation. Thomas Aquinas had argued in the thirteenth century that self-killing was a sin as it went against our God-given natural inclination for self-preservation. But still suicide represented something of a puzzle, as it seemed to require an 'overcoming' of this most natural and God-given instinct. The Reverend Charles Moore's *A Full Inquiry into the Subject of Suicide* (1790) has the following: 'But the species of suicide … deviates so widely from the first principles of human nature, that fortified, as mankind are, by the strong and prevalent impulses of self-love and self-preservation, one should think all enlargement on the subject would be needless, as well as all caution against its commission futile and nugatory' (p. 3).

The instinct of self-preservation is most often represented, by medicine as well as theologians, as the strongest force in man, and its overcoming needed to be accounted for in some way. Nineteenth-century mental medicine offered two explanations; (i) a greater force or impulse able to overwhelm the instinct for survival or (ii) a weakening of the instinct of self-preservation so that death is not so feared or is even sought. These ideas come to the fore towards mid-century, with the suicidal impulse postulated as an internal force that could, in those possessing an innate propensity to suicide, or those of weak will and constitution, be stronger than the instinct for self-preservation. At the same time it was argued, as notions of degeneracy began to appear on the horizon, that the instinct for life itself could become diseased or perverted, and suicide result.

The terms 'impulse' and 'instinct' take on a distinct medical meaning in the hands of alienists. Initially (for example, Esquirol's 1821 article) they are rarely drawn on in the medical discourse on suicide. Burrows (1828) talks of suicide 'committed under very opposite impulses' (p. 413), but here the meaning is analogous to that of 'motives', and Ellis (1838) asserts that suicides can sometimes take place from a 'sudden impulse' (p. 125), but the nature of the impulse is not speculated on.

The use of 'impulses' and 'diseased instincts' within mental medicine can be traced to Prichard's *A Treatise on Insanity and Other Disorders Affecting the Mind* (1835). Prichard much influenced Esquirol (and vice versa – Prichard's book contains a glowing dedicatory message to Esquirol), particularly with regard to the notions of 'moral insanity' and 'moral perversion'. For Prichard the minds of those suffering from 'moral insanity' were 'strangely perverted and depraved', with the consequence that 'the power of self-government is lost or greatly impaired' (p. 4). As Barbara Gates notes, such thinking enabled the linking of crime with illness, for, as Prichard asserted with regard to 'moral insanity', '[h]omicides, infanticides, suicides of the most fearful description have been committed under its influence' (in Gates, 1980, p. 13). Prichard, in his

Treatise (1835), reasoned that the 'propensity to suicide is simply a moral perversion, and ... there is a perversion of the strongest instinct of nature, that of self-preservation', continuing that it is the 'characteristic of moral insanity to pervert the natural instincts or propensities, and suicide displays the most signs of these perversions' (p. 401).

Such language and concepts were readily taken up, in England as well as France. In Bucknill and Tuke's 1858 *Manual of Psychological Medicine*, instincts can be conceived of as 'perverted' and 'diseased' (p. 201). Here, the instinct of self-preservation, 'deeply implanted in the inner recesses' of the individual constitution, is 'overborne' – becomes perverted – by the diseased actions of other faculties or instincts. Similarly, in Copland's huge *A Dictionary of Practical Medicine* (1858), there is talk of a 'morbid impulse', 'suicidal impulse' (here linked to 'congestion of, or of inflammatory determination of blood to, the brain', p. 552).

In Bucknill and Tuke (1858) the notions of instinct and impulse are brought together; 'there are cases in which the instinct of self-preservation is more especially diseased, being, as it were, reversed in its operation. There is here a blind, unreasoning, irresistible impulse to commit suicide – a true suicidal monomania' (p. 201).

The terms come to overlap in meaning, and coincide frequently as descriptors of internal forces. For Morselli (1882), there is even an 'instinctive impulse' which 'makes itself so much the master of the individual will as to draw the worthy man to homicide, the prudent and courageous to suicide'. This impulse 'has power to weaken and conquer ... the reflective and sensitive faculties', leading the individual to act against his will and better judgment (p. 281). Suicide thus comes to be read as caused by forces located deep within the individual that are conceived as unhealthy, diseased, abnormal and perverse. Reason is 'conquered', the worst in 'man' defeats that which is most noble, and suicide results.

A distinct 'suicidal impulse' comes to be postulated, whereby patients 'in an acute and unmistakeable state of insanity, and in one that is hardly recognizable as being insanity except in this one feature, have a violent desire and longing to commit suicide' (Fielding Blandford, 1871/1976, p. 182). This impulse is only ever sketchily presented, though, and its origin, boundaries and form are never clearly explicated. At best we learn that it is a force that can differ 'vastly in its intensity and persistency' (Wynter, 1875, p. 312) although it is most often 'of a temporary nature' (p. 313). It is a force known almost entirely from its effects. An analogy is made with epilepsy. Thus the suicidal impulse may be, 'of convulsive nature sudden in its onset, transient in its course, and followed by immediate and complete relief; its analogy to the epileptic state being still further indicated by the occurrence of an aura, usually an aural hallucination' (Bevan Lewis, 1889, p. 187). Henry Maudsley (1892b) also makes use of the image of the impulse as manifesting itself in the form of a convulsion, explaining that an urge to suicide may arise in those patients who had 'the insane neurosis':

which displayed its morbid energy in a convulsive idea, not otherwise than as the epileptic neurosis, to which it is closely allied, displays its morbid energy in convulsive movement. Looking at their mental state from a strictly pathological point of view, it is entirely consistent with experience, for as the function of the motor centres is movement, so the functions of the supreme nerve-centres is thought, and as a morbid state of the motor centres occasions convulsion of movements, so, in like manner, a morbid state of the mind-centres occasions what, for want of a more appropriate term, may be called a convulsion of idea. (p. 137)

Medical knowledge from one domain (epilepsy), centring on a discourse of nerve and motor centres, of morbid states leading to convulsions, is brought to bear on another (suicide). Such a move acts to strengthen medical authority in relation to possible challenges, making clerical and judicial views on the subject appear unscientific and outdated by claiming to have located the truth of the cause of suicide in the disordered or diseased body of the afflicted. Such a position was not without moral or legal ramifications, however. For, if the effects of a 'suicidal impulse' are 'almost identical with the automatic acts performed by epileptics during periods of temporary unconsciousness, which acts are frequently either suicidal or homicidal' (Strahan, 1894, p. 116), it followed that, 'there is nothing more voluntary, in the proper meaning of the term, in the death of such a one by his own act than there is in the silence of the mute, the jibbering of the idiot, or the convulsion of the epileptic' (p. 116).

What is of particular interest here, in terms of exploring what sort of suicide mental medicine creates by reference to the notion of an impulse, are the implications in terms of agency and responsibility. For, as Maudsley writes, 'as the will cannot restrain a convulsive movement, of which the patient may all the while be conscious, so the will cannot always restrain, however much it may strive to do so, a morbid idea which has reached a convulsive activity, although there may be all the while a clear consciousness of its morbid nature' (1892a, p. 138). Charles Mercier also talked of a 'suicidal insanity', where there existed a 'persistent suicidal impulse' but without 'appreciable disorder of the intellect'. In these cases:

The patient is quite aware of his morbid state, deplores it, struggles against the horrible temptation, but in the end, unless very closely watched, is hurried into suicide by it. ... Nevertheless, his intellect is at times so completely the slave of his morbid impulse that it is constrained to watch for opportunities and to devise means to carry it into effect. (Mercier, 1890, p. 353)

There are echoes here, in the formulations of Maudsley and Mercier, of Esquirol's original assertion that although a patient may be aware of the 'wrongness' or immorality of his actions, he is nevertheless powerless to prevent them. For Esquirol, it was passions that could overwhelm the will and reason, now it was another form of internal force, this time conceived as a 'morbid energy', or an impulse of a 'convulsive' nature. Maudsley also writes of a distinct 'impulsive insanity', whose nature also compromises the patients will:

it is a fact that in a certain state of mental disease a morbid impulse may take such despotic possession of the patient as to drive him, in spite of reason and against his will, to a desperate act of suicide or homicide; like the demoniac of old into whom the unclean spirit entered, he is possessed by a power which forces him to a deed of which he has the utmost dread and horror. (Maudsley, 1892a, p. 188)

Mental medicine, towards the end of the century, seems to have arrived at an interesting point. The standard view within medical circles is that suicide is no longer to be conceived of as a voluntary act, but there is a struggle to provide a scientifically plausible account as to why this might be. An internal force of some nature is postulated, that takes possession of the person, overpowers their reason and will, and impels them to suicide. Thus Maudsley (1892a), in an echo of his sentiments above, relates how the 'suicidal propensity' could spring into activity and 'display itself in a convulsive energy', one that 'seems as if it were independent of the operations of the mind, which is otherwise rational, as if it were a demon that had taken possession of the man, and ruled him in spite of reason and will' (p. 140). The possession, though, is no longer by a demon that entered from without; instead a force arises from deep within the individual, and finds expression as a morbid, destructive energy able to overwhelm all internal restraint. Thus, the intellect, the will and even the instinct of self-preservation become weakened, diseased and perverted in their actions.

What is not established clearly is a source or site of this impulsive force. There appears instead, within the discourse of mental medicine, an energy that could be entirely absent one moment, strike with full force the next, then disappear again; one that arises from somewhere but also seemingly nowhere; a force that is ultimately knowable only through its manifestations – most often those otherwise inexplicable acts of violence, suicide and homicide. Yet, at the same time as they were asserting the existence of such an intangible force, alienists remained wholeheartedly committed to a 'physicalist' dogma that insisted that all phenomena relating to insanity had a physical 'seat' in the diseased body. This was a necessary requirement for the maintenance of medical and scientific authority. As Roger Smith (1981) writes, 'physical explanations were the prerogative of scientific medicine; physicalism was therefore also central to claims for medical expertise' (p. 40). Maudsley (1863, in Smith, 1981, p. 11) had written that 'medicine deals with matter, force, and necessity', but it also, primarily, dealt with the body, and as the idea of an 'irresistible impulse' gained in currency, there was an expectation that the concept would find some sort of corporeal 'home'. Use of the analogy with epilepsy had allowed talk of 'explosions of nerve force' and 'muscular convulsions', but there is a distinct lack of speculation on where this energy sprang from, and how it then translated into apparently organised, purposeful actions. These descriptive shortcomings, though, were more than made up for by the utility of this impulse when it came to explaining otherwise inexplicable actions. Psychiatry could define its social function and justify its practices by reference to apparently motiveless and impulsive destructive acts, and an 'irresistible impulse' allowed for a physicalist, medical, scientific-sounding explanation, albeit one that lacked a certain specificity. But this was also its strength, for such a nebulous object was one that was particularly hard to refute as it did not present much of a target to opponents, the only evidence of its existence being the impulsive act itself.

In terms of defining suicide by reference to insanity, we can see that various forms were created by medical discourse during the nineteenth century. While it was initially conceived as resulting from the actions of diseased organs, later ideas of morbid impulses and instincts come to predominate. At each point the authority of the theories rests on the use of a medical and scientific vocabulary, for no positive evidence is found for the existence of morbidity beyond the assertions of the doctors themselves. What decreases in importance in medical descriptions as the century wears on is an 'external' context of suicide beyond the confines of the individual body. Also lacking is the idea of suicide being in any way a voluntary act, with its own motives derived from the cultural context and the life of the individual. Deterministic, physicalist descriptions prevail. These trends culminate in the constructing of suicide from a discourse of degeneracy – whereby death by suicide comes to be read as a form of natural selection, arising from an innate, inherited morbidity. Here, the suicide is understood to be constitutionally unfit to live, and death is both inevitable and necessary. Nature determines the suicide, and individual will and social restraints are rendered powerless (see in particular Strahan, 1894, pp. 30, 65–6, 78–9).

The would-be suicide, as a victim of such pathologies, continues to be constituted as a figure without speech within psychiatric discourse – not only in that it was believed that they lacked the means to communicate the cause of their desire to die (for the blind forces that impelled them to death are not read as knowable let alone communicable by doctors), but also in that their deaths were, within psychiatric discourse, ascribed to a constitutional defect, an internal impulse, or some form of intellectual or emotional derangement, each acting in some way to diminish the patient's authority to speak with reason and sense.

How suicide came to be constituted as a kind of madness in the nineteenth century has been mapped. It is also possible to trace a reciprocal effect – that is the means by which ideas around suicide were drawn upon in defining the nature of madness.

Defining insanity by reference to suicide: what suicide revealed of madness

In asserting that suicide arose as a consequence of some form of internal pathology, alienists reconstituted suicide as a type of insanity. At the same time, this redescription of suicide also changed, in part, what it was to be mad. Suicide showed madness to be individual, internal, and private. In addition, the madman, possessing a propensity to suicide but also able to conceal it, was revealed to be dangerous and cunning. These themes will be outlined in turn.

Madness is internal

Alienists, as we have seen, did not confine *pathologie interne* only to diseases of the bodily organs. The moral and intellectual faculties could also be diseased, and these were understood to interact reciprocally with the body's organs. What is clear in these formulations regarding suicide and insanity is that while there may be observable external manifestations of madness and associated destructive propensities, fundamentally they arise as a consequence of pathological processes occurring within the person. Reason, passions, dispositions and desires, read as internal attributes or possessions of the individual, could each be diseased. Later, following Prichard (1835), are added impulses and instincts. Descriptions varied as to the exact nature of these interior phenomena, but that suicide followed as a consequence of internal pathology was a constant in medical constructions of suicide throughout the century. Madness, of which suicide was a manifestation, could thus be constituted as arising from within the diseased interiority of the patient, and explanations that located the causes of insanity and suicide outside the individual patient came to possess less currency.

Madness is individual, private and hidden

Suicide came to be constituted, by means of medical/psychiatric discourse and practices, as individual in nature. The keeping of individualised case notes, the writing up of case studies, the interrogation and diagnosing of patients, the dividing up and dispersal of patients within the asylum according to their perceived 'management' needs as well as the prescription of specific regimes of treatment – in short those individualising techniques noted by Foucault (2006) – all served to create a regime of truth in relation to both madness and suicide centred on the individual patient. Additionally, once the cause of such an act is taken to reside within the individual patient it comes to be somewhat hidden and private – the propensity to self-destruction is located within the patient, unseen and unobservable, and the act itself is inexplicable except by reference to a specialised knowledge of pathology. Madness, as in the case of an impulse to suicide, could be hidden, and detecting insanity became a question of looking for concealed signs of its presence. Mental medicine became in some measure the art of reading the body for signs of a not-yet-manifested madness.

Madness is dangerous

That suicides were mad confirmed that madness was dangerous. Further, suicide and homicide were continually brought together in the writings of alienists and psychiatrists to illustrate the hidden dangers of madness. Thomas Mayo (1838), for example, wrote that if 'the tendency to suicide occasionally requires the supposition of insanity for its explanation, this hypothesis is requisite in an equal degree to enable us to explain the wish to kill others' (pp. 80–1), and concludes that 'insanity is, in some sort, productive of the homicidal *act*, and is itself the consequence of the homicidal *tendency*' (p. 81). Insanity thus comes to be read as both explanation and cause of murder and suicide (see for examples Forbes Winslow, 1840, p. 39; Millingen, 1839, pp. 211–12; Morison, 1848, p. 223; Copland, 1858, pp. 551 and 556; Fielding Blandford, 1871/1976, p. 180; Maudsley, 1892a, pp. 131–2). Propensities or impulses are presented as responsible for both suicide and homicide, but the similarities or differences between the acts are not explicated in any detail. It remains sufficient to assert 'impulses' as both explanation and cause of destructive acts, and a strong connection comes to be forged between dangerousness, madness and medicine.

The madman is cunning

Given that the propensity to suicide (and homicide) was largely unobservable, its uncovering was of some importance. Here, the doctor sought, by careful observation, or by sheer force of his will when confronting a suspected suicide, to make visible what was hidden within. That patients resisted revealing their propensities and intentions, that they did not confess what they knew to be true, was proof of their cunning, and evidence of the deceit inherent in insanity. Esquirol remarked that mono-maniacs knew how to 'repress the expression of their delirium, and to dissemble the disorder of their understanding' and in so doing deceived all, and that the 'same is true of some individuals, over whom the purpose to commit suicide holds complete sway' (1845, p. 267). The frustrations felt by the physician faced with the certain knowledge of the presence of madness, but the inability to make it visible for all to see is illustrated by Forbes Winslow (1840). He writes of 'the singular cunning of lunatics; how extremely difficult it is in many cases where *we know* the individual to be unquestionably mad, to make his delusions apparent' (p. 230).

A form of dangerous madness is conceived, the premonitory signs of which are hidden even from the eye of the expert, and whose first mani-festation may be lethal. Foucault (2002a), in discussing the interest of alienists in such violent acts, writes of an attempt 'to grasp a type of derangement that manifested itself only in the moment and in the guise of a crime, a derangement that would have no symptom other than the crime itself and could disappear once the crime had been committed' (p. 182). For Foucault, '[n]ineteenth-century psychiatry invented an entirely fictitious entity, a crime that is insanity, a crime that is nothing but insanity, an insanity that is nothing but a crime' (p. 182). Foucault discusses for the most part acts of homicide, but the 'psychiatric reason-ing' with regard to suicide was the same – there is created an all but inexplicable act that could only be understood by notions of hidden propensities and impulses, the consequence of internal pathology. Thus the madness that emerges from the discussions of suicide is internal to the individual, hidden but potentially lethal in its effects – the madman a threat to society, dangerous and cunning.

The reciprocal redescriptions of insanity and suicide were in part con-ducted by means of an ongoing debate within medical circles. Throughout the nineteenth century medical men did not discuss whether suicide could be conceived, in some instances, as a manifestation of madness – this was held to be a fact and was not seriously contested, even outside medicine – but rather they focused on the limits of this construction, on cases where the sanity or otherwise of the suicide was in doubt, as well as on establishing the percentage of suicides who could be considered insane. In so doing, physicians and alienists were involved in a process of defining and redefining the nature and boundaries of insanity, as well as the nature and function of the emerging psychiatric profession. Madness, constructed through a discourse on suicide, was individual, private and dangerous. Esquirol, following Pinel, had broadened the scope as to what constituted insanity, so that by the end of the eighteenth century and into the nineteenth it was no longer purely derangement of the intellectual faculties that constituted madness. The boundaries of insanity did not remain fixed, however, and ongoing discussion amongst nineteenth-century 'mental medics' as to whether all suicides were mad, and the consideration of those cases of suicide that were seen to fall outside the reach of insanity, helped define the nature and set the limits for what constituted insanity. Set the boundary broadly enough and all suicides were insane (albeit temporarily), a more narrow definition and some suicides could be considered sane. At the same time, in setting out a view of suicide as a manifestation of certain types of madness, notions of what constituted insanity were reshaped. This continual forming and reforming of the truths of madness in relation to suicide, and vice versa, can perhaps be most usefully analysed not by attempting to establish their correspondence to some ahistorical or acultural truths of mental illness or suicide but rather by attempting to discern a strategic logic in the workings of psychiatric power in this period.

Defining psychiatry by reference to suicide: what suicide tells us of the function of psychiatry

A recognisable psychiatric profession, characterised by a distinct 'psychiatric' style of reasoning, began to emerge around the middle of the nineteenth century (Davidson, 2001). The formation of such a professional group can be traced to late eighteenth-century and early nineteenth-century alienists and practitioners of mental medicine (Scull, 1981; Porter, 1987; Foucault, 2006). The nature of this profession, and its social function, has been the subject of much debate (see, for instance, Scull, 1993, or Shorter, 1997, for differing interpretations). Here, what the 'psychiatric' approach to suicide might tell us of the function of psychiatry, at least in terms of its emergence in the nineteenth century, will be discussed in relation to the following themes:

- psychiatry as a moral enterprise;
- psychiatry as public hygiene and control of the dangerous individual;
- psychiatric discourse as formative of notions and practices of self-restraint.

It is argued that psychiatry formed an object of study – essentially an unseen and dangerous force within the individual that could impel the person to commit terrible acts – and then sought not only to define and explain such 'impulses', but to confine and contain them as well.

Additionally, psychiatry also sought to instil within the dangerous individual the means for self-restraint.

Psychiatry as a moral enterprise

The pathologisation of suicide, the process whereby suicide came to be read as a matter of medical concern rather than as a sin or a crime, is usually presented as a relatively benign process, a move away from religious and legal condemnation to a more humane and scientific understanding of suicide (Gates, 1980; Jamison, 1999; O'Connor and Sheehy, 2000; Colt, 2006). Porter (2000), for instance, speaks of a shift in status of the suicide 'from pariah, malefactor or sinner to object of pity' (p. 219). There is also a view that doctors played a key role in this process by offering a less severe, more rational approach to the problem (Berrios and Mohanna, 1995; Goldney and Schioldann, 2000, 2002; van Hooff, 2000). According to this analysis doctors sought to medicalise suicide as a way of humanising the treatment of suicides in the face of religious and legal persecution. Such a reading, however, ignores the often passionate condemning of suicide and the would-be suicide by medics throughout the century, particularly those specialising in lunacy. Nineteenth-century medical writings on suicide are often marked by their abhorrence of the act.

From the start, medical writings on the subject are in part formed from a Christian, moral discourse. Burrows, after consideration of the physical causes of suicide, concludes 'that there is frequently much of vice and caprice too, even in the commission of so awful an act as suicide' (1828, p. 440). For Burrows little should be done with regard to suicide to 'diminish the detestation which ought to be felt at the mere contemplation of acts so repugnant to GOD and derogatory to man' (p. 448). Forbes Winslow gleefully took up this theme. In a chapter entitled, 'Suicide a Crime against God and Man. – It Is Not an Act of Courage' Winslow (1840) writes:

Among the black catalogue of human offences, there is not, indeed, any that more powerfully affects the mind, that more outrages all the feelings of the heart, than the crime of suicide. Our laws have branded it with infamy, and the industry which is exerted by surviving relatives to conceal its perpetration evinces that the shame which is attached to it is of that foul and contagious character, that even the innocent consider themselves infected by its malignity. (p. 36)

Such a stance was not necessarily taken to be contrary to a medical or scientific view. Later Winslow writes, '[t]hat the act of suicide must be most offensive in the sight of God is evident, since it is that which most directly violates those laws by which his providence has formed, and still directs, the universe' (p. 38).

Throughout the century, this mix of the medical, scientific and moral continued. Even with those doctors involved in the collation and presentation of statistics morality and judgement were never far from the surface (Rimke, 2005). As Hacking (1990) has documented, the 1820s and 1830s saw in France the 'counting of suicides', that is the beginnings of a statistical approach to understanding suicide, and the British followed suit a little later. In 1858 William Farr, the Registrar-General, began to tabulate suicides separately from other deaths, and others, notably John Netten Radcliffe (1859, 1862), began to write on the subject of suicide using statistics to illustrate their arguments. Radcliffe, an epidemiologist with the Medical Department and later appointed as Public Health Inspector, was employed between 1858 and 1863 as subeditor of the *Journal of Psychological Medicine*, owned and edited by Forbes Winslow (Anderson, 1987). The views expressed by Radcliffe were overtly moral in tone. Radcliffe, like Burrows before him, was influenced by the writings on suicide by *aliénistes* in France, in particular Brierre de Boismont's *Du suicide* (1856). Radcliffe, like Burrows and Winslow, saw immoral living, intemperate habits, 'defective or perverted morality', in short *vice*, as leading to suicide. 'In somewhat more than 40 per cent (42.7) of the cases examined by M. Brierre de Boismont the morality was bad, the individuals having been drunkards, gamblers, or thieves, or lived in concubinage or adultery' (Radcliffe, 1862, p. 705). Worried that the reader may get the impression that nearly 60 per cent of suicides may therefore be people 'leading a regular life', Radcliffe makes it clear that among this number are 'lunatics, weak-minded, and exalted spirits, hypochondrias, sick, and persons reduced to poverty and misery'. He concludes that those who abandon themselves to vice 'have in prospect poverty, a prison, sickness, insanity, and suicide' (p. 705). Lest we be in doubt as to the true nature of suicide, Radcliffe makes it clear that lack of morality is at the heart of the issue and that 'whatever tends to weaken our notions of the sinfulness or criminality of the deed will of necessity render man most prone to it' (p. 705). Moral instruction is necessary to prevent suicide, Radcliffe concludes: '[n]o influence, therefore, can be conceived more powerful to hold in check the self-infliction of death than such as indelibly fixes upon the act the character of an evil far surpassing in gravity any, even the sharpest or bitterest, ill to which any man may be subjected' (p. 705).

As for medicine proving protection against the severity of the law, Radcliffe bemoans the use of the 'temporary insanity' verdict in cases of suicide:

The mischief of this is of course great; for at the same time that it removes the stain of criminality from the act, it also sets aside the notion of sinfulness, thus sweeping away the two great obstacles to the commission of self-murder. It begets, moreover, a seemingly legitimate ground of sympathy with suicide, which is most objectionable and injurious. (Radcliffe, 1862, p. 708)

Barbara Gates (1980) has argued that 'later Victorian medical attitudes became less harsh than those of earlier decades, when moral standards were more absolute. This trend, of course, has become our own legacy from the Victorians' (p. 173). Gates singles out both Henry Maudsley and S. A. K. Strahan, as doctors who demonstrated a compassionate attitude to suicide. Such a reading is sometimes difficult to support in the light of some of their pronouncements on the subject. Here is Maudsley writing in 1861: '[a]ny poor creature from the gutter can put an end to himself; there is no nobility in the act, and no great amount of courage required for it. It is a deed rather of cowardice shirking duty, generated in a monstrous feeling of self, and accomplished in the most sinful, because wicked ignorance' (Maudsley, 1861, p. 201).

For Strahan (1894) we should 'grieve in silence' when an act of suicide is prevented (p. 78), 'for,' he argues, it is the 'careful and deliberate cultivation of the unfit which is responsible for a really large proportion, not only of the suicides of to-day, but of the insane, epileptic, idiotic, drunken, mute, scrofulous, and criminal; indeed, for a large proportion of all that is worst in suffering humanity' (p. 79). Indeed, if one were to persist in caring for such creatures 'infantile death, sterile idiocy, barrenness and self-destruction will appear and extinguish the stock' (p. 78). One has to search hard to find compassion in the writings of Maudsley and Strahan, but not look too far to find fears of 'hereditary taint' and concern over racial contamination.

It is perhaps tempting to suggest that medicine was merely reproducing commonly held beliefs and attitudes, but as MacDonald (1997) and Anderson (1987) have convincingly argued, the views of laymen, on the evidence of verdicts reached by coroners' juries, were often more tolerant and compassionate towards suicide than those of medical men. And when the penalties for self-murder were removed by stages in 1823, 1870 and 1882, few doctors argued for a relaxation of the law, and many remained opposed to reform (MacDonald, 1997). Alienism, and later psychiatry, operated in a moral space, and as such its function in the nineteenth century tended to be as much about the control of unwanted conduct as the cure of sickness (Foucault, 2005; Rimke, 2005). The study of the medical/psychiatric formation of truths in relation to suicide offers the possibility of understanding this function in more detail, for here it may be possible to discern a strategic logic in the discourse and practices of mental medicine and psychiatry in relation to suicide in the nineteenth century. The circular relationship between the discursive constitution of the 'dangerous individual', and the establishment of an institutional apparatus concerned primarily with the containment and restraint of dangerousness at both the population and the individual level, will now be considered.

Psychiatry as public hygiene and control of the dangerous individual

By emphasising the dangerousness inherent in insanity, alienists could justify their practices of incarcerating and controlling large sections of the population by arguing that they were engaged in protecting society from a potentially lethal peril (Foucault, 2002a). To this end, throughout the century, suicide was represented as a threat – not only to individuals but also to the population at large. Suicide was discussed in terms of contagion and there were fears expressed of suicide epidemics. Burrows (1828) cites examples of outbreaks of suicide in Malta amongst British soldiers, amongst women in Lyon who threw themselves down a well, and the suicides of 1,300 people at Versailles in 1793. For Burrows, these were epidemics and he concludes, following a discussion of a number of deaths in the French village of St Pierre Monjou, that were it not for the 'interposition of the civil authorities, the contagion would have spread' (p. 438). Burrows stops short of attributing physical causes to 'imitative suicide', unlike the French physicians Burrows often looked to for guidance, seeing instead, once again, vice at work. For Winslow (1840) too, suicide 'prevails epidemically' (p. 108), but he is more sympathetic to French thinking than Burrows when it comes to attributing physical causes to outbreaks of suicide. Copland (1858) discusses epidemic suicide, attributing many such acts to '*mental sympathy or imitation,* and somewhat even to a passion for *notoriety*' (p. 554, emphasis in original). Bucknill and Tuke (1858) comment also on the 'epidemic character of the disease' (p. 206), but in their book fear of contagion is identified less with airborne diseases, or with mental propensities, than with the threat of hereditary transmission. Burrows, Mayo, Winslow, Morison and Radclifffe each outline examples of suicides that seem to run in families, but towards the end of the century fears of inherited suicidal propensities come to predominate and the threat is now not only to individuals but to the whole race.

We have seen already how suicide comes to be formed as degenerate in the writings of both Strahan (1894) and Maudsley (1892a). For Strahan, degeneracy undermined the vitality of the race, and the suicidal, along with 'the blind, deaf, dumb, idiotic, insane, epileptic' (1894, p. 72), were but symptoms of the declining health of the nation as a whole. Strahan laments 'all these weaklings are permitted and at times even induced to contaminate the race by the propagation of their unfitness' (p. 72).

The family could be construed as both under threat from such 'contamination', and as its source. Maudsley (1892a) noted how 'strongly hereditary' suicidal insanity often is (p. 138). He argued that the suicidal propensity was 'inherited like the tricks of movements which run in families' (p. 139), but also he expressed concern about the 'infective effect' that the suicide of a friend or relative can have. Non-medical remedies to the threat of suicide were scorned upon. Both Maudsley and Strahan, as well as Tuke (1892), were much influenced by Italian Henry Morselli's 1882 book, *Suicide: An Essay on Comparative Moral Statistics*, and Morselli quotes approvingly of Maudsley's disdain for engaging the suicidal in talk; '[i]t would be of much use, as Maudsley wisely says, to preach moderation to the whirlwind as to talk philosophy to a man whose predilections and antecedents lead him to the border either of madness or violent death' (p. 373). By the end of the century suicide had come to be seen as inevitable, determined by ancestry and the forces of natural selection. Psychiatrists argued that it was only by excluding the weak and unfit from society, by preventing propagation, that there was any hope for the survival of the civilised peoples. Strahan urged vigilance. Not 'all members of every family, one member of which has sought death voluntarily, are so degenerate as to be unfit to propagate their kind', but he maintains that 'all such should be looked upon with suspicion'. Signs of degeneration should be looked for 'and if sought will frequently be found'. The amount of degeneration discovered will give the investigator a clue as to the degree of danger faced by descendents. He concluded that the 'suicide by his last act places the bar sinister upon the escutcheon of his family, and the man or woman who marries into such a family runs a terrible risk' (1894, p. 90).

The individual, the family and the nation were thus all under threat from suicide, and it was argued that medicine could provide solutions – both in terms of the insights doctors were able to offer by means of their understanding of epidemics, contagious diseases, and hereditary transmission, and with regard to the exclusion and containment of the threat. Such a power-knowledge nexus ensured the continuing authority of medicine in relation to suicide by providing grounds for the continuation, even extension, of the practice of confinement, as well as a rationale and opportunity for the accumulation of more medical/psychiatric truths. As Foucault (2002a) has argued, alienists were not slow to represent insanity as inherently dangerous. By emphasising the threat posed by insanity (to individuals, to families, to social order, to civilisation, to the healthiness of the race) alienists could argue that their practices (incarceration, observation, restraint) were a necessary defence against a real danger to society. It is dangerousness, Foucault (2002a) argues, that provides the emerging psychiatric profession with its *raison d'être* – that is they function as a form of control or protection from the dangers inherent in the population. Foucault, in discussing the development of the link between the concepts of dangerousness and madness in the early nineteenth century, dismisses the idea that the encroachment of psychiatry into new domains could be seen as merely 'imperialism' on the part of psychiatrists, or that it can be understood simply as a rationalisation of a chaotic moral situation. Rather, Foucault understands psychiatry during this period as being a form of public hygiene – a manifestation of a bio-politics played out at both individual and population levels. In the eighteenth century the process of urbanisation, the huge growth of the industrial workforce, and the development of demography raised questions, in medical and biological terms, of human 'populations' – how people lived, their conditions of existence, their nutrition, birth and death rates and their 'pathologies'. In the context of such bio-political concerns, Foucault believes a new set of techniques and practices emerged that sought to manage the health of the population as a whole, but also acted on individual bodies to maximise their health, efficiency and productivity (Foucault, 1981). Foucault talked here of 'bio-power', and it was within such a network of relations and concerns that the social 'body' became a biological reality and thus the object of medical intervention – with the doctor as technician and medicine a public hygiene (Foucault, 2002a). By the turn of the nineteenth century, Foucault argues, psychiatry could develop and flourish because it sought to concern itself with the dangers inherent in this social body. Insanity was seen to be linked, by numerous social commentators, to issues such as debauchery, alcoholism, overcrowding and urban life. Equally, madness was conceived as a source of danger for oneself, for others, for one's contemporaries, and for one's descendants through heredity. Either way, social 'danger' was implicated. Indeed, to justify its practice of enforced confinement psychiatry sought to demonstrate that 'madness, by its nature, and even in its most discrete manifestations, was haunted by the absolute danger, death' (p. 185). Psychiatry, Foucault argues, in seeking to claim those perceived as threats to the social order as objects of medical intervention was attempting to justify its primary function – the 'control of the dangers hidden in human behavior' (p. 185). During the nineteenth century doctors specialising in lunacy assumed a position of authority in relation to suicide not because of any medical discoveries on their part, nor because they were persuasive in arguing for more humane treatment of the suicide or would-be suicide, but rather because they offered the possibility of a more effective form of control than the sanctions of Church or state. That the means of prevention offered opportunities for the production of knowledge, and that the truths of suicide thus formed justified such measures enabled medical power in relation to suicide and the suicidal to be established, consolidated and extended over time.

Psychiatric discourse as formative of notions and practices of self-restraint

The insane patient was often presented in medical texts as an individual who lacked internal restraint, which manifested itself in improper and inappropriate behaviour. Late eighteenth- and early nineteenth-century moral treatment sought to rectify this state of affairs by recourse to moral instruction. Proper conduct, it was assumed, would follow from correct guidance. As Foucault sets out in *The History of Madness* (2005), the founding asylums at Bicêtre, and The Retreat at York, were less the product of philanthropic sentiments than of moral certitude. These asylums, and the others that followed, were decidedly moral spaces; William Tuke (at The Retreat) sought to establish a community based on Quaker values and practices, and under Pinel, Bicêtre was a place of uniform morality (without the religion), where work and correct social relationships were seen as essential to the re-establishment and maintenance of proper conduct.

Foucault sought to demonstrate in *The History of Madness* that the apparent 'liberation' of madness enacted at Bicêtre and The Retreat by Philippe Pinel and William Tuke respectively was no more than an appearance, an illusion of liberation. In place of chains and physical restraint, the patient was subjected to moral regimes that sought to reform and reshape his/her very being:

the partial suppression of physical constraint at the Retreat was part of a whole, of which the essential element was the constitution of 'self-restraint', where the freedom of the mad, checked by work and by the gaze of others, was constantly threatened by an acknowledgement of guilt. What at first glance seemed to be a simple negative operation that loosened bonds and freed the profound nature of madness turned out to be a positive operation that enclosed madness in a system of rewards and punishments, including it into the movement of moral consciousness. (Foucault, 2005, p. 487)

It was the instilling of a moral conscience within the individual that would lead to the containment of the dangers inherent in madness. The moral managers thus preached self-restraint in place of physical restraint, and the asylums worked towards the positive formation of an interiority fearful of transgression rather than control and domination of the body. Moral education and guidance were often prescribed (e.g. Mayo, 1838; Winslow, 1840; Radcliffe, 1862), and James Duncan's *Popular Errors on the Subject of Insanity Examined and Exposed* offers an example of this line of reasoning:

> I think it is not unreasonable to suppose that, even over those who are already labouring under partial insanity a certain influence for good may be exerted, which will have the effect of restraining some of them, at least from the commission of suicide. I have already stated … my firm conviction that certain classes of lunatic are capable of exercising some degree of self-control, and of restraining their passions within proper bounds: and everything which tends to lead any of these unfortunate beings to act in conformity with the dictates of right reason must be attended with the greatest advantage …. [I]f lunatics are capable of practicing self-restraint, under any circumstances, why should it be thought unreasonable to suppose them capable of exercising it in reference to this tendency to self-destruction? (Duncan, 1853, p. 97)

It was to self-control as well as to external restraint that such men looked in the prevention of suicide. By such thinking, however, suicide came to be conceived as a failure of internal control, a lack of self-restraint and insufficient moral character on the part of the deceased. The causes of suicide are once again read as located within the interiority of the individual patient, and prevention as a matter of correction or treatment of internal abnormalities or pathology.

As has been discussed, in this period the truth of suicide was formed by reference to insanity, and reciprocally, the truth of insanity was in part constituted by ideas on suicide. The changing formulations regarding the truth of the relationship between insanity and suicide evident throughout the nineteenth century can be explained less by reference to a gradual uncovering of true knowledge concerning suicide and mental illness, but rather by the accumulation of knowledge proceeding hand in hand with the extension of medical/psychiatric practices in a circular fashion that enabled the consolidation and strengthening of medical/psychiatric power. The notion of the inherent dangerousness of madness, illustrated repeatedly by reference to suicide and the suicidal, provided a rationale for psychiatric practices, and those self-same practices facilitated the production of ever more knowledge of the nature of the dangerous (suicidal) individual. What will be considered next are 'truth effects' – in particular the ways in which certain subjectivities came to be formed in relation to production of truths of suicide.

Subject formation

An argument has been made in this book that new forms of self-accomplished death began to emerge in the early nineteenth century.

The medical redescription of suicide in terms of interior pathology not only created new concepts and ways of responding to suicide, but also new subjectivities constituted in part from the discourse and practices of alienism and mental medicine. This section outlines some of the forces at work in the formation of the 'pathologised' 'suicidal subject', and also traces the development of the 'responsible, accountable and culpable clinician'. The processes of subject formation are illustrated by reference to primary medical/psychiatric texts as well as reports from coroners' inquests quoted in secondary sources. The coroners' reports drawn upon in Olive Anderson's *Suicide in Victorian and Edwardian England* (1987), from East Sussex, the City of London and Southwark, provide evidence of the increasing 'interior' nature of suicide, of the move away from understanding suicide mostly in terms of socially situated motives and towards seeing suicide as arising from internal, pathological causes.

The underlying argument of this section is that processes of subjectivation went hand in hand with those of objectivation (Foucault, 1998). That is, as new truths of suicide came to be formed, new ways of being in relation to suicide were created. Individuals with a desire to die become patients, victims of disease, and are thus taken to have a diminished responsibility for their actions. In relation to the suicidal patient, the responsible and accountable (and possibly culpable) clinician is formed. Additionally, those deemed to be insane are positioned as potentially dangerous, to themselves or others. These points will be discussed in turn. First, an example of how the creation and dissemination of new medical/scientific truths of suicide acted to form a different kind of suicide, and suicidal person, will be set out.

An example

That new forms of suicide came into being in relation to the production and dissemination of medical truths can be illustrated by reference to the death of the painter Benjamin Haydon in 1846. Haydon himself kept a detailed journal and wrote an autobiography (collected together in three volumes by Tom Taylor as the *Life of B. R. Haydon, from his Autobiography and Journals*, 1853), and from these a picture of sorts can be formed of the relationship between the medical/psychiatric discourse on suicide and the constitution of a 'suicidal subjectivity'.

Foucault (1998), in an overview of his work originally written as part of an introduction to his *History of Sexuality* but not included in the final text, discusses the ways in which modes of objectivation and subjectivation relate. He notes that 'this objectivation and this subjectivation are not independent of each other. From their mutual development and their interconnection, what could be called the "games of truth" come into being' (p. 460). Foucault was not particularly concerned with 'games of truth' read as involving 'the discovery of true things' but rather he was interested in the ways by which the subject could come to be constituted as an object of knowledge within the 'human sciences', but also have knowledge of itself in relation to those authoritative truths produced by such sciences. Haydon's journals provide a way of mapping the formation of a subject in relation to the production of medical/psychiatric truths in the first half of the nineteenth century.

Obviously, many forces were at work in Haydon's suicide (disappointment over the reception of his paintings, debts, etc.) but in part at least an interconnection between Haydon's thoughts (if we take his journal as a record of such), his actions and the truth of himself as constituted by medical/psychiatric discourse and practices can be discerned. What also can be mapped, if only incompletely, are those ways by which certain truths circulate within a culture. Haydon's suicide was much discussed, particularly after the publication of his journals and autobiography, within 'professional' texts such as the *Journal of Psychological Medicine*, but also more widely in publications such as the *Quarterly Review*. Newspapers also covered the story, and through such means certain authoritative knowledges of suicide were reproduced and disseminated. The suicide of Haydon was in part informed by reference to medical knowledge, and subsequently this event acted to further disperse or distribute such truths.

In 1846 'historical painter' Benjamin Haydon shot himself in the head and then cut his throat. His friend, the poet Elizabeth Barrett remarked to a friend, on hearing of the death, that he must have succumbed to a 'suicidal impulse', '[f]or he was mad if he killed himself, of that I am as sure as if I knew it. If he killed himself, he was mad first' (in Gates, 1989, p. 15).

Historian Barbara Gates (1989) writes that Haydon was 'morbidly interested' in the relationship of the 'physical brain to the act of self-destruction' (p. 15). In a journal entry of 1821 he had written:

I am inclined to imagine that much of the pain and anxiety of mind I have suffered for the last few days arose from nothing more or less than *indigestion*. My stomach was heated and affected my brain. Suppose in that humour I had shot myself! Would a superior Being have destroyed my soul, because, my brain being irritated by an indigestion, I had in a state of perturbation put an end to a painful existence? Surely not! (in Taylor, 1853, vol. II, p. 17)

Haydon evidently had an awareness of how the viscera and brain were held to be connected within medical thought. There is perhaps more than a touch of Hippocratic 'humoral' medicine here as well, but it is interesting that Haydon attributes his 'perturbation' to his 'heated' stomach affecting his brain, and that these are linked to thoughts of self-destruction.

As has been documented in this chapter, early nineteenth-century medical writings on suicide concerned themselves with notions of pathological anatomy, particularly with regard to the brain, as explanations for suicide. Haydon believed the suicides of Sir Samuel Romilly (in 1818) and Castlereagh (in 1822) were due to medical reasons, namely an excess of blood in the brain, writing that 'the two must have achieved relief when they cut their throats and the blood began to flow, removing the pressure built up in their brains' (in Gates, 1989, p. 15). Haydon considered himself the victim of too much blood on the brain, and it is believed that he cut his own throat in an attempt to relieve such pressure (p. 15). In his diary Haydon had written: '[i]t may be laid down that self destruction is the physical mode of relieving a diseased brain, because the first impression on a brain diseased, or diseased for a Time, is the necessity of this horrid crime. There is no doubt of it' (in Taylor, 1853, vol. III, p. 169).

Haydon believed he was suffering from a 'diseased brain' that required relief through blood letting. It can of course be argued that Haydon's death was a singular act and therefore unrepresentative of suicides in general at this time (Anderson, 1987, p. 107), but the fact that Haydon could conceive of self-destruction in terms of pathological anatomy, that the 'truth' of his troubles were to be found in medical theories of organic disease that necessitated a drastic physical remedy, points to the formation of new ways of thinking, acting and experiencing in relation to suffering and suicide. Medical science was not involved solely in the discovery or uncovering of the facts of suicide; rather there was a production and circulation of new truths that acted to form new objects of study (the diseased brain, 'suicidal monomania', etc.), and new modes of being in relation to such objects (suicidal patients with an excess of blood on the brain, the 'suicidal monomaniac'). Haydon's life and death can be read as an example of the interconnectedness of modes of objectivation and subjectivation discussed by Foucault (1998, pp. 459–63).

At the inquest held after the discovery of Haydon's body the coroner, Mr Wakley, asked the painter's daughter, Mary Haydon, if her father had 'complained of his head in any way of late?' (*Annual Register*, 1847, p. 92). She replied that he had, and that 'during the last two or three days I recollect to have seen him frequently put his hand up to his head' (p. 92). Extracts from Haydon's diaries were also read out to the jury in order to 'throw any light upon the state of deceased's mind recently' (p. 93). Jurors heard of Haydon's anxieties about his financial situation and his disappointment over the number of visitors to a recent exhibition of his works. It was concluded by the jury that Haydon was in 'an unsound

state of mind when he committed the act' (p. 96). Thus suicide is reproduced as an act of insanity, and the ensuing publicity that surrounded
Haydon's death, the reporting of the inquest and, later, the publication of
his journals and autobiography, further acted to reinforce such a view
(although much was also made of Haydon's 'artistic' temperament, his
'genius' and the failure of the English people to fully appreciate his talents.
See, for instance, the obituary in the *Annual Register*, 1847, pp. 262–4).

If we look to Hacking's notion of 'dynamic nominalism' (1999), those
processes whereby people, as 'interactive kinds', can 'become aware of how
they are classified and modify their behavior accordingly' (p. 32) then
Haydon's reported experiences and actions would seem to conform to
Hacking's (and Foucault's) notion that subjects are formed in relation to
authoritative knowledge. For Hacking (1999), 'dynamic nominalism' also
involved what he termed a 'looping effect', whereby the changes undergone
by people in response to being classified then affect the systems of classifications themselves. The writings on Haydon's suicide can help illustrate
these processes. Although much was written in the 'popular' press and in
periodicals such as *Bentley's Miscellany*, the *Gentleman's Magazine*, *Fraser's
Magazine* and the *Quarterly Review*, of particular interest here are the
discussions within professional circles as to the exact nature of his physical
and mental problems. The publication of Haydon's journals in 1853
prompted a certain amount of debate, and these allowed for a 'looping
effect' of sorts, despite the absence of the author. Haydon's text 'feeds
back' into psychiatric discourse and shapes, if only in a small way, the
formation of medical truths in relation to suicide.

The *Journal of Psychological Medicine* (Anon. 1853) contained a lengthy
article 'Haydon: – a psychological study', written in response to the
publication of Haydon's journals. Here, the painter's suicide is attributed,
interestingly, to 'his own follies', 'a weak and delusive faith' (p. 502), and
later to the lack of '*sound religious principles*' (p. 521, emphasis in original).
A mixture of the moral and the medical continue throughout the article,
and the next line refers to that 'morbid cerebral condition which at last led
him to self-destruction' (p. 521). The author notes that three of Haydon's
children died of 'hydrenchephalus' ('probably begotten when he was in a
state of cerebral irritation') and 'considering the wear and tear recorded, it
is not surprising that his own brain at last gave way' (p. 521). The
'disordered state of poor Haydon's brain' is once again remarked upon
in relation to a journal entry that recorded his brain as 'harassed and
confused' (p. 522), yet it was an 'undisciplined will' in the face of 'impulsive ideas' that is read as his undoing (p. 524). As a consequence the
'material organ – the cerebrum – was too tired and shaken by his undisciplined conduct … It was physically incompetent to the task; it tottered

from time to time ... when unusually weighed, and at last ... it failed under the pressure' (p. 524). The author concludes that '*suicidal* monomania may not, indeed, be the specific form of the cerebral disease, but cerebral disease in some form' is linked to suicides such as Haydon's (p. 524). The author, finally, posits that it was moral failings that best account for his 'self-commanded plunge'. As Foucault (2005) argued, psychiatry was, from the first, primarily a moral endeavour. 'Moral therapy', for Foucault, involved the instillation of bourgeois values into those deemed idle or unproductive by means of the development of a 'moral consciousness'. Haydon's suicide afforded a chance to reinforce the necessity of such moral work. Here, in the conclusion to the piece, the virtues of 'mental discipline – self-control – self-denial – mastery over the passions' are spelt out. The author concludes:

> The moral of Haydon's story lies upon the surface. It is none other than that drawn by his own pen. He says, when analyzing the character of his intellect, '*My mind wanted the discipline of early training. I trace all the misfortunes of my life to this early and irremediable want.*' What a lesson does this confession teach us! Early training – early mental discipline – self-control – self-denial – mastery over the passions – how much of our happiness depends upon the steady cultivation of such habits of mind! (p. 527)

Haydon, influenced by the truths of organic medicine, in turn influences, through his suicide and journals, medical theories on suicide and insanity. His suicide is constructed as both a failure of the brain and of the will. A lack of discipline in the face of destructive impulses is read as leading to a 'tired' and 'shaken' cerebrum and an inevitably sorry end. In terms of the discursive formation of the subject in relation to suicide, Haydon's experiences are in part shaped by theories of cerebral weakness and failure, and in turn his act of suicide comes to further reinforce the truths of mental medicine – namely, that self-mastery and self-discipline are necessary for the healthy functioning of the brain, and through such means suicide could be warded off. This truth of his death was formulated and reformulated many times over, with the same mix of morality and medicine evident. In France, Brierre de Boismont's *De suicide et de la folie suicide* (1856) discussed Haydon's life and whether or not his death should be considered voluntary or an act of 'alienation' over several pages (pp. 510–13). In England *Bentley's Miscellany* (1846, volume XX, pp. 212–16), the *Quarterly Review* (1853, pp. 295–318), and the *Gentleman's Magazine and Historical Review* (August, 1853, pp. 140–7) all carried articles relating to his death.

Undoubtedly, Haydon's suicide was, as Olive Anderson (1987, p. 107) remarks, in many ways unrepresentative of the time. He was educated, literate, and had a degree of renown; obviously not all suicides could be so described. Yet in conceiving of suicide as pathological, in understanding the cause of his suffering in terms of disease and sickness, and in formulating this truth of himself by reference to the truths of medicine and science Haydon represents not so much what suicide was but more what suicide was in the process of becoming.

The changing nature of the suicidal subject

Anderson's own research here supports such a claim. Her *Suicide in Victorian and Edwardian England* (1987) draws on the records of numerous coroners' inquests throughout the nineteenth and early twentieth centuries to document changing social attitudes to suicide. Her findings add credence to the notion that suicide came to be read as an increasingly private, internal and medical concern throughout the Victorian and into the Edwardian era. Not only were medical men increasingly called upon to act as experts in coroners' courts, but also medical/psychiatric concepts and theories were more frequently used to explain suicide. Further, and importantly in light of the arguments made in this book, the act of suicide itself came less to involve concerns that centred on issues around one's social standing (in terms of shame that may have accompanied the revelation of debt or sexual impropriety, etc.) or financial security (e.g. loss of work and the threat of destitution) and more 'an introspective agony', a 'brooding and long drawn out' affair, essentially an 'escape from depression, disappointment and self-reproach' (Anderson, 1987, p. 420). A desire to die could be formed, by the turn of the twentieth century, in relation to medical and psychiatric truths of the self and suicide that would have been alien a hundred years before. Anderson uncovered inquest papers for the City of London for 1911, and here suicide notes left by the deceased are suggestive of increasingly medical explanations for their actions, but also point to attempts to locate the source of their suicidal promptings and actions within their own interiority: one writes, for example, 'this instinct keeps saying why do you live why not end it all'; others indicate that the reasons for suicide were no longer clear even to the person themselves, that interior sufferings could arise for which no explanation could be found: a publisher's clerk described at the inquest as 'deeply retiring' wrote of 'the agony I have been through for no reason whatever' (p. 171). Anderson concludes that it was not

severe pain, or hardship, or dishonour which unnerved these people, but rather some threat, real or imaginary, to their comfort or self-esteem. Fanciful introspection, disproportionate anxiety, deluded judgement do indeed all seem to have played a much larger role than in 1861; and this, together with the disappearance of drunken suicide, means that subjective factors more than objective ones, and ingrained personality patterns to have counted for more than external circumstances among these Edwardian City suicides. (Anderson, 1987, p. 172)

Anderson finds a similar story in Southwark for 1911. Here again 'worries had come to loom larger: dread of disease, of insanity, or of professional inadequacy. More often than before, suicide presented itself as a tempting escape – and an escape not from tragic sorrow or suffering, but rather from worry, depression, and self-dissatisfaction' (1987, p. 173).

Yet the stories had been different only fifty years or so earlier. Here, Anderson (1987) notes that a heterogeneity of motives for suicide were recorded by coroners in both London and the more rural Rape of Hastings district in the papers she studied for the periods 1861–2 and 1859–66 respectively.

As suicide changed, new subjectivities came to be formed. Of interest here, in examining the effects of the formation of suicide as pathological and medical, is the creation of a relationship between suicidal patient and doctor (as well as 'auxiliary' asylum staff) charged with preserving their life.

Responsibility, accountability and culpability in preventing suicide

As noted in the previous chapter, Pinel and Esquirol's formulations of moral responsibility in relation to alienation threw into question the extent to which free agency/choice could be attributed to acts such as suicide (see Gauchet and Swain, 1999, p. 164). As a kind of madness, self-destruction could be said to be determined, in part at least, by insanity. No longer read solely or unproblematically as perpetrators of a crime or of an unpardonable sin, suicides could now be positioned as victims of disease. Obviously, the status of the deceased was often muddied, with moral/judicial readings of the act persisting alongside the newer medical/secular readings in the nineteenth century (Anderson, 1987; Andrew, 1988; Gates, 1989; Healy, 2006), but an underlying trend of secularisation can certainly be detected, as suicide moved from being constituted as a sin to a form of insanity (Watt, 2004), and the suicide from perpetrator to victim. As a victim of an illness or disease, the suicide's responsibility for certain actions was read as lessened in important ways, and alongside this diminution there is a growing realisation that doctors and other authorities (justices of the peace, police, lunatic attendants, etc.) were to be held, to varying degrees, responsible for the prevention of suicides (Anderson, 1987, part IV).

Obviously of importance here, given the centrality of the asylum with regard to suicide in this period, is the relationship between alienist/psychiatrist and patient. Foucault, in his 1973–4 lectures at the Collège de France (published as *Psychiatric Power*, 2006), speaks of a particular dynamic involving responsibility immanent in such encounters:

> My impression is that at the bottom of every psychiatric interview there is always a sort of transaction taking the following form. The psychiatrist says to the person before him: Well, here we are, you are either here of your own free will or at the behest of someone else, but you have come here because people are uneasy and complain about you; you say certain things, you have done certain things, you behave in a certain way. I am not in any way questioning you about the truth of these facts and I do not want to know the truth or falsity of the reproaches made against you, or even the malaise you feel. (p. 273)

What is at stake in the psychiatric interview, in exchanges such as this, Foucault argues, is not so much the investigation of the nature of the illness, its 'reality' or otherwise, rather it is the status of the participants themselves. The doctor offers the removal of responsibility, legal and moral, in exchange for the patient offering up the events in his life, or his experiences, as symptoms. For by so doing the patient can be constituted as suffering from an illness that diminishes the possibility of his/her being held to account for certain actions, however criminal or morally reprehensible, and in turn the psychiatrist can be constituted as a doctor – can have his medical status, his authority to diagnose and to treat, to detain and release, confirmed. Foucault's account of such a transaction continues:

> I am prepared to relieve you of legal or moral responsibility ... on the one condition that you subjectively accept the reality of all this, on condition that you give all these facts back to me as subjective symptoms of your existence, of your consciousness. I want to find all these elements again in your account and confessions, more or less transformed, no matter, as elements of your suffering, as the force of a monstrous desire, as the signs of an irresistible impulse, in short, as symptoms ... Give me the symptoms: I will remove the fault. (p. 273)

The doctor, in receipt of symptoms, divests the patient of responsibility, accountability and thus culpability, and assumes himself the responsibility, as physical and moral guardian, of ensuring the return to health of the patient as well as (more importantly in Foucault's estimation) protecting the public, and the patient, from the dangers taken to be inherent in madness. With a suicidal patient, however, such a transaction is fraught with ambiguities and complications, for what such an exchange opens up is the possibility of the failure of the patient to keep his/her side of the bargain, and to behave as a patient should – namely, to make the effort to get better, or to allow him/herself to be protected. The greatest danger to the authority and status of the doctor, as guardian and restorer of health, lies in the refusal of the patient to continue living – for even in the face of near total domination the possibility of resistance remains.

One can understand the need to maintain a moral condemnation of suicide on the part of doctors – the patient may have been a victim of disease and sickness, but they could be blamed for the vices that led to the illness – for such a move insulated them a little from charges of failure and shared out the blame for the death. Also, there is a desire to constitute the various forms of illnesses as not just dangerous but unpredictably so. Thus suicide is often read as the first sign of insanity, a symptom of a dangerous illness that comes from nowhere and carries no other traces. Here again, the culpability of the doctor is lessened by such a formulation, for the foe they battle is lethal in its effects but virtually undetectable before it strikes. Finally, one can see that in the manoeuvres played out between patient and doctor suicide would represent the strongest possible move the patient could make in relation to the forces rallied against them – a form of resistance in response to the threat of total domination or subjection. Here, suicide could represent a refusal (of being constituted as a patient, of various treatments, of submission to the will of the doctor, of containment, confinement and restraint). The stakes here were obviously high, and no victory would ever be experienced by the patient (cf. Osborne, 2005, pp. 284–5), but that such a move was possible each participant in the psychiatric encounter was acutely aware.

There appear in many medical texts of the period fears amongst those who worked with the suicidal that, although they accepted responsibility for the prevention of patient suicides, they would be held accountable and blamed for such deaths. With suicide constituted as a matter of illness and disease, diagnosis and treatment, containment and restraint, issues of responsibility, accountability and culpability in relation to acts of self-destruction came to the fore in medical texts, asylum inspection reports, coroners' judgments, and more widely in periodicals and newspaper reporting.

As early as 1822, not long after Esquirol's publication of his 'Suicide' article, and in a review of Falret's book on 'hypochondriacism and suicide', the *Monthly Gazette of Health* asked whether Castlereagh's recent suicide should have been averted by his physician:

Is it not most extraordinary, that no active means were adopted by his physician, to quiet his [Castlereagh's] brain, or by his friends about him, to prevent the commission of an act of violence? His Lordship complained of great confusion of head, *attended with pain*. Dr. Bankhead *ordered seven* ounces of blood to be abstracted by cupping, and a saline purgative to be administered ... Now, on such a subject as the late Marquis of Londonderry, with such an affection of the brain, what effect could the learned Doctor expect from the loss of *seven* ounces of blood? If the Doctor had any doubts as to the condition of the brain of his patient, which, from the appearance of his eyes, and the presence of acute pain in the head, was clearly inflammatory, why did he not order the operation of cupping to be repeated, and a quantity to be abstracted, proportioned to his Lordship's habit, and the importance of the organ which was effected, after the effects of bleeding had removed all mystery from the case? (*Monthly Gazette of Health*, 1822, p. 255)

After detailing the treatments Castlereagh should have been in receipt of, the article asks: '[h]ad such active treatment been employed at the time the Doctor ordered him to be cupped, might not His Lordship have been at this time in the enjoyment of health?' (p. 255). With the act of self-destruction constituted as a medical issue, taken to be analogous to other physical diseases or illnesses, suicide became read as preventable, and failure to do so could lead to censure, as in the case of Castlereagh. For doctors this could be damaging, for they could be positioned as the perpetrator of acts (or of sins of omission) that lead to the death of the patient (the victim of illness as well as of the doctor's failings). Forbes Winslow (1840) bemoaned the fact that many a good physician's career had been ruined by a suicide, and John Burdett Steward (1845) talked of 'suicidal cases' being 'the most painful to have charge of' (p. 92). Such pained feelings were probably not lessened by the attention often given to cases of suicide by the publication of coroners' reports in journals and newspapers and, for those employed in an asylum, the publication of the findings of investigations carried out by the Lunacy Commission. Olive Anderson writes:

[f]rom the first, the Commissioners in Lunacy as well as the public regarded the prevention of suicide as one of the most important duties of the officers in every asylum, and failure provoked not only critical comment in the local press, but searching official investigations and the apportioning of blame by name in the published annual reports of the Commissioners to the Lord Chancellor. A series of suicides would ruin any asylum career. (Anderson, 1987, p. 402)

Charles Mercier sums up the difficulties and fears presented by the threat of suicide to doctors once such acts are constituted in terms of illness, dangerousness and containment/restraint:

Of all the tasks of the alienist physician none is more difficult, of all his responsibilities none is more onerous, than that of determining when the tendency to suicide in any individual case has so far subsided to allow of the patient being restored to home, to friends, to society, and to liberty. A patient is admitted in deep melancholia; he improves in health, he becomes cheerful, he becomes active, his delusions subside; he says that he feels better, that his former fancies have departed, that he recognises their falsity. He is watched for days and weeks, and as his improvement is maintained and he seems quite recovered he is allowed to go home. Next morning he is found hanging from a gas-bracket. Such, with variations in non-essentials is the history with scores of cases. Nothing is more difficult than to tell when the tendency to suicide has faded out. The patient seems well, seems cheerful, happy, and active. His friends are clamouring for his discharge. The basest and most sordid motives are attributed to his medical custodian for his caution and prudence. At length he yields; the patient is discharged, and forthwith commits suicide. Then is the wrath of his friends more bitter than ever against the doctor who, at their own persistent solicitation, gave the patient the chance of destroying himself. Then a coroner's jury gravely censures the doctor for his want of care, forethought, and skill. (Mercier, 1890, pp. 351–2)

In the asylum the doctor could face censure for holding a patient against his/her will, and later be criticised for not adequately protecting the same patient on his/her release. So, whereas Foucault (2006) saw a mostly mutually beneficial trade-off between symptom-giving on the part of the patient and responsibility removal by the psychiatrist, the relationship constituted within medical discourse also served to trap each, physician and patient, in a potentially damaging oppositional relationship. Suicide, or the threat of suicide, could become a tactical manoeuvre, a way of resisting psychiatric power, of the patient asserting his/her will, once and for all, in opposition to that of the doctor. The doctor is constituted as accountable and culpable, and the patient absolved of responsibility due to his/her illness.

One solution in the asylums, from the doctors' perspective at least, was the delegation of responsibility to others. Most of the tasks seen as contributing to the prevention of suicide were medically prescribed but were not usually undertaken directly by the medical staff. Instead these tended to be delegated to asylum attendants who were given responsibility for the day-to-day prevention of suicide (Shepherd and Wright, 2002). Consequently, when a suicide occurred it could be attributed to the negligence of the attendant rather than any medical shortcoming (Benham, 1903). Attendants faced penalties, from fines to demotion or dismissal if found to be negligent in preventing a suicide (Shepherd and Wright, 2002). An attendant's handbook from the end of the century outlines some of the duties handed down to staff, and the worries that went with them:

Acutely suicidal cases are a great worry to all who have to deal with them. They are a constant strain upon the mind, and the anxiety about them is at times very harassing. The knowledge that you are responsible for the safe keeping of a woman who requires, during the whole twenty-four hours, to be kept under continuous notice because she is just waiting for an opportunity of injuring herself, is very wearing. If, in addition, the patient is, as is frequently the case, uneasy, worrying, and always wishing not to do those things which ought to be done, the life of the nurse in whose care she is placed is not a happy one. In such cases the nurses receive a printed or written notice with the patient, which informs them of the suicidal tendency, and warns them that she must never be permitted to escape from observation. (Harding, 1894, p. 94)

Responsibility for the safety of the patients was thus passed down, along with a good deal of the worry that suicidal patients engendered in staff. With the transfer of responsibility from patient to doctor, and from doctor to attendant there was also a passing on of a considerable amount of anxiety. The strategies developed in the asylums to deal with the problems presented by suicidal patients will be explored in the next chapter.

9 Managing the problem of the suicidal patient: containment, constant watching and restraint

Asylum practices

As has been outlined, alienism constituted a form of insanity that involved the moral as well as intellectual faculties. Thus, 'the passions' could act to incite a propensity to suicide. Later, diseased and perverted impulses and instincts come to the fore as explanatory concepts within mental medicine. What remains fairly constant, though, throughout the nineteenth century is the formulation and reformulation of suicide as a madness that is characterised by the eruption of an internal, destructive force. Thus, in the asylums

it is no longer a question of recognizing the madman's error, but of situating very precisely the point where the wild force of the madness unleashes its insurrection: What is the point, what is the domain, with regard to which the force will explode and make its appearance ...?

Consequently, the tactic of the asylum in general and, more particularly, the individual tactic applied by the doctor to this or that patient within the general framework of this system of power, will and must be adjusted to the character-ization, to the localization, to the domain of application of this explosion and raging outburst of force. (Foucault, 2006, p. 8)

This dangerous force, with its potential for destruction, was taken by alienists and psychiatrists to reside within the insane patient, and the asylum was designed to contain and restrain its action. For Foucault (2006) the asylum becomes the site where such a force could be enclosed, where signs of its possible action could be detected, and where, in the event of it being 'unleashed', it could be controlled by the administration of a greater force. Medical/psychiatric strategies with regard to the suicidal can be seen as falling within this broad strategy, and can be summarised fairly succinctly:

- containment;
- constant watching; and
- restraint.

Containment primarily was achieved by confinement in the asylum. Once there the suicidal patient could be placed within a ward or dormitory (sometimes a dormitory specially designated for suicidal patients) and closely observed (Shepherd and Wright, 2002). Any sign of destructive propensities or impulses was mostly met by the patient being physically restrained from harming him/herself (although such a move was not formally sanctioned due to the insistence of a dominant philosophy of 'non-restraint' in the asylums, doctors often admitted that, in practice, physical or mechanical restraint was necessary (see Anderson, 1987, p. 404).

Such means of preventing patients harming themselves were utilised in the establishments presided over by Pinel at Bicêtre and Tuke in York, but it was Esquirol who perhaps most clearly articulated the functions of the asylum in this respect. In *Des maladies mentales* (1838) he writes: '[p]ersons who have a propensity to suicide, should occupy apartments on the ground floor of a building, cheerful, and pleasantly located' (p. 309). But it was also, Esquirol makes clear, a place of confinement, observation and restraint:

They should be guarded night and day by attendants, vigilant, and having experience to meet the wiles of suicide, usually exceedingly skilful in baffling the watchfulness of the most active. If it be necessary at any time, to have recourse to the camisole, this should not operate as a motive to security, for patients have made use of it to strangle themselves. (pp. 309–10)

Asylum superintendents in England also advocated similar practices. Sir William Ellis, previously superintendent at Wakefield County Asylum, and at the time of writing his *Treatise on Insanity*, superintendent at Hanwell County Asylum, Middlesex, advised that 'early and unceasing watchfulness' was an 'absolute requisite' (1838, p. 115) in cases where the propensity to suicide was present. Forbes Winslow (1840), although never employed in a public asylum, owned and managed two private 'madhouses' in Hammersmith, London. He lamented: 'how difficult it is for the medical man to persuade the friends of a person who has evinced a disposition to suicide, of the absolute necessity of his being confined and carefully watched!' (pp. 204–5).

Where necessary, 'bodily restraint' (Ellis, 1838, p. 128) was also required. This point is emphasised by Winslow:

In cases in which the disposition to suicide has been evinced, the patient ought to be carefully watched, and, under some circumstances, placed under restraint. Men who talk loudly of the effects of moral coercion, and who repudiate the idea of strait-waistcoats &c., have but little practical experience of the treatment of the insane. Moral discipline has done much good. Deeply should we regret to see the system which has been in force within our own recollection again introduced into our lunatic asylums. In endeavouring to avoid Scylla we have fallen into Charybdis. How many lives are lost in consequence of the patients not being properly secured when they have exhibited a desire to commit self-destruction. (Winslow, 1840, pp. 205–6)

George Savage and Fielding Blandford also publicly admitted to such practices towards the end of the century (Anderson, 1987, p. 404), the implication being that they never really went away.

An attendant's handbook from 1894 suggests that the practices of confinement, constant watching and restraint continued to be considered the best means of preventing suicide at the end the century. The following detailed advice was given to staff on the observation and supervision of the suicidal patient:

It will be necessary to examine such patients' clothes each evening at bed time, to see that nothing has been concealed in them which might be used for the purpose of self-injury. There are attempts made by lunatics to smuggle tapes, string, pieces of corset steel, etc., into bed with them, in the hope of being able to attain their end under cover of the bed-clothes. The teeth of a small buckle have been used for this purpose. Male patients, who have not been thought suicidal, have smuggled sharp instruments into bed, and destroyed themselves during the night. Of course, in cases where no warning has been given by the patient in any way, such accidents are liable to happen. Some patients try to conceal such things in the mouth, the armpits, and between the buttocks.

In the case of women, tapes and apron-strings must be borne in mind; among men, neckties are always a danger. Patients will frequently tear their clothing into strips, and either attempt strangulation or choking by pushing the pieces into the back of the throat. Handfuls of hair, pulled from the patient's own head, have been used in this way. The fact that injury may be attempted by precipitation down a flight of stairs should be borne in mind. I have known a patient to push his head through a window, and attempt to cut his throat by sawing his neck against the jagged fragments of glass that remained fixed in the wood. A special word of caution with regard to scissors is needed in the female wards. They are such everyday articles that the chance of their becoming dangerous weapons is apt to be forgotten. The ways in which very suicidal cases will try to effect their purpose are numerous. A woman, who appears to have no idea of anything in the world, will all the while be pondering methods of putting an end to her existence. The only way of meeting such cases is by continuous and careful supervision. (Harding, 1894, pp. 95–6)

Obviously, a rationale for the containment and restraint of dangerous impulses and propensities was not hard to find. As Savage argued, he was prepared to do whatever 'was best for the individual' (1884), and the prevention of harm required, at times, physical means as well as moral. Confinement, constant watching and restraint are presented as self-evidently necessary and without alternative (or the only alternative being injury or the death of the patient). Thus, as Foucault (2002a) argues, the control of dangerousness could act as the rationale for a whole host of repressive practices, as well as providing the opportunity for the production of knowledge. Foucault's (2006) account of the workings of psychiatric power also offers the possibility of a different analysis; as a constituting element in an unequal power relationship between doctor and patient, such measures could be read as at times raising the stakes in an ongoing, and potentially lethal, battle of wills, with the physician and patient attempting, by any means possible, to effect their purpose – death for the patient (a form of escape as well as resistance), the continuation of life and achievement of health through medical means on the part of the physician.

Asylum suicides

As the century wore on, the number of asylums in England increased at a great rate (and this increase was mirrored in other industrialised countries), as did the number of people certified as insane (Scull, 1993). The arguments as to why such rises occurred are beyond the scope of the present study, but what is of interest are the numbers admitted to asylums considered suicidal, and whether or not the means of prevention developed there were successful. The answer to the first question has been answered, in part, by historians studying the period. Shepherd and Wright (2002) estimated that; '[d]uring the course of the nineteenth century, between one-quarter and one-third of all admissions to lunatic asylums were described in their admission papers as "suicidal" even though "dangerousness" (either to self or others) was not a criterion for confinement required by English law' (p. 193).

Given such numbers, was suicide a common occurrence within asylums? Anderson (1987), as well as Shepherd and Wright (2003), suggests not. Anderson writes that 'although each year thousands of patients were admitted with "suicidal" against their names, only a dozen or so successful suicide attempts were annually made within asylum walls' (1987, p. 405). Shepherd and Wright (2003), similarly, note that 'although patients were commonly described as suicidal in admission records, suicides within the walls of the asylum were rare and becoming less common' (p. 193). Shepherd and Wright offer the graph shown in Figure 9.1 of reported suicides for the period 1861 to 1881.

Archival research carried out by the author into the records of the Kent County Lunatic Asylum, Chartham, bears out the findings of Anderson (1987) and Shepherd and Wright (2002) with regard to low numbers of suicide, and is perhaps worth a brief digression here, as the

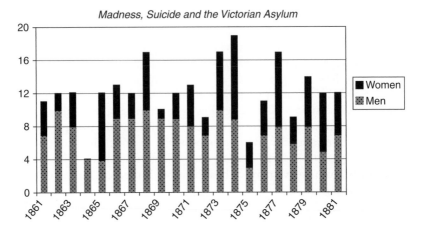

Figure 9.1 Reported suicides in licensed institutions for the insane, England and Wales, 1861–81.
Source: Annual reports of the Commissioners in Lunacy, 1862–82 (Shepherd and Wright, 2002, p. 177).

figures for the number of suicides would seem to be typical, and the steps taken to prevent such acts are illustrative of measures generally undertaken within the asylums of this period.

The Kent County Lunatic Asylum had opened in 1875, having been constructed in the previous three years to designs by John Giles & Gough. The first patients arrived on 5 April, transferred from the nearby Barming Heath Asylum, Maidstone (East Kent Archives: EK/MH/T3/Ar19). Designed to accommodate 870 patients, the asylum admitted 383 patients in the first year, with staff consisting of a medical superintendent, sixty nurses, a chaplain, a clerk/steward and ten tradesmen. The following year the number of patients increased to 485 (EK/MH/T3/Ka1; Ka16).

The first suicide occurred in 1882, and by then the asylum held nearly 870 patients, and had received around 1,500 admissions since its opening in 1875 (EK/MH/T3/Aa2; CA1–4). The asylum would not see another suicide for another six years, and the first quarter of a century of the asylum saw only three suicides in total (EK/MH/T3/Aa2; Aa3–38; Ab). In the first seventy years, Kent County Lunatic Asylum had only seven suicides, including a run of thirty-one years (1896–1927) without a single self-inflicted death (EK/MH/T3/Aa2; Aa3–38; Ab1–2; Ca1–4; Kr2–5; Kr14–17; Ks1–4; Ks5; Ks8–11; Ks12; Kz2–3; Mc; Md; Mj; Mk; Mp).

Figure 9.2 Kent County Lunatic Asylum, Chartham, *c.* 1900
(photograph in author's possession).

The first suicide was commented upon by Medical Superintendent
Robert Spencer in his journal:

Suicide – I much regret to state that a patient named William Webb committed
suicide yesterday morning by hanging. The patient went out into the airing
ground about 9 O'clock. Shortly after ten it began raining and they came in –
by mistake this patient got to 7 ward. One of the attendants of the ward asked
him which ward he belonged to and he said 2. He was taken by the Attendant
to 2 ward. A little before 12 he was missed by Albert Austin charge attendant
of W1, whose patient he was. On seeking for him he was found on the upper
part of the staircase suspended by his neck handkerchief to the hand railing. He
had been dead but a short time as he was quite warm. The Charge Attendant
Austin was in fault in not counting his patients when they returned from the
grounds.
    A Coroners Inquest was held the same evening and the verdict of the jury was
'Hanged himself when in a state of mental derangement.' This is the first suicide
since the opening of the Asylum now over seven years. (14 July 1882, EK/MH/
T3/Ca2)

The asylum was designed, built and administered with one of its primary
functions being to prevent the patients from killing themselves. Each
patient on admission was assessed as to whether they presented a danger
to themselves, to others, or both (EK/MH/T3/Mc). Any patient

considered to possess a propensity to suicide was constantly watched, day and night, by attendants. Initially the patient would be placed in one of the two (male or female) admission wards, and closely observed for any behaviour that might indicate they were dangerous to themselves. At night suicidal patients were placed together in special open dormitories (again male and female sides), and watched throughout the night by an attendant (EK/MH/T3/Aa2). The need for such measures was stressed time and time again by the Lunacy Commissioners in their annual report on the running of the asylum. In 1877 they noted: '[t]he epileptics are at present 27 males and 35 females. We are glad to report that these are now brought together at night, and placed with a certain number of suicidal patients in a dormitory. They are under continuous supervision by a special night attendant of each sex having no other duty' (EK/MH/T3/Ab1). The report for the following year stated: '[t]he arrangements for the special case of suicidal and epileptic patients during the nights continue to be carried out with efficiency and complete success. No accidents of any kind have occurred since these were established and Dr Spencer is strongly impressed with their importance' (EK/MH/T3/Ab1).

The report for 1881 gives a more detailed picture of the procedures that had developed for the management of suicidal patients: '[t]he attendants are by day 26 men and 32 women – at night there is an attendant in each of the dormitories set about for epileptic and suicidally defined patients, another sits there who visits the blocks in which these dormitories are and a third is in each division acting as general night attendant' (EK/MH/T3/Ab1).

As suggested previously, not only were the patients constantly watched, but the attendants themselves were subject to observation – a system of hierarchical surveillance characterised by Foucault (1977) as a constitutive element of disciplinary forms of power. A few weeks after the death of William Webb, the attendant in charge of the male side epileptic and suicidal dormitory was found asleep by the acting superintendent on his rounds of the asylum, and subsequently transferred to day duty. Albert Austin, the attendant deemed culpable by the medical superintendent for the suicide of William Webb, was moved to another ward and placed on a lower grade (EK/MH/T3/Ca2). It is also of interest to note that this suicide occurred following a breakdown in the practice of constant watching, and the movement of the patient outside of the rigidly ordered routine set for him.

To return to the main theme of the section, preventing suicide was apparently a primary aim of the asylums, and, on the surface at least, the institutions were successful in their endeavours. To what can their success be attributed? Shepherd and Wright conclude:

Part of the apparent success had to do with the emergence of refined preventive measures. Earlier in the century, restraint was commonly used – either in the form of straitjackets or manacles. But in the wake of the lunacy reform movement, which attacked mechanical restraint, medical superintendents were obliged to employ other means to prevent suicides within their institutions. During the period under question, strict surveillance and the frequent use of sedatives, became more commonly employed. Penalties – such as fines and dismissal – for attendants on duty during a suicide, coupled with the publicity and coroner's report resulting from a 'successful' suicide, made medical superintendents and staff eager to avoid such occurrences within the walls of the asylum. (2002, pp. 193–4))

It would seem that in the battle of wills between asylum staff and a suicidal patient, it was the staff that mostly – nearly always – prevailed. Yet there is need for caution, too, in the interpretation of such figures. As Anderson (1987) notes, it was often enough to gain admission to an asylum to display 'quite slight suicidal tendencies'. 'Bucknill and Savage ... agreed that certification documents exaggerated the extent of suicidal propensities' (p. 405). Savage estimated that only around five per cent of the patients under his care at the Bethlem had made 'serious attempts at suicide or seemed likely to repeat such attempts, although between 20 and 30 per cent were always registered as suicidal' (p. 405). Thus it may have been, as Foucault (2002a) argued, that madness was presented as inherently dangerous to serve the purposes of the emerging psychiatric profession, and that the risks of suicide in those diagnosed as insane were in actuality always rather less than made out.

The low rates of asylum suicides are interesting to compare with present-day in-patient suicides (while remaining fully aware of the difficulties of making such comparisons). Healy *et al.* (2006) compared suicide and suicide attempt rates for 741 admissions for schizophrenia and 1,303 admissions for psychoses to the North Wales Asylum between 1875 and 1924, with first admissions for psychosis in north-west Wales between 1994 and 1998, and concluded that current rates of suicide for schizophrenia and other psychoses appear twenty-fold higher.

As detailed above, my own research into the casebooks, mortality records and Lunacy Commission reports for the Kent County Lunatic Asylum suggested that between 1875 and 1945 there were seven suicides – that is one a decade. Recent figures suggest that there are now around five in-patient suicides a year for the area of Kent roughly comparable to that covered by the old County Asylum (East Kent Community NHS Trust, NHS Performance Ratings, July 2002).

The very low suicide rates in the asylum give pause for thought, for a number of interpretations are possible here. The most obvious is that the disciplinary measures in the asylums worked: that is, they were effective in their purpose of confining and containing those considered to possess the potential for self-destruction; such people, under a regime of constant watching, were unable to effect their purpose; and where the attempts to instil a degree of self-restraint through the cultivation of a moral conscience did not succeed, physical restraint was employed to thwart their plans. The near total domination of the patient by the asylum staff could ensure no self-destructive act could arise. Add in a poor diet and the use of sedative drugs such as chloral and opium, and there remained a diminished possibility of the suicidal patient acting on his/her desire to die. Olive Anderson (1987) also points to the 'treatability' of those confined as suicide risks, arguing that 'melancholics', who made up the majority of suicide cases, were considered to be the ones most likely to be discharged cured. Healy *et al.* (2006) suggest that methods used in the late nineteenth century to prevent suicides were mostly similar to those used today – 'the removal of sharp utensils, belts and shoelaces, the dispersal of groups of suicidal patients, and observation' (p. 226) – and that the greatest difference between 1900 and 2000 was the fact that 'Victorian period patients could more readily be kept on locked wards, were not discharged until the risk of suicide was thought to have completely passed and were not discharged on recently instituted psychotropic medication' (p. 226).

Healy *et al.*'s interpretation, and to an extent Anderson's, rely on the belief that patients, as well as suicide itself, are largely unchanging phenomena – that is the patients have remained the same, as has the nature of suicide, so the only variables to be considered in determining the reasons for the different rates of suicide are the different treatments administered. Locked/open wards; long/short stay; institutional/deinstitutionalised care; 'old' drugs/'modern' psychotropic medication become the identified variables that could account for such differences. The possibility that mental illness and forms of self-accomplished death might vary according to time and place is not greatly considered. To conclude that asylums were effective is to take at face value the belief in the dangerousness or destructiveness of mental illnesses – the idea that it is something inherent in the illnesses that leads to death by suicide. Equally, it is to take acts of suicide as unchanging. In so doing, the variable nature and meanings of the act are lost to analysis. However, by drawing on Foucault's ideas concerning the 'deployment' of dangerousness in the formation of psychiatry (2002a), and his work on the particular relationships of power between doctor and patient in the asylums (2006), a different analysis is perhaps made possible.

A high proportion of those taken to be in some way insane were said to be in possession of a propensity for suicide – thus up to a third of admissions to the asylums were recorded as suicidal (Shepherd and Wright, 2002). However, many of these recorded 'suicide cases' may have been in little danger of harming themselves – a few asylum superintendents eventually came to admit as much. Instead, the high number of 'cases' perhaps reflected the continual deployment of the threat of suicide. As noted earlier, Foucault (2002a) argued that the concept of the 'dangerous individual' was of importance in the establishment of a function for the emerging psychiatric profession in the nineteenth century. By positing notions of an insanity that 'remains invisible until it explodes; that for this reason no one can forecast it, unless he has considerable experience and a trained eye' (p. 185), psychiatry could justify its practices.

It is possible to argue that insanity during this period was not, as was asserted over and over again by alienists and psychiatrists, by its nature dangerous, but came to be constituted as such. Through the continual stating and restating of the truth that the potential for self-destruction often resided within the insane, that to be mad was to be dangerous, a 'looping effect' (Hacking, 1999) was effected whereby the 'insane' came to recognise within themselves the dangerous impulses and propensities they were told were there, and over time learnt to report such leanings back to their doctors, who duly noted their existence, the forms they took, the intensity of the forces involved, the moments when such forces were most likely to break out, etc. The insane thus came to recognise the truth of themselves as possessing internal, destructive impulses and urges – the internalisation of a medical truth – acted in a manner consistent with such truths (but rarely to the extent that they endangered themselves), and were subjected to practices that further reinforced such truths (confined, contained, constantly watched for an 'eruption' of destructiveness, restrained in their actions). Through such means madness could be constituted as dangerous, asylum practices justified, yet suicide rates kept at low levels. The constitution of madness as dangerous possessed a strategic logic in terms of the consolidation and expansion of psychiatric power, and such power facilitated the accumulation of authoritative knowledge that further reinforced the perceived dangerousness of madness, and such a power-knowledge relationship should not be overlooked in the analysis of suicide rates in the asylums.

If we ignore relations of power-knowledge and assert instead that suicide and mental illness have remained essentially unchanged in the modern period (from the early nineteenth century on) then we must account for the very low rates of suicide evident in the Victorian asylums in relation to the comparatively high rates of in-patient suicide found now by reference to different regimes of treatment, and conclude that treatment in the asylums was more effective. Yet contemporary practices of hospitalisation, constant observation and restraint represent similar forms of suicide prevention to those undertaken in the asylums. Other variables such as length of stay or drug treatments have changed and may well be important factors in the comparative suicide rates, as suggested by Healey *et al.* (2006). However, by postulating suicide and mental illness as changeable, a different form of analysis is made possible, one that can take into account the ways in which dominant discourse and practices act to form and shape the objects and subjects of study and the processes by which concepts of dangerousness and suicidality may be deployed for strategic ends arising out of certain relations of power. The lines of force that act to constitute the relationship between doctor and suicidal patient could be said to be multiple and tangled. The usual picture of, on the one side, the insane patient possessed by a malign destructive impulse and, on the other, the doctor able to uncover this hidden madness, who then acts to confine, contain and, if necessary, restrain such a force, glosses over the complexities involved. Rather, psychiatry needed such a force to justify its practices of confinement yet also was threatened by it. It incited its presence but feared its effects. What was required was the possibility of suicide but not its actuality. Thus, in the asylums there came to be high numbers of 'suicidal cases', but low numbers of death by suicide. Within the walls of the asylum this arrangement of forces was, for the most part, safely managed. With the closing of the institutions, however, once the protective function of the asylum was lost, the relations of power shifted, and the dangers of madness came to be realised in increased numbers of self-inflicted deaths by mental health patients. As Healy *et al.* (2006) argue, deinstitutionalisation, the use of newer drug treatments and shorter stays in hospital all potentially lead to higher numbers of patient suicides. From this, however, we do not necessarily need to conclude that mental illnesses are innately dangerous, nor do we have to believe in the existence of malign, unseen, explosively destructive forces as cause or explanation for the self-accomplished deaths of those designated mentally ill.

Conclusions

The previous two chapters have argued that rather than discovering previously hidden truths of suicide, mental medicine came to form the suicidal patient as an object of study and in so doing created a number of objects and concepts to account for the apparent existence of a desire to die in their patients. Initially notions of pathological anatomy were called upon in a style of thought imitative of general medicine. Later, unlocated and unseen impulses were proposed. Neither furnished psychiatry with firm foundations upon which to diagnose and treat suicidal patients, but they did enable the emerging profession to assert the necessity of their calling – namely the protection of individuals and the population from the dangers inherent in madness. In the absence of effective medical interventions, confinement, containment, constant watching and restraint remained the mainstay of psychiatric management of the suicidal patient. Such disciplinary measures worked in that asylum suicides remained rare occurrences, but it could also be argued that the dangers of insanity were always overplayed for strategic reasons.

What is clear is that psychiatric formulations came to dominate understandings and practices in relation to suicide by the end of the nineteenth century. How such dominance was extended, challenged, and then reasserted, is the subject of the next chapter.

10   Towards the 'normatively monolithic' – 'psy' discourse and suicide: 1897–1981

The challenge to, and later reassertion of, psychiatric dominance in relation to suicide

By the latter decades of the nineteenth century doctors had come to assume positions of authority in managing the suicidal across a number of sites and in a variety of roles – in asylums particularly, but also outside the asylums as police surgeons, as general practitioners in their surgeries or in patients' homes, in gaols as prison medical staff, as hospital doctors, as expert witnesses in court and at inquests, or as lecturers within schools of medicine (Anderson, 1987). As Anderson notes, their expertise was contested in some areas more than others, but for the most part the medical knowledge produced and circulated was taken to be authoritative, and certainly in relation to the control and management of the suicidal, medical practices, particularly in the more recognisably psychiatric forms they had assumed in the asylums from mid century on, were dominant (Gates, 1989; Berrios and Mohanna, 1995). Moral tracts condemning the act appeared infrequently (e.g. the Reverend Gurnhill's *The Morals of Suicide*, 1900), and the severest laws against suicide had been repealed by 1882 (Anderson, 1987). Suicide had come to be 'regarded with sympathy rather than with abhorrence. It is spoken of as a "misfortune" rather than a crime' (Henson, 1897, in Gates, 1989, p. 166). Sociological, psychological and psychoanalytic 'challenges' were yet to materialise (Durkheim's *Le suicide* was published in 1897; Freud's *The Psychopathology of Everyday Life* in 1901). Within the confines of the asylum, practices of containment, observation and restraint effectively managed suicidal patients to such an extent that suicides were a rare occurrence (Shepherd and Wright, 2002; Healy, 2006; see also previous chapter). In professional journals and books the main debate was whether all, or just nearly all, suicides were insane at the time of death. Adjustments and refinements to psychiatric categories continued, and so there could be talk of suicide in terms of 'melancholia' (Maudsley, 1892b), 'maniacal states' or 'delusional insanity' (Savage, in Tuke, 1892), and as the century neared its end suicide came to be discussed in relation to fears of degeneracy and moral decline (e.g. Strahan, 1894). What remained constant was the assertion of a causal link between individual pathology and suicide.

Psychiatric formulations gradually came to reshape 'everyday' understandings and actions in relation to suicide. Olive Anderson, from her analysis of coroners' papers in her *Suicide in Victorian and Edwardian England* (1987), notes that the meaning of dying by suicide changed over time from the mid-Victorian to Edwardian period:

Some coroners' papers for Edwardian London demonstrate that by then alcoholism, loss of work, and brushes with destitution were less important than they had been fifty years earlier. In the early twentieth century people worried more about their own health and adequacy, and saw suicide as an escape from depression, disappointment, and self-reproach, in a way which a present-day psychiatrist might not find unfamiliar. (p. 420)

The reasons given for suicide changed, but so did, according to Anderson's analysis, the act itself. For Edwardians, she wrote, 'their approach to suicidal action was more brooding and long drawn out, and less casual and impulsive, than that of their mid-Victorian predecessors', and concludes that suicide could now be characterised as 'essentially an introspective agony over private fears and feelings' (p. 420). Medical/psychiatric knowledge of suicide, gleaned from observations of asylum patients (their actions, gestures, bodily state, etc.) all read as symptoms of pathological states and recorded in case books, came to be reproduced and disseminated through multiple channels (textbooks and journals, as well as articles in ever more widely read periodicals, books, and newspapers) and acted to gradually redefine the meaning of suicide. Through such means, acts of self-destruction came to be increasingly associated with individual pathological states, and it is possible to map the emergence of a form of suicide recognisable today – the tragic act of the mentally unwell individual. Psychiatric power was, of course, reinforced by the production and deployment of such knowledge – for the medical truths of suicide (as essentially an unpredictable act of pathology) confirmed the necessity of the confinement, watching and restraint of the insane (suspected of harbouring dangerous propensities or impulses) and the suicidal (suspected of possessing traits of madness, or constitutional defects) in order to nullify, or at least contain, the threat posed to the patients themselves, to others, and in the latter stages of the century, to the population as a whole through the transmission of such pathology and abnormalities along family lines.

The early twentieth century does, however, also mark something of a change in that new forms of therapeutic intervention emerge that in many ways complement, but in others challenge, the authority of psychiatry with regard to suicide. Nineteenth-century psychiatrists looked to the patients' bodies (their movements, gestures, expressions, etc.), made visible through their confinement and regulation in the asylum and understandable by means of the development of systems of classification and theoretical speculations, as well as after death through autopsy, in order to accumulate expert knowledge as to the causes of suicide. With the emergence of psychoanalysis new theories of self-destructive behaviours could be formulated and new practices undertaken – for the speech of the patient came to be considered of potential use in uncovering the reasons for suicidal thoughts, desires and behaviours. With suicidal behaviour rethought as a problem that arises in the 'psyche', a dialogue of sorts could arise, for the truth of suicide could potentially be uncovered by means of an exploration of this 'deep', internal space of the patient. Numerous 'talking cures', initially Freudian psychoanalysis, later all manner of approaches under different names (Jungian, Adlerian, Kleinian, Gestalt, Rogerian, existential, etc.) emerged, each regarding the patients' reporting, or perhaps confessing, of their thoughts, feelings, dreams, imaginings and memories as an important part of the treatment process. What did not change, however, with the proliferation of various schools of therapy in the twentieth century, was the emphasis on pathologies located within the interiority of the individual as explanations for suicidal behaviours. Instead, there arose a multiplication of the deficits and pathologies that were said to be the properties of the individual, leading to an increase in the ways in which suicides could be constituted as 'sick' or 'abnormal'.

What is perhaps challenged with the emergence of psychoanalytic and psychological discourse and practices in relation to suicide and the suicidal is the idea that these are solely or necessarily the domain of the psychiatrist, in particular the asylum doctor. The practices of these later forms of 'psy' discourse were based less on disciplinary measures of confinement, surveillance or restraint but more on technologies that Foucault characterises as 'pastoral' (Rose, 1998). These techniques of confession and self-disclosure, that are extended into the relationship of the self to itself by means of 'self-inspection, self-suspicion, self-decipherment, and self-nurturing' (p. 26), open up new ways of relating to suicidal patients. The patient, certainly within analytic settings, is encouraged to 'look within' themselves, to seek out the emotional or psychological cause of their suicidal propensities, to disclose their fears and desires to the analyst or therapist, who in turn offers an interpretation of the true meaning of the patient's suicidal promptings. Such a figure need not be medical, and as the twentieth century progresses therapists of all theoretical persuasions come to proliferate, all offering the possibility of treatment for the suicidal, and although a portion of such therapeutic work is undertaken by medics, it is by no means all. Psychologists, psychiatric nurses, social workers, occupational therapists and counsellors all emerge as distinct professional groups within the century, each offering their own versions of 'pastoral' care. Importantly, though, when suicide is thought to be likely, the psychiatrist is again called for and the asylum (later remodelled as 'psychiatric units' or wards) required, with the right and responsibility of doctors to forcibly detain and treat those deemed mentally ill and a danger to themselves or others enshrined in law (for example in the UK the Mental Health Acts of 1959 and 1983). Pastoral power does not supplant the disciplinary with regard to suicide, but emerges in conjunction as a set of supplementary techniques, ones that enable different ways of thinking and acting in relation to suicide, but with their 'safety' underwritten by the continuation of the possibility of detention and restraint if required.

Of course psychiatry itself does not remain the same during the twentieth century. For Nikolas Rose (1986), these changes are primarily territorial, a shift from asylum to community, a 'proliferation of sites for the practice of psychiatry' (p. 83). As a consequence, new populations could come under the auspices of psychiatric care, and the focus widened from 'insanity' to the 'neurotic' (sometimes pejoratively referred to as 'the worried well'). Whole new sections of the population thus came to be 'psychiatrized' (p. 83), but the psychiatric practices that emerged in relation to this opening up of new sites were no longer exclusively based on segregation and coercion, or 'dominated by a narrow organicism at the level of theory and treatment' (p. 82), but rather could be characterised more as 'administrative'. Such a 'managing' role – in Nikolas Rose's (1996) phrase, 'less that of curing illness than of administering pathological individuals across an archipelago of specialist institutions and types of activity, and simultaneously engaging in a prophylactic and preventative work of maximising mental health' (p. 5) – enabled an extension and diffusion of psychiatric power across a number of sites, and here again one can note the deployment of the threat of suicide as a strand that in part enables and justifies such a process. As was noted in chapter 8, the management of social threat had underpinned the formation and development of the psychiatric profession – the asylum functioned as a solution to the problem of what to do with those who violated social norms of conduct and facilitated the production and accumulation of knowledge that not only enabled the creation of a distinct medical speciality dealing with various 'mental maladies', but also provided the rationale for many asylum practices through the propagation of the belief in the inherent dangerousness of insanity, with suicide a visible manifestation of such danger.

Similarly, degeneracy was in part constituted by reference to suicide, and through such deaths not only were individuals threatened but also the population as a whole through the transmission of constitutional defects and propensities that could lead to further self-destructive acts. The new forms of psychiatric practice that characterised the move out of the asylums also deployed the threat of suicide as a rationale for their existence and extension. The mental hygiene movement that emerged in the 1920s and 1930s in the UK sought to intervene to prevent the possibility of danger arising as a consequence of mental disturbance, suicide being one identified threat. More recent 'community' approaches for mental health patients since the 1980s could also be justified by reference to the prevention of suicide. Suicide prevention strategies, a feature of national and international health policy in the last two decades, have sought to target a wide range of 'at risk' populations across a number of locations, including not just psychiatric wards, but also prisons, schools, colleges and universities, hospital Accident and Emergency (A&E) departments, drug and alcohol services, and rural farming communities (see, for instance, the *National Suicide Prevention Strategy for England and Wales*, Department of Health, 2002), and represent something of an extension and diffusion of psychiatric power with administrative 'pastoral' practices supplementing more longstanding disciplinary techniques.

Psychiatric dominance in relation to suicide does meet with some resistance during this period, however, with the emergence of sociology as a distinct discipline with a theoretical interest in the causation of self-destructive acts. Whereas the findings and arguments of the nineteenth-century 'moral statisticians' had tended to be used to bolster the claims of psychiatry (Hacking, 1990), the publication of Durkheim's *Le suicide* in 1897 opened the door to a sustained challenge (theoretically, if not in practice) to psychiatric truths of suicide. Durkheim sought to show how regularities in the suicide rates of nations and cultures across time could best be explained by reference to social rather than individual factors, and his theories have been taken up on many occasions since (e.g. Halbwachs, 1978 [originally published 1930]; Henry and Short, 1954; Hendin, 1964; Taylor, 1982, 1988). Social, rather than individual, pathology emerges as a truth in its own right, albeit one without the currency to seriously challenge the basis of psychiatric practices. The influence is felt more at a population/social policy level, where statistical facts relating to the social characteristics of completed suicides have guided policy-making (e.g. United Nations/World Health Organization, 1996; Department of Health, 2002).

The rest of this chapter looks to map some of the ways in which the truth of suicide as primarily a matter of individual pathology comes to be reinforced and extended (theoretically and in practice), but also challenged, in the twentieth century. Once again the focus is on how truths in relation to suicide are produced and reproduced, as well as mapping the effects of such ways of thinking. The emergence of the various 'psy' disciplines is briefly touched upon, and an example, drawn from the psychoanalytic literature (Karl Menninger's *Man Against Himself* (1938) and a related paper) of the ways in which an individual can come to be constituted as suicidal is set out as illustrative of a process of subject formation in relation to a certain mode of objectivation (Foucault, 1998). Also, the development of the use of 'psychological autopsy' to demonstrate the almost ubiquitous presence of mental illness in suicides is outlined and then critiqued. Challenges to 'psy' truth claims from sociology and from Thomas Szasz are discussed in relation to their effectiveness to act as points of resistance to the dominant formation of suicide as an individual and pathological act.

Extending the possibilities for the 'pathologisation' of suicide

Nikolas Rose's *Inventing Our Selves* (1998) traces the formation of a 'psychological' style of thought from the latter part of the nineteenth century on, and argues that the 'psy' disciplines (psychiatry, psychology, psychotherapy and psychoanalysis) can be discussed in terms of a collective 'psychology' in that they each contributed to the formation of an 'internal universe of the self' characterized as a 'profound inwardness' whereby 'conduct, belief, value, and speech were to be interrogated and rendered explicable in terms of an understanding of an inner space that gave them form' (p. 4). The development of psychoanalysis, abnormal psychology and psychological therapies in the twentieth century certainly led to an increase in the different kinds of mental pathologies and abnormalities that were said to exist, and these frequently came to be linked, aetiologically, to suicide in the theoretical writings of experts.

Evidence for such connections was sought and located by means of the analysis and interpretation of the content of the patient's speech. Whereas nineteenth-century psychiatry had, for the most part, not encouraged the patient to speak, Freudian psychoanalysis and later psychological therapies were founded on the notion that treatment necessitated the revealing of the patient's innermost thoughts and feelings. The suicidal patient was no longer just to be confined, contained and restrained, but was now, within these new treatment modalities, required to confess. The resulting patient–therapist dialogues opened up new possibilities for constituting pathological and suicidal identities. Analytic theory, certainly the classical

Freudian variety, proposed a subject driven by unconscious impulses and urges, and through the processes of analysis the patient was exposed to the belief that these were inherent traits residing deep within, and that actions and behaviours could be understood as manifestations of an internal battle between creative and destructive instincts. These theories are outlined by reference to Freud's writings, and then processes of subjectivation are illustrated by examination of a case study presented in Menninger's 'Psychoanalytic aspects of suicide' (1933/1996). These texts are examined in order, again, to cast light on the relationship between the creation of certain truths of human nature, the constitution of a suicidal subjectivity, and relations of power.

Psychoanalytic constructions of the suicidal subject

Freudian psychoanalysis emerged in the first decades of the twentieth century, and looked to build a new objective science of the individual subject. Founded on notions of perverted instinctual drives largely inherited from nineteenth-century psychiatry these were newly described and elaborated upon in psychoanalytic discourse, and suicide came to be seen as arising from these internal impulses and instincts. Much of the discussion that follows concerning Freud's theories of suicide rely to a large extent on their treatment in Robert Litman's 'Sigmund Freud on suicide' originally written in 1970 and also to be found in Maltsberger and Goldblatt, 1996. There follows an analysis of Karl Menninger's *Man Against Himself* (1938), for here influential formulations of suicide were set out, and it is possible to trace certain 'truth effects' in terms of the creation of the suicidal subject formed in relation to the authoritative knowledge of the analyst.

In *The Psychopathology of Everyday Life* (1901) Freud writes of an instinct of self-destruction that he considered by no means rare, '[f]or the trend to self-destruction is present to a certain degree in very many more human beings than those in whom it is carried out' (in Litman, 1996, p. 206). A theory of a universal death instinct was not to be formulated until late in his career, however. Freud did discuss suicide at two meetings of the Vienna Psychoanalytic Society on 20 and 27 April 1910. Here, other well known analysts such as Alfred Adler and Wilhelm Stekel spoke at length of the problem and how it related to analytic theory and practice, emphasising for the most part the aggressive aspects of suicide. Freud said little, confining himself to a few concluding remarks, and expressing himself somewhat dissatisfied with the proceedings:

I have an impression that in spite of all the valuable material that has been brought before us in this discussion, we have not reached a decision on the problem that interests us. We are anxious, above all, to know how it becomes possible for the extraordinarily powerful life instinct to be overcome; whether this can come about with the help of a disappointed libido or whether the ego can renounce its self-preservation for its own egoistic motives. (in Litman, 1996, pp. 206–7)

The nineteenth-century psychiatric debate on how the instinct of self-preservation can be overcome is reworked, in Freudian psychoanalytic terms, as an internal drama of competing forces between destructive libidinal drives and egoistic self-preservation. Freud concludes his remarks with the advice to his colleagues to suspend their judgement until 'experience has solved this problem' (Litman, 1996, pp. 206–7). Litman believes that Freud struggled to integrate his ideas on suicide into a coherent and comprehensive theory: '[a]ccording to Freud, human behaviors are derived ultimately from needs to satisfy instinctual drives. In his early theory the basic, conflicting instinctual drives were thought to be libido (sensuality, sexuality) and self-preservation (hunger, aggressive mastery). How could suicide satisfy the needs either of sexuality or self-preservation?' (p. 207).

It was not until late in his career that Freud believed he was able to articulate a satisfactory theory. Eventually, notes Litman, Freud came to revise his notions of the workings of the instincts in order to emphasise the importance of self-destructiveness. Specifically, a death instinct came to be conceptualised that supplemented the theory of the libido. Freud came to believe that human nature encompassed both a life instinct – 'Eros' – and a death force or instinct – 'Thanatos'. As he wrote in 1923:

After long hesitancies and vacillations we have decided to assume the existence of only two basic instincts, Eros and the destructive instinct. The aim of the first of these basic instincts is to establish ever greater unities and to preserve them thus – in short, to bind together; the aim of the second is, on the contrary, to undo connections and so to destroy things. In the case of the destructive instinct we may suppose that its final aim is to lead what is living into an inorganic state. For this reason we also call it the death instinct ... In biological functions the two basic instincts operate against each other or combine with each other ... This concurrent and mutually opposing action of the two basic instincts gives rise to the whole variegation of the phenomena of life. (in Litman, 1996, p. 212)

The destructive instinct is taken to be an inherent aspect of human nature. The primary forces of creation and destruction are placed within the interiority of the individual, and actions and behaviours seen as manifestations of the outcome of the struggle between them. Before Freud arrived at these final formulations, he had found it difficult to account for suicide and self-harming behaviours. But in each of his attempts an interior drama is proposed; in 'Mourning and melancholia' (written in 1915, published in 1917), for example, a whole array of internal forces are proposed and set in motion in order to explain suicide. Most interesting, when examining the trend towards increasingly 'interior' explanations (that is those approaches that sought the causes of self-destruction within the 'deep' interiority of the individual), is the move initiated by Freud to see suicide as an expression of murderous impulses turned inward:

> We have long known it is true that no neurotic harbors thoughts of suicide which he has not turned back upon himself from murderous impulses against others, but we have never been able to explain what interplay of forces can carry such a purpose through to execution. The analysis of melancholia now shows that the ego can kill itself only if, owing to the return of the object-cathexis, it can treat itself as an object – if it is able to direct against itself the hostility which relates to an object and which represents the ego's original reaction to objects in the external world. (in Litman, 1996, p. 208)

What is of interest, in relation to the questions posed in this book, are the effects of such statements, disseminated through professional, expert writings, and more particularly in the analyst's room, with regard to the formation of subjects, and what relations of power-knowledge can be discerned. Psychoanalytic theory and practices (there were obviously many, discussion is limited here to the theories and practices discernable in the writings of Freud and Karl Menninger) opened up new possibilities in relation to suicide, both for the 'profession' itself as well as for their subjects. New objects could be formed, and new subjects constituted, in relation to the truths generated through analysis. The powers of the analyst in relation to the patient – to elicit confession, to name the true meaning of what is spoken (in particular to decide on the normality or otherwise of what is said), to locate the source of problems, and to advise on the means of resolving such problems – were considerable. Such relations of power opened up the possibility of reasons for destructive urges being 'uncovered', of there arising a shared understanding between analyst and analysand that could lead to the resolution of the internal drama, through therapy, in favour of the life force – in short, there arose possibilities for the alleviation of suffering. The practices of psychoanalysis also facilitated the production of knowledge – more and more could come to be known, it was argued, of the psychopathological causes of suicide as analysts recorded and published their patients' phantasies and their dreams of and desires for destruction and death. Theories focused in particular on issues around sexuality and childhood experiences, and thus biographical details and information on the sexual desires and functioning of the patient could come to be the material from which accounts as to the causes of suicide could be constructed. Obviously, this allowed for numerous possibilities, certainly in relation to the rather limited organic, 'physicalist' explanations demanded of nineteenth-century psychiatry.

Through the practices of therapy, and by the production and circulation of such knowledge, it was believed acts of self-destruction could be understood and potentially averted.

The locating of such destructive urges within the individual subject, and the linking of suicidal impulses to the sexuality of the patient and his/her history, could also be said to be problematic, however. Patients subjected to analytic procedures (the authoritative interpretation of their confessed dreams and desires) could come to be exposed to the belief that they possessed an interiority inherently pathological and destructive. What is more, analytic theory held that such an interiority was only partially accessible to the subject through introspection. Patients could absorb the notion that their thoughts, feelings and actions were determined by unconscious (and destructive) processes that required expert analysis to uncover and interpret. The patient was always subject *to* as well as subject *of* the analytic process, relatively powerless when it came to formulating the truth of their dreams, imaginings, desires and actions. From such a position patients came to be constituted by reference to an authoritative, pathologising set of discourses and practices that individualised their suffering by locating its cause firmly within their own psyche, read as inherently unknowable yet profoundly destructive.

Such means of constituting the analytic subject in relation to suicide can be traced in the work of Karl Menninger. *Man Against Himself* (1938) begins with Freud and a lengthy description of the workings of the death-instinct: 'Thanatos; there exists from the beginning in all of us,' he writes, 'strong propensities toward self-destruction' (p. 5). Menninger bases his thesis on Freud's theory of opposing primal forces, the life and death instincts. The finer details of Menninger's position vis-à-vis Freud are beyond the scope of this book, but Menninger's account is of interest as illustrative of a kind of truth-telling in relation to human nature, and also in that suicide, as set out in *Man Against Himself*, remains pathological and individual, but is now read as almost entirely an issue of internal forces. Here, the interiority of the patient, the 'psyche', is constructed as the scene of a mighty battle, with death the result of the ascendancy, or victory, of the death instinct. As with Freud, the 'death-instinct, or primary impulses of destructiveness are opposed by a life-instinct or primary impulses of creativeness and constructiveness; it is various phases of interaction between these two which constitute the psychological and biological phenomena of life' (p. 71). From such a position Menninger can redescribe a very wide range of behaviours and conditions ('martyrdom', 'invalidism', 'alcohol addiction', 'psychosis', 'impotence', 'purposive accidents', 'malingering' and even becoming physically unwell) as being caused by internal destructive forces. In the preface he writes, '[i]t is true ... that in the end each man kills himself in his own selected way, fast or slow, soon or late' (p. vii). All deaths, by this account, can be accounted for by reference to an innate self-destructive force.

In Menninger 'external' factors in suicide are relegated to a secondary role, and are read as manifestations of internal, unconscious, forces:

For we know that the individual always, in a measure, creates his own environment, and thus the suicidal person must in some way help to create the very thing from which, in suicide, he takes flight ... In other words, if for one's own unconscious purposes, one brings about an apparent justification in external reality for self-destruction, the unconscious purposes are of more significance in understanding the suicide than the apparently simple, inevitable, external circumstances. (Menninger, 1938, p. 18)

Menninger attributes 'three internal elements' to suicide: 'the element of dying, the element of killing, and the element of being killed' (p. 24). The notion of destructive impulses underlies each of these, as Menninger summarises later in considering the deeper motives for suicide:

These are, (1) impulses derived from the primary aggressiveness crystallized as a wish to kill, (2) impulses derived from a modification of the primitive aggressiveness, the conscience, crystallized as the wish to be killed, and (3) I believe there is evidence that some of the original primary self-directed aggressiveness, the wish to die, joins hands with the more sophisticated motives and adds to the total vectorial force which impels the precipitate self-destruction. (p. 72)

The means by which such theories could, through the practices of psychoanalysis, act to constitute, in part, a certain kind of suicidal patient, and a particular form of self-accomplished death, will now be considered. Such processes can best be illustrated by analysis of a case study presented by Menninger in an earlier paper 'Psychoanalytic aspects of suicide' (Menninger, 1933/1996). This paper introduced Menninger's 'suicide triad' outlined above ('the wish to die, the wish to kill, and the wish to be killed'). In the paper the following story is recounted:

Another illustration which might be added is that of a thirty-five-year-old son of a travelling salesman, whose parents had taken him in early childhood on many railroad trips and permitted him to sleep with them in the berth. Riding on the train has always had for him a great fascination and no doubt gratified some incest phantasies in association with the above memories, and also the satisfaction of father identification, his father having made his living by travelling. (pp. 29–30)

Here, biographical details of the patient's childhood are brought together with questions of sexual desire. Unconscious 'phantasies', such as the 'incest phantasies' mentioned in the text, are taken to lie outside the patient's consciousness but, in Menninger's account, are understood to influence behaviour. Through the process of analysis such unconscious elements of the patient's psyche are said to be brought into consciousness, and the patient comes to believe that he must act against this concealed enemy within – his unconscious:

At a time when his analysis was in reality progressing very favourably, he one day had the feeling, suddenly, as he rode on the suburban train, that it was senseless, unnecessary, futile, and there came a strong impulse to kill himself, 'because my unconscious plays such tricks on me; I just thought, "Hell! I'll show it! I'll jump out of the train."' The analytic material of the next few days became chiefly lament and self-reproach for the feeling 'that I have so constantly – of course unintentionally – deceived the analyst and tried to fool him and play tricks upon him, all of which reacts only, of course, to my own harm'.

The idea of an unconscious (a hidden part of himself able to play tricks on him) has, presumably, been formed in conversation between analyst and analysand, as a reality to be confronted in some way. Things are further complicated as the impulse to harm himself is reinterpreted as a form of aggression against the analyst and his own father; '[o]ne can see in this impulse to jump from the train, first of all a direct aggressive threat toward the analyst and toward the father whom the analyst represented. Jumping from the train meant the end of the analysis, not only symbolically, but in reality. It was also casting the father out of the train, an obvious symbolic parricide'. Menninger goes on to consider the motives for the patient's impulse to die:

The reasons alleged for his contemplated suicide are equally significant. His conscious thought was that his unconscious had played tricks upon him and he would take revenge on his unconscious. Obviously his 'unconscious' was the analyst; he was justifying his attack upon the analyst by charging him with having played tricks. As a matter of fact, however, such an allegation had no basis in reality and was an inverted charge, a charge against himself that he had projected upon the analyst. He had indeed played tricks upon the analyst, as he well knew, and felt guilty about it. He was anxious to shew that these tricks had harmed him and the need for punishment is also fulfilled in the jumping from the train. 'Punishment of the unconscious' represented punishment of himself.

What is being formed here in terms of the subject? The patient's 'psyche' seems to be represented as a site of battle and conflict over which he has little or no insight or control. The internal, destructive impulses impel him to act in ways he can neither understand nor effectively restrain. Further into Menninger's interpretation the patient is said to have an unconscious desire to be 'homosexually attacked':

But one can also infer from this (as was clearly brought out in the patient's subsequent material) that he actually wanted the analyst to play these said tricks on him. By playing tricks on him he had unconscious reference, of course, to the erotic motive, i.e. the wish to be homosexually attacked. But against this wish by way of defence (dictated by the super-ego), and against the indignity of the attack (directed by the ego), there arose the outwardly directed destructive tendencies of projection. Thus, 'It is not I who plays tricks upon the analyst, it is he who plays tricks upon me. He attacks me. Therefore I hate him, I want to kill him, I do kill him. But for killing him I also feel guilty and must suffer a like fate myself.'

Menninger summarises the forces taken to be at work in the patient's impulse to suicide: '[i]n other words, this man feels guilty for (1) this parricidal wish, (2) his hostile wishes against the analyst, (3) his deception or attempted deception of the analyst, and (4) his homosexual wishes. The guilt for all of these demands punishment of a similar sort, namely, an attack directed against himself. Hence the suicidal impulse'.

One way to understand the formulations set out in Menninger's account is that, in asserting the truth of internal, 'intrapsychic' conflict as causative of suicide, a certain kind of suicidal patient and form of death is produced. Such discourse, enacted in therapeutic practice, is formative as much as representative. Psychoanalysis, at the time of Menninger's writing, possessed authority with regards to the understanding of human nature. Through conversation in therapy, a subject comes to be formed, one apparently beset by hidden desires, impulses and fears. That is not to suggest that the patient did not experience difficulties and distress prior to therapy, or that therapy was not of benefit (there is no way of knowing) but more that the process of therapy could lead, as is suggested by the account set out above, to the production of beliefs about an opaque interiority full of dangerous desires and impulses (to be 'homosexually attacked', to kill and be killed) that could become known only through acts of confession and expert interpretation. The idea of an internal, 'naturally' arising destructive force, identified by the analyst and rendered harmless by means of expert guidance and interpretation, perhaps underplays the complexity of relations between therapist and patient.

The production and circulation of expert truths of suicide through the process of psychotherapy, as illustrated by Menninger's account, can also be analysed in terms of relations of power-to-knowledge and knowledge-to-power. As noted above, the formulation of expert knowledge relies on imbalances of power within the therapeutic relationship itself. Within accounts such as Menninger's one can discern some of the processes through which a subject can come to be constituted by reference to the 'objective' knowledge of the therapist. The possible effects of being subjected to objectifying practices are discussed by David Halperin:

To be, and to find oneself being, known and described – rationally (or so it can be made to seem) and therefore definitively, more objectively (or so one is told) than one is capable of describing oneself and therefore irrefutably, resistlessly, and with an instantaneous finality that preempts and defeats any attempt on one's own part to intervene in the process by which one becomes an object of knowledge, and that renders one helpless to stave off the effects of a knowledge one has had no share in creating – that is an experience whose peculiar terror is hard to convey to those who have never suffered from the social liabilities that cause the rest of us to be continually and endlessly prey to it. (Halperin, 1995, p. 176)

It is not being suggested that by their nature all such encounters between analysts and patients were necessarily problematic, more that for the patient at least, to be constituted in relation to authoritative, essentially pathologising discourse has its dangers.

Psychoanalysis, as practice and theory, flourished in the United States and in Europe, and came to be hugely influential, alongside other 'psy' disciplines, in shaping modern conceptions of what it is to be human. The extension of 'psy' power relied on the production and circulation of expert knowledge of the human condition, and the practices of therapy facilitated such a process. 'Psy' formulations, often in the shape of case studies or descriptions of the process of therapy (as exemplified by Menninger's above), drew on suicide as an issue of concern, and the suicidal individual as a subject worthy of study. As the number of therapies specialising in the treatment of individual cases of psychopathology multiplied (Adlerian, Jungian, Kleinian, Winnicottian, Gestalt, Rogerian, etc.), the suicidal subject was taken up time and again as object of knowledge, and the truths produced and disseminated constituted suicide as an individual, pathological phenomenon, one that required expert 'psy' understanding and intervention, a relation of power-knowledge that was simultaneously productive and constraining – productive in terms of knowledge, but constraining in that increasingly suicide came to be read in terms of a compulsory ontology of pathology.

Challenging psychiatric dominance

As noted in the introduction to this chapter, 'psy' disciplines such as psychoanalysis offered more an extension of the possibilities of conceiving suicide in terms of individual pathology than a concerted challenge to the central doctrine produced and refined by psychiatry during the nineteenth century. Two ways of approaching the subject, however, can be discerned that did not seek to reduce suicide merely to a question of individual sickness or abnormality. Emile Durkheim's *Le suicide* (1897) heralded the beginnings of a sociology of suicide that looked to social, rather than individual, causes of such acts. Later, in the second half of the twentieth century, an anti-psychiatry movement arose that, while not specifically targeting suicide as an area of concern, did question some of the foundational ideas and utility of psychiatric practice. A central figure here was Thomas Szasz, and he addressed his concerns about psychiatric approaches to suicide in a series of articles (1971, 1986, and 1989) and in a book *Fatal Freedom* (1999). The arguments set out by both Durkheim and later sociologists, as well as Szasz, will be outlined, and the extent to which they could be said to have challenged psychiatric dominance in relation to suicide considered.

Sociological discourse on suicide

Any discussion of sociological approaches to suicide almost certainly needs to address Emile Durkheim's *Le suicide*. First published in 1897, it has exerted a considerable influence, both in terms of the study of suicide and with regard to the formation of sociology itself as a separate academic discipline. It is not the purpose of this section to offer an overview of sociological contributions to what has come to known as 'suicidology', or even to review in detail Durkheim's book, but rather to point to general areas where the primacy of psychiatric thought and practices in relation to suicide have been challenged. Durkheim's work here is illustrative (and was indeed formative) of a certain 'sociological' style of thought that stands in contrast to medical approaches to suicide, for he explicitly rejects the work of Esquirol and his followers in positing individual, pathological causes of suicide, and instead argues for the existence of a rather complex social aetiology for such acts.

As is well known, Durkheim suggested there were four basic suicide 'types': egotistic, anomic, fatalistic and altruistic (although fatalistic suicide is not much discussed). These classifications were said by Durkheim to emerge from analysis of the causes of suicide – established by reference not to the theories of *aliénistes* such as Brierre de Boismont, or information contained in statistical reports (which he suggested reflected only the opinions of the officials who collated the figures), but rather by looking to different states of 'social environments', namely 'religious confessions, family, political society, occupational groups, etc.' (Durkheim, 1951, p. 151). Analysis of these would lead to the identification of 'suicidal currents' (p. 145) that could be said to account for the formation and variation in the social suicide rate. Once such causes could be established, Durkheim argued, different types could be identified – thus egotistic suicide was characterised as arising, in Durkheim's analysis, due to 'excessive individualism' in relation to social norms, altruistic suicide to 'insufficient individuation' (p. 217), and anomic suicide to insufficient social regulation of an individual's 'passions' and behaviour (p. 258).

In order to substantiate his arguments for the primacy of a social aetiology of suicide, Durkheim first attempts to despatch with the theories of those, beginning with Esquirol, who had posited 'extra-social' factors such as 'psychopathic states' as causative of suicide. Addressing directly the belief that suicide arises only as a consequence of insanity, Durkheim argues that such a position can be defended in two different ways: 'Suicide itself is either called a disease in itself, *sui generis*, a special form of insanity; or it is regarded, not as a distinct species, but simply as an event involved in one or several varieties of insanity, and not to be found in sane persons' (p. 58). Durkheim deals with the first by asserting that such a view depends on providing evidence of there being a specific *suicidal monomania*, and then by arguing that monomania itself does not exist, and 'if then there are no monomanias, there cannot be a suicidal monomania and, consequently, suicide is not a distinct form of insanity' (p. 62). The second, that suicide occurs only in a state of insanity, is erroneous, Durkheim argues, because there are 'suicides, and numerous ones at that, not connected with insanity' (p. 67), and further, since 'no psychopathic state bears a regular and indisputable relation to suicide' (p. 81), it was thus necessary to look to other factors, namely those social currents that acted on the suicide rate: '[w]e have in fact shown that for each social group there is a specific tendency to suicide explained neither by the organic-psychic constitution of individuals nor the nature of the physical environment. Consequently, by elimination, it must necessarily depend upon social causes and be itself a collective phenomenon' (p. 145).

As Mike Gane (2005) notes, 'once the debate began on Durkheim's study it has never ceased' (p. 226). Numerous studies have sought to test the thesis put forward in *Le suicide* (two recent examples being Baller and Richardson, 2002 and Stockard and O'Brien, 2002), without ever arriving at a definitive conclusion as to the correctness or otherwise of Durkheim's arguments, perhaps due as much as anything to the difficulty in isolating or specifying the variables he studied. Although *Le suicide* could be said to have successfully launched a whole programme of research, it was less successful in repudiating the claims of the alienists and psychiatrists as to the contribution of individual pathology to the aetiology of suicide. For although Durkheim argued that suicide could not be considered a form of psychopathology in itself, this was a position that was no longer seriously defended by the time *Le suicide* appeared. Similarly, to argue for the non-existence of suicidal monomania was, by 1897, to construct something akin to a straw man to attack. Durkheim's repudiation of the thesis that suicide occurs secondarily to different forms of insanity equally carried little weight; that some suicides could not be considered insane was a point already conceded by psychiatrists, who were happy to assert that although some were not mad, the overwhelming majority of suicides were. Finally, the lack of a 'regular and indisputable' association between a singular 'psychopathic state' and such acts could also be safely ignored, for the arguments of the psychiatrists did not depend on such a relation – many states could be implicated (melancholic, manic or delusional for instance), and thus Durkheim's assertion of the absence of one state in the causation of suicide was hardly injurious to their position.

Sociology has continued to look to identify social factors that could explain rates of suicide, without ever seriously challenging the dominance of psychiatric practice in relation to suicide and the management of the suicidal. One of the problems faced by social approaches to the prevention of suicide is identifying points of intervention. Whereas psychiatry has the individual body as a focus for preventative measures, and confinement and restraint possess an obvious rationale, sociology has had to work with a much more diffuse and complex set of variables – 'suicidogenic currents' in Durkheim's vocabulary – without a similarly clear justification for intervention. Durkheim considered religion, the family, political life and education as possible means to restrain those destructive currents present in society, but rejected them all as ineffective. It was the work environment, Durkheim argued, organised as a moral 'space' that could act to prevent suicide. Yet here, perhaps, another of the difficulties in establishing social solutions in relation to suicide is highlighted – for, in contrast to individual approaches, the universality of the target for intervention is harder to claim. Psychiatry can declare the psychopathology of suicide unchanging, but sociology must admit that social life is subject to a degree of change that means that its targets are rarely stationary. The moral organisation of 'occupational groups' as a means to prevent suicide, as advocated by Durkheim, would seem to possess little currency today. Developing a coherent and plausible rationale for social interventions that could rival those of 'individual' medicine represents a challenge to sociology, and in its absence psychiatry has continued to dominate practices of suicide prevention.

Thomas Szasz on suicide

Thomas Szasz, a long-time critic of coercive psychiatric practices, has written on matters relating to suicide for over three decades. In 1971 he argued that the suicidal 'patient' was not ill:

he has no demonstrable bodily disorder (or if he does, it does not 'cause' his suicide); he does not assume the sick role: he does not seek medical help. In short, the physician uses the rhetoric of illness and treatment to justify his forcible intervention in the life of a fellow human being – often in the face of explicit opposition from his so-called 'patient'. (Szasz, 1971, p. 10)

For Szasz, suicide prevention practices are problematic when any form of coercion is involved – such measures are an attack on individual freedom, for each person has a right to choose to die at the time and in the manner they wish. 'For a long time,' Szasz (1999) writes, 'suicide was the concern of the Church and the priest. Now it is the business of the State and the doctor. Eventually we will make it our own choice, regardless of what the Bible or the Constitution or Medicine supposedly tells us' (p. xii). This is the nub of Szasz's argument; individual autonomy is paramount, and attempts to limit our freedoms need to be resisted in order to safeguard our rights and liberty. Neither medicine, neither the Church nor the state should be given the authority to intervene to prevent a person's voluntary death – be it from suicide or by refusal of life-saving or life-prolonging treatment (the discontinuation of haemodialysis is Szasz's (1999) example).

Szasz's book on suicide, *Fatal Freedom* (1999), is polemical and uncompromising in its sustained attack on the legitimacy of medicine to act coercively to limit individual choice in relation to death. Szasz also addresses medicine's role in 'voluntary' euthanasia ('death as treatment') as well as in 'involuntary' cases ('killing as treatment'). Psychiatry, in particular, as elsewhere in Szasz's work (e.g. 1974), is singled out for particular criticism for its coercive practices. For while Szasz has little difficulty with treatment so long as it is freely consented to by the patient, any intervention that compromises the free choice of the individual is positioned as illegitimate.

Few, however, have taken up Szasz's ideas. Reviews of his work tend to be critical, or else he is ignored within psychiatric circles. His views on suicide, however, came to prominence more recently when Szasz, who has continued to practice as a psychiatrist, was sued in 1994 over his handling of a patient under his care who killed himself. The story is related in Kay Redfield Jamison's *Night Falls Fast*:

The legal complaint filed against Szasz charged that he instructed and advised his patient to stop taking lithium in June 1990 ... The complaint further charged that Szasz had failed to render 'psychiatric medical care and treatment in conformity with the customary and accepted sound standards of medical care,' 'failed to properly diagnose and treat manic depression,' and 'failed to provide proper therapy to treat manic depression,' and 'failed to keep adequate and proper medical records'. Although Szasz's attorney maintained that the patient had stopped taking lithium of his own accord and Szasz himself did not concede he had committed malpractice, the court ruled that the widow was to receive $650,000 in settlement. Szasz, despite his distaste for the psychiatric establishment, was a member of the American Psychiatric Association, and it was the organization's malpractice insurance carrier that ended up paying the settlement. (Jamison, 1999, pp. 254–5).

The story illustrates the degree to which the truths of suicide – as an act of individual pathology that necessitates confinement and restraint – are underwritten in law.

Sociological approaches to the study of suicide represent something of a challenge from 'outside', but have for the most part lacked sufficient discursive currency to unsettle the accepted truths of the causes of suicide formulated in terms of individual pathology. Durkheim's reliance on official statistics has been subjected to some criticism, most notably by Jack Douglas (1967) and J. Maxwell Atkinson (1978), but sociology has continued to seek correlations between rates of suicide and certain social factors such as marital or economic status, religious affiliation, levels of employment, etc. (see Taylor, 1988, for a review of post-Durkheimian sociological approaches to the study of suicide). Such research has been drawn upon in formulating suicide prevention strategies at international and national levels, but Durkheim's attempt to establish a discipline that could rival or overturn the dominance of psychiatry, theoretically and practically in relation to suicide, has not been successful.

Similarly, Thomas Szasz's attempts to force psychiatry to confront its history of coercive practices with regard to the treatment of the suicidal have met with little success. Szasz essentially takes an ethical and political position with regard to self-accomplished death, which for him always is an act of freedom and the right of each individual regardless of circumstance. Placed in relation to the medical and scientific truths of psychiatry such a stance lacks purchase. Szasz cannot prove that mental illnesses are not real diseases, nor that suicide is always the voluntary act of a responsible and autonomous agent. Psychiatry can almost always find traces of psychopathology in the lives of those who go on to kill themselves (see discussion below on the psychological autopsy study of Robins *et al.* 1959/1996), but critics such as Szasz are unable to demonstrate their absence. Szasz can attempt to provoke a political/ethical debate on psychiatric practices with regard to suicide, but if the other 'side' ignore him (as has generally been the case) there is little he can do to force change. Legally, medically and scientifically his position is relatively weak, and politically the threat of 'danger' in relation to mental illness often carries more weight than calls for greater freedom. Szasz predicts that one day 'death control' will be understood as a personal decision in the same way as birth control now is, but for the present the realisation of such a hope would seem to be quite some way off. Understood as a criticism from 'within', Szasz's polemics have had as little influence as those sociological ones from 'without'.

Reasserting psychiatric dominance

In this section the processes by which suicide came to be associated with modern definitions of mental illness are reviewed. In the second half of the twentieth century psychoanalytic approaches to suicide gradually began to wane in influence in the UK and in the United States (albeit less markedly so), and the subject increasingly came once again to be read as primarily a medical/biological issue. As psychiatry began to formulate a standardised nosology (the first edition of the American Psychiatric Association's *Diagnostic and Statistical Manual of Mental Disorders* (DSM) was published in 1952) it became possible to categorise suicides according to agreed-upon psychiatric diagnoses. One approach that sought to classify suicides retrospectively according to psychiatric categories became known as the 'psychological autopsy'. Eli Robins and colleagues' 1959 study of 134 people who killed themselves in St Louis is reviewed, as this continues to be read as an important piece of research in that it was the first to establish a correlation between categories of mental illness and suicide (see Jamison, 1999, p. 31 and below). Analysis of the St Louis study can illustrate the ways in which the truth of the link between psychopathology and self-accomplished deaths could come to be formed through psychological autopsy, and how such an approach to the study of deaths by suicide could act to strengthen psychiatric power through the production of knowledge that confirmed the 'almost ubiquitous presence' (p. 31) of psychopathology in a sample of community suicides, thereby demonstrating the necessity (in order to save lives) of extending psychiatric practices beyond the confines of the asylums and hospital wards and into the community. The effects of the productive power-knowledge configuration centring on psychiatric investigations into deaths by suicide are addressed.

Demarcating the normal and pathological in relation to suicide: psychological autopsy, St Louis, 1959 and 1981

As noted earlier, psychological autopsy studies are most often drawn upon when claiming a link between mental illness and suicide. One of the studies cited in support of this claim was conducted by Eli Robins and colleagues in St Louis in 1956–7, and published in 1959 in the *American Journal of Public Health* as 'Some clinical considerations in the prevention of suicide based on a study of 134 successful suicides'. Robins, a psychiatrist at the Washington University School of Medicine, together with his team interviewed surviving family, friends, colleagues and acquaintances of the deceased. A full-length book, *The Final Months: A Study of the Lives of 134 Persons who Committed Suicide* (1981), was later published, detailing the background to the original study, the methodology employed, and case vignettes of each of the 134 people included in the study.

The stated aim of the original survey of consecutive suicides was to 'reach the most accurate possible psychiatric classification of the sample' (Robins, 1981, p. xiii). To this end a number of research questions were formulated, the first two give a good indication of the direction the research took:

- What proportion of persons who commit suicide are clinically ill prior to death?
- What is the nature and frequency of the illnesses from which these people suffer? (p. 3).

Robins's book details the ways in which the interviews were structured to answer the research questions:

In order to determine the presence or absence of a psychiatric disease in each of the subjects and to diagnose the disease as accurately as possible, the interviewers' questionnaire was designed to lead the interviewees through a step-by-step description of the subject's last months. Questions concerning general behavior followed the questions about onset and duration; these in turn were followed by further questions with emphasis on more specific symptomatic behavior. The last were grouped in order to elicit information about specific symptoms considered to be commonly associated with various psychiatric illnesses. (Robins, 1981, pp. 17–18)

Interviewees were asked to provide information about the 'duration and onset' of the deceased illnesses, of their 'symptomatic behavior', and of 'specific symptoms ... associated with various psychiatric illnesses'. In the context of such a priori assumptions of pathology embedded within the interview structure, the findings of high rates of mental illness were perhaps not surprising. Much of the information provided by the interviewees came to be interpreted as evidence of pathology in the sample – in his book Robins provides a list of the 100 most frequent 'symptoms occurring in suicide subjects' (p. 19), and here the range of behaviours, gestures, attitudes and events that came to be read as evidence of illness is set out. Symptoms included:

- weight loss;
- fatigue;
- less talkative;
- family objection to subject's drinking;

- drifting from job to job ten years prior to suicide;
- dizzy spells;
- indecisiveness;
- back pain;
- complete silence at times;
- without work for periods of more than six months;
- not as clean as usual;
- change in ordinary lifestyle;
- trouble with police;
- being fired from at least one job;
- more thought than usual about religion;
- arrests for traffic violation;
- 'strange' behaviour;
- thoughts out of the ordinary;
- wearing dirty clothes;
- loudness, noisiness;
- worry about being 'poverty stricken';
- loss of voice;
- difficulty with simple arithmetic;
- a lot of talk about sex;
- change in way of dressing.

A wide range of disparate behaviours and events could be affirmed as symptomatic of underlying pathology by their placing into discrete illness categories – 'affective disorder, alcoholism, antisocial personality, anxiety neurosis, drug-dependence, homosexuality, hysteria, mental retardation, obsessive-compulsive neurosis, organic brain syndrome, phobic neurosis, and schizophrenia' (Robins, 1981, p. 4). Interestingly, the authors of the original paper were concurrently involved in the creation of standardised psychiatric diagnostic criteria – as with alienism in the early nineteenth century, the redescription of suicide in terms of mental illness proceeded hand in hand with the reformulation of what it was to be mentally ill. The reported behaviours of the subjects in the St Louis study were constituted within a field of pathology that was in the process of being redrawn and redefined. This was acknowledged in the 1981 book:

Systematic description of psychiatric disease had been an ongoing interest in my group at Washington University who undertook the study of suicide. The diagnostic criteria finally drawn up for use in the study were in part based on DSM-1, but in larger part were based on our own clinical experience with psychiatric patients manifesting a wide range of symptoms of psychiatric diseases. Careful descriptions of the various courses of these diseases played a major role in our diagnoses and this aspect was emphasized in devising the criteria. (Robins, 1981, p. 11)

The introductory comments to a reprint of the original 1959 paper (Robins *et al.*, 1959/1996) also documents how Robins and his colleagues at Washington University were engaged in the creation of diagnostic criteria for psychiatric illnesses concurrently with their investigations into the prevalence of these illnesses in cases of suicide: 'much of the impetus for the contemporary revision of the American psychiatric nomenclature came from the Department of Psychiatry at the Washington University School of Medicine in St Louis, of which Robins was the chairman'. That Robins and his co-researchers, in investigating the suicides in their study, discovered 'something remarkable – that 98 per cent of them were clinically ill, and that 94 per cent had a *major* psychiatric illness' (p. 143) reflects perhaps the broad boundaries of their definition of illness.

Through the practice of conducting psychological autopsy studies, questions as to what constituted mental illness were again answered in part by reference to suicide, and suicide once more came to be redescribed in terms of changing definitions of psychopathology. The oscillation between constituting suicide by reference to pathology, and pathology by reference to suicide once more proved to be productive. New knowledge could be produced through psychological autopsy studies that in turn cast light on the nature of mental illness, and research into mental illness could be utilised to analyse and understand acts of suicide. Robins concluded his 1981 book with an epilogue that suggested that the 'broader our knowledge of suicide, in terms of numbers, the less likely we are to overlook clues to a biological cause', but equally, '[w]e must be prepared to use the accumulated clinical knowledge in an effort to uncover the biological nature of those psychiatric illnesses most commonly associated with suicide' (p. 431).

The circular relationship between the production of knowledge and the constitution of psychopathology and suicide (as exemplified by the work of Robins *et al.* at the Washington University School of Medicine in the 1950s) could also be said to contain a strategic logic, for psychiatric practices could be justified by the truths uncovered by such means, and with regard to suicide the necessity of psychiatric approaches reinforced. By such means, suicide was again deployed to strengthen psychiatric power, this time outside the asylum and hospital psychiatric wards. The discovery of pathology in almost all suicides outside psychiatric care could justify the calls for more psychiatric staff across a wider range of sites, as well as the need for more research. Numerous psychological autopsy studies have since been undertaken and published ('in excess of 150' according to Cavanagh *et al.* (2003, p. 396)) with each in agreement that in virtually all suicides the presence of severe mental illness could be identified. Similarly, the expansion of psychiatric diagnostic categories has increased apace (Gergen, 1994, p. 148), for the application of broader criteria for constituting categories of mental illness did not stop with the first edition of the *Diagnostic and Statistical Manual* of the American Psychiatric Association. With every new edition (the most recent is DSM-IV-TR) new ways of being classified as mentally ill are added, and with such an increase the possibilities for retrospectively uncovering evidence of symptoms of psychopathology by means of psychological autopsy increase. The 'regime of truth' in relation to suicide, formed around a compulsory ontology of pathology, has a history, one formed through circular and productive relations of power-knowledge.

Conclusions

In the study by Robins *et al.* (1959/1996), suicide is constructed by reference to mental illness, and concurrently, notions of what constitutes mental illness are formed in relation to suicide. Through such means a wide range of gestures, behaviours and attitudes could come to be redescribed as symptomatic of individual illness, their pathology confirmed (retrospectively in the case of psychological autopsy studies) by the act of suicide. Similarly, in the case of the psychoanalytic formulation of a self-destructive act presented here, various behaviours and speech acts of the patient are constituted as pathological in line with the analytic theory expounded, and are taken to confirm the truths of such a theory. Whereas the study by Robins *et al.* enabled a certain 'broadening' of notions as to what constitutes mental pathology, the psychoanalytic formulations exemplified by Menninger's case study allowed suicide to be conceptualised according to metaphors of depth, with pathology and abnormalities read as residing within the 'deep' interiority of the individual suicidal subject – an interiority constituted by reference to innate (sexual or destructive) impulses and drives, taken to be shaped by early childhood experiences. Such formations of suicide and the suicidal subject have been analysed here in order to illustrate the ways in which almost all self-accomplished deaths came to be constituted as pathological by means of a broadening of the number of individual attributes, behaviours, gestures, beliefs, etc. taken to be indicative of mental illness through the practice of conducting and publishing psychological autopsy studies. Analysis also focused on how acts of suicide could come to be individualised and pathologised through the formulation of theories of inherent destructive impulses and unconscious desires located within the 'psyche' of the subject of psychoanalytic practices. The formation and circulation of truths of suicide also acted to produce power-effects. Relations of power produced knowledge which in turn extended and strengthened power. The effectiveness of these circular relations of power-to-knowledge and knowledge-to-power acted to restrict and contain challenges from both outside and within psychiatry that arose in the form of non-medical 'talking cures', from research into the social causes of suicide, and from individual critics such as Thomas Szasz.

The effects of the reproduction of psychiatric truths and the consolidation of psychiatric power with regard to suicide throughout the twentieth century can be mapped. Clinicians remained responsible and accountable in relation to the actions of their suicidal patients, and potentially culpable in the event of their deaths. The truth of suicide continued to be sought primarily in relation to the individual patient. The introduction of more 'pastoral' techniques and strategies of power supplemented the disciplinary measures introduced in the previous century, which remained quietly accepted as necessary in the face of the threat of suicide, with few dissenting voices raised against their continuation.

11 The discursive formation of the suicidal subject: Sarah Kane and *4.48 Psychosis*, 2000

Introduction

Foucault, in his much discussed essay 'What is Enlightenment?', writes of how a historical ontology of ourselves would need to address a series of questions, namely: 'How are we constituted as subjects of our own knowledge? How are we constituted as subjects who exercise or submit to power relations? How are we constituted as moral subjects of our own actions?' (2000a, p. 318). The emphasis until now in this book has for the most part been on those modes of subjection whereby individuals are constituted as subjects in relation to the truths of suicide espoused within psychiatric and other 'psy' discourses, and the relationship between the production and dissemination of authoritative knowledge and relations of power. The economies and forms of power identified – the emergence of a bio-political rationality, and the implementation of disciplinary and pastoral techniques – have been taken as largely productive in their effects, creating knowledge and forming subjects in relation to such knowledge; the 'responsible and accountable clinician', as well the 'suicidal patient'. What has been less developed is the notion of individuals acting in opposition to such modes of subjection. The ways by which acts of suicide can be read as resistance to psychiatric power need also to be addressed.

The different ways in which the subject can be constituted, as discussed above, do not necessarily exist separately. Processes of subjection and subjectivation (the term sometimes employed to denote the ways in which an individual comes to act on itself as a reflexive being) can co-exist, it is argued – the subject may at one and the same time be constituted within a certain 'regime of truth', yet also act to subvert or resist such a regime. In relation to the suicidal subject this can mean an act of suicide could be read as both a consequence of certain modes of subjection (the formation of a pathological or suicidal identity) and resistance to being so subjected. Such a reading is possible of Sarah Kane's play *4.48 Psychosis*, which deals with a death by suicide. The play will be discussed in more detail below but before then the question of first-person accounts of suicidal states will be addressed.

Suicidal subjectivities and first-person accounts

It was argued in chapters 3 and 4 that suicide has come to be read as the tragic act of a 'mentally unwell' individual. As Hill (2004) notes, suicide 'is understood primarily as an act arising out of intense, morbid, and pathological states of mind, representative of the furthest extreme of human misery' (p. 1). Those disciplines that concern themselves with these pathological interior states, principally psychiatry and psychology, would contend that the rigorous application of scientific methods has rendered such states knowable. The argument tends to run that these pathological states of mind have always existed, but were misrepresented or misinterpreted by earlier cultures. From such a perspective it is possible to say that a 4,000-year-old Egyptian poem reveals that the author was a 'severely psychotically depressed man with feelings of persecution and self-deprecation who also undoubtedly shows strong suicidal tendencies' (Thomas, 1980, p. 285), and that '[t]he seven sheets of the papyrus ... describe an interior landscape not unlike that of almost any lonely, despairing person considering suicide today' (Colt, 2006, p. 205). Similarly, it is possible to write that the author of another Egyptian poem from roughly the same period 'gives a detailed description of negative thoughts, hopelessness and helplessness, which are characteristic of the state of mind of a person contemplating suicide', that the 'poem presents an accurate picture of depressive mood, and the negative thought pattern that accompanies it', and to conclude that 'the Ancient Egyptians appear to have had a significant grasp of the psychopathology of suicide' (Royal College of Psychiatrists, 2006. See also, Pahor, 2006). Similar pathological states of mind are thus taken as having existed in all cultures across all time periods. This book, however, has argued against understanding these illnesses or diseases of the mind as universal phenomena, interpreting them instead as variable cultural and historical constructions. So psychiatry and psychology, rather than first discovering then accurately portraying these states, as is often claimed, have instead played a significant role in the creation of these truths of 'mental life'. As medical and scientific artefacts, the representations of mental life formed by psychiatric and psychological discourses possess a certain degree of authority and truth value, and as a consequence, can affect how people view themselves and how they behave. As outlined earlier, Ian Hacking (e.g. 1986, 1999) talks of a 'looping effect', whereby people come, albeit imperfectly, to resemble descriptions of themselves and their categorisation. Hacking suggests that a form of dialogue is set in motion – a process of co-construction whereby psychiatry and psychology observe changes in beliefs and behaviour, and over time descriptions and categories are altered to account for these, with old elements modified and new ones added. Consequently, people can come to resemble expert descriptions of 'suicidal patients', understanding themselves, for instance, as possessing a 'propensity' or 'impulse' to suicide. One way this process can be examined is through analysis of first-person accounts of suicidal states. These, it is argued, can offer insights into the ways in which psychiatric and psychological constructs can come, in part, to form suicidal subjectivities.

As was noted in chapter 3, however, such accounts are few and far between. A few do exist, and these tend to reproduce (as would be expected) expert formulations. Given the difficulties involved in speaking of suicide in any way other than by the reproduction of authoritative, expert discourse, Sarah Kane's *4.48 Psychosis* (2000) is remarkable. It is a deeply affecting piece of theatre, a rich, multi-layered text, poetic and strident, and quite unforgettable either seen or read. However, the analysis here focuses less on any consideration of the artistic merits of the play, and more on what it could be said to reveal in terms of how contemporary suicide and suicidal subjectivities can be formed, and the relations of power at work between those charged with preventing suicide and those with a desire to die.

Sarah Kane, suicide and *4.48 Psychosis*

Sarah Kane was a British playwright who gained a certain degree of notoriety during her lifetime for the violence, 'depravity' (Jack Tinker (1995) of the *Daily Mail* described her first play, *Blasted*, as '[t]his disgusting feast of filth') and the challenging and disturbing themes she sought to portray on stage. Kane completed five plays in her lifetime; the last, *4.48 Psychosis*, was produced posthumously the year after her death by suicide in 1999.

Suicide was a recurring theme in Sarah Kane's work. In each of her plays a character attempts, with or without success, to commit suicide. In her own life, Kane was hospitalised following an overdose of antidepressants and tranquilisers shortly after completing *4.48 Psychosis*, and while in King's College Hospital, south-east London, she hanged herself.

In the words of her brother, Simon Kane, *4.48 Psychosis* concerns 'suicidal despair' (quoted in Sierz, 2000). Sarah Kane herself wrote of the play being 'about a psychotic breakdown and what happens to a person's mind when the barriers which distinguish between reality and different forms of imagination completely disappear, so that you no longer know the difference between your waking life and your dream life. And also you no longer know where you stop, and the world starts' (Kane in Saunders, 2002, pp. 111–12).

The play itself is hard to summarise – there are no named characters and time is not represented in an obviously linear way. One reading of *4.48 Psychosis* is that it seeks to represent in language an 'inner landscape', one full of despair and suicidal impulses. David Greig, in the introduction to Kane's collected plays, emphasises this interiority in her work: 'Kane mapped the darkest and most unforgiving internal landscapes: landscapes of violation, of loneliness, of power, of mental collapse and, most consistently, of love' (Greig, 2001, p. ix), and he writes of *4.48 Psychosis* as describing 'the internal landscape of a suicidal psychosis' (p. xvi). He continues:

4.48 Psychosis is a report from a region of the mind that most of us hope never to visit but from which many people cannot escape. Those trapped there are normally rendered voiceless by their condition. That the play was written whilst suffering from depression, which is a destructive rather than a creative condition, was an act of generosity by the author. (Greig, 2001, p. xvii)

Others have read the play in the same light. A review in the *Daily Telegraph* talked of 'Sarah Kane's astonishing *4.48 Psychosis*' that 'shows us what suicidal depression feels like from the inside' (*Daily Telegraph*, 14 May 2001). The reviewer continued: '[w]hen *4.48 Psychosis* was first performed at the Royal Court last year, Kane's family were anxious that it should not be seen as a suicide note. Yet it is impossible not to view it as a deeply personal howl of pain, a work ripped not just from its author's churning brain, but from the core of her being'. The quote suggests that Sarah Kane looked inside herself and drew out the truth of her inner being – that the work (and her pain) emerge from a source deep within. Such a stance can act to separate in our understanding the experiences of individuals from the cultural and historical milieu out of which they are formed. An alternative position is to reject the notion that suffering and its expression arise solely from 'inside' an isolated self, and instead take *4.48 Psychosis* to be a historically situated cultural product, constructed, in large part, from psychological and psychiatric discourse. From this perspective, the play can be interpreted as exemplary of contemporary representations of suicide – individual, private and pathological in nature. An analysis of the text will attempt to draw out these aspects, and an argument is put forward that *4.48 Psychosis* illustrates the process whereby individuals can come, albeit imperfectly, to resemble descriptions of pathological identities produced in relation to 'psy' truths and practices. In addition, the play can also be read as critique and subversion of dominant formulations of the self and suicide; critique by means of its representation of the cold comfort sometimes offered by psychiatry, in terms of how those in distress are constituted by psychiatric discourse (the main character explicitly rejects the notion that his/her experiences can be explained solely by reference to 'illness'), and how, more practically, in terms of the effects of certain practices of psychiatric institutions. The text can also be read as subverting discursive formations of the self found within governing psychiatric and psychological discourses as singular, transparent and autonomous, by portraying instead the self as fragmented, contingent, even illusory, and subversive also in the way that suicide becomes, through the play, a public rather than a private act to which we, as reader or audience, are asked to bear witness.

4.48 Psychosis as constituted by 'pathological' discourses on suicide

The play is constituted in part from 'psy' discourse. In places specific 'mental health' texts are quoted, but also reformulated. An example of this is the appropriation of the Beck Depression Inventory (BDI). This, an assessment tool used by mental health practitioners to measure the severity of depression, is a twenty-one-item self-administered question-naire that asks the respondent to 'choose one statement from among the group of four statements in each question that best describes how you have been feeling during the past few days' (Beck *et al.*, 1961). Kane initially quotes almost verbatim from the available answers in the inventory:

I am a complete failure as a person
I am guilty, I am being punished
I would like to kill myself (Kane, 2000, p. 4)

The BDI is usually understood to be a measure of a pre-existing illness or condition (see Beck *et al.*, 1988), but an alternative reading is to see it as in some way performative, in that it acts, at least in part, to produce (and reproduce) what it purports only to name. Thus, it could be said that a certain view of the person, the world, and what it is to suffer and to be mentally ill is formed in relation to the measure.

The BDI assumes the following:

- the existence of a discrete condition, 'depression';
- that this depression consists of two components, 'psychological' and 'somatic';
- that the psychological elements of depression are 'pessimism', 'past failures', 'guilty feelings', 'punishment feelings', 'self-dislike', 'self-criticalness', and 'worthlessness';
- and that the somatic elements consist of 'sadness', 'loss of pleasure', 'crying', 'agitation', 'loss of interest', 'indecisiveness', 'loss of energy', 'change in sleep patterns', 'irritability', 'change in appetite', 'concentration difficulties', 'tiredness and/or fatigue', and 'loss of interest in sex'.

As a self-report questionnaire the BDI asks that a person 'look inside' themselves and report on the degree of worthlessness, pessimism, self-dislike and criticalness found within, as if these were transparent, acultural, and uncontested notions, analogous to the symptoms of a physical disease or illness. However, if we take seriously the critique of the Enlightenment ideal of the 'unified, coherent, and independent' self (Martin and Barresi, 2006, p. 268), which can be observed and accurately described, then the assumptions embedded in the BDI become problematic – for if a sense of self is discursively formed not merely found, then such descriptions of a pathological interiority acts to create as much as represent such 'states'. This is not to propose that the BDI causes depression, but rather that what is suggested is a more subtle, long-term, cultural formation of 'reality' – of certain ways of understanding and experiencing the world. For people presenting with depression, distress obviously pre-exists exposure to the BDI, but the BDI, and similar tools, also discursively reconstitute a certain view of 'internal pathology' that can be hard to resist. In Kane's play the character personalises the generalities found in the original test, and is thus constituted in part by notions of self-hatred, pessimism and failure.

The 'patient' character does not merely reproduce the phrasing of the BDI, however, but paraphrases and plays with it as the list is expanded upon:

I cannot make love
I cannot fuck
I cannot be alone
I cannot be with others
My hips are too big
I dislike my genitals (Kane, 2000, p. 5)

Almost every statement, as with the BDI itself, begins with a personal pronoun, and each negative aspect is taken to be part of the self – a self thus constituted as deficient and pathological. Other examples from the text illustrate the ways in which experiences of the self can come to be formed, and identity in part constituted, in relation to expert discourse. Here, Kane draws on elements from American suicidologist Edwin Shneidman's *The Suicidal Mind* (1996). Shneidman, much influenced by Henry A. Murray's formulation of 'psychological needs' found in his *Explorations in Personality* (1938), theorised that when these needs were frustrated psychological pain would arise, 'which in turn drives suicidal thought' (Shneidman, 1996, p. 21). Shneidman condenses Murray's ideas to some twenty needs (e.g. abasement, achievement, affiliation, aggression, etc.). Each need is accompanied by a brief prose descriptor (e.g. 'INVIOLACY To protect the self and one's psychological space', p. 21). These, as well as the BDI, are played with in *4.48 Psychosis*:

to achieve goals and ambitions
to overcome obstacles and attain a high standard
to increase self-regard by the successful exercise of talent
...
to win affection of desired Other
to adhere and remain loyal to Other
to enjoy sensuous experiences with cathected Other
to feed, help, protect, comfort, console, support,
    nurse or heal
to be fed, helped, protected, comforted, consoled,
    supported, nursed or healed
to form mutually enjoyable, enduring, cooperating and
    reciprocating relationship with Other, with an equal
to be forgiven
to be loved
to be free. (Kane, 2000 pp. 31–3)

Works such as Shneidman's (1996), as expert readings of the truth of our being, possess authority in defining what it is to be a person – subjects are constituted in relation to these expositions of the truths of our nature. Such texts can act as resources that enable individuals to manage the difficulties of life (through providing a vocabulary that allows people to make sense of the world and experiences, by positioning individuals as subject to 'known' psychological or psychiatric phenomena that offer the possibility of diagnosis, treatment and cure). But they can also be problematic. Such ways of presenting human nature – as driven by needs – can form subjects who experience themselves as in some way deficient in the meeting of these needs. In the play, for instance, a need for love is placed alongside references to an absent 'Other', a lover seemingly irremediably lost:

Sometimes I turn around and catch the smell of you and I cannot go on I cannot fucking go on without expressing this terrible so fucking awful physical aching fucking longing I have for you. And I cannot believe that I can feel this for you and you feel nothing. Do you feel nothing?
(*Silence.*)
Do you feel nothing?
(*Silence.*) (Kane, 2000, p. 12).

The absence of the 'Other' (and the associated 'unmet need') seem to heighten the pain experienced by the suicidal character in the text, who, just prior to the play's conclusion, talks of:

this vital need for which I would die
to be loved
(pp. 40–1)

From a different perspective these needs can be understood less as demanding internal 'pulls' inherent to our nature, requirements that must somehow be appeased or fulfilled, and instead are taken to be cultural products or creations that can come to be 'doubled' or 'interiorised' – that is, an 'outside' force forms an 'inside' that in turn can act on the body or the world (to make use of Gille Deleuze's (1999) formulation of Foucault's position). The belief that we are in possession of a nature that has requirements and needs that must be fulfilled (beyond the basics of food, air, shelter) is fairly pervasive, and can lead to feelings of deficiency and inadequacy, even a sense of desperation – for a thing that is 'needed' is presented as a necessity rather than as just a desirable possibility. The result is that we can come to be defined in relation to what we lack, our life's work dedicated to seeking that which eludes us but that we cannot stop searching for. Relations of power-to-knowledge and knowledge-to-power are also implicated here, for the constitution of deficient subjects reinforces the necessity for expertise, for the production and dissemination of knowledge through the development of research programmes, the delivery of conference papers and the writing and publication of journal articles, etc. The knowledge generated in turn provides a rationale for existing practices, and 'psy' power can be consolidated, strengthened and extended.

Another pervasive aspect of modernity is the requirement to find 'one's true self', 'to be true to oneself', or simply to 'be yourself' – the idea that one is engaged, and needs to be engaged, in the tasks of self-discovery and self-expression (Taylor, 1989). In Kane's play, as well as the search for an absent Other, there is a seeking for an 'essential self', one that is to be found by means of an 'inward' looking. In the play, the closest the central character appears to come to finding or experiencing such a 'real' self is the time when she is considered, by others, to be most out of touch with reality – that period in the early morning alluded to in the title:

– At 4.48
  when sanity visits
  for one hour and twelve minutes I am in my right mind.
  When it has passed I shall be gone again,
  a fragmented puppet, a grotesque fool. (Kane, 2000, p. 27).

An 'essential self' cannot then be found, and this inability to locate a 'real' self seems to lead in the play to a need to find validation in the eyes of another. As the play approaches its end – the apparent act of suicide – the character asks, or demands:

Validate me
Witness me
See me
Love me (Kane, 2000, p. 41)

There is a need to be seen and loved, even if it is in the moment of leaving:

watch me vanish
watch me

       vanish

watch me

watch me

     watch (Kane, 2000, p. 42)

But the validating, witnessing Other remains absent from the play, as does the self, the play's penultimate line being:

It is myself I have never met, whose face is pasted on the underside of my mind (Kane, 2000, p. 43)

The causes of suicide, and the 'suicidal subject', in Kane's play, are constituted for the most part from 'psy', mostly psychiatric, discourse. Suicide is understood to arise from unmet needs (a 'citational' act of borrowing from Shneidman (1996)) that are located within the person. The suicidal person is taken to be disturbed in some way, and a pathological identity, drawn in part from a widely used assessment tool (the BDI), is constructed. The suicide is also represented as disconnected from others and their own 'essential' self. Suicide is thus reconstituted in Kane's text as a pathological and individual act. But the play does not merely restate such commonplaces, for there can also be found within the text a critique of psychiatric discourse and practices with regard to the 'suicidal patient'.

4.48 Psychosis as a critique of, and resistance to, psychiatric discourse and practices

4.48 Psychosis can be read as critique, and as casting light on the cold comfort sometimes offered by psychiatry to those diagnosed as mentally ill and the suicidal. As Graham Saunders (2003) writes: 'for the most part [4.48 Psychosis] is an impassioned critique of the hospitalization and treatment of those with mental illness, in which the individual is questioned, diagnosed and treated with powerful combinations of antidepressants and anxiolytics as part of a process likened to being "fattened up, shored up, shoved out"'. Three passages in the play are here highlighted:

- the depiction of an experience of humiliation during a ward round or case review;
- interactions between a doctor and patient that cast light on imbalances in relations of power;
- an ironic redescription of case notes regarding medical treatment.

The ward round or case review

Near the beginning of the play, there is a description that reads as a recollection, from the patient's point of view, of a ward round or some form of multi-professional case review. It is clear from the beginning that it is not a happy memory:

It wasn't for long, I wasn't there long. But drinking bitter black coffee I catch that medicinal smell in a cloud of ancient tobacco and something touches me in that still sobbing place and a wound from two years ago opens like a cadaver and a long buried shame roars its foul decaying grief. (Kane, 2000, pp. 6–7)

The cause of that shame is revealed:

A room of expressionless faces staring blankly at my pain, so devoid of meaning there must be evil intent.

Dr This and Dr That and Dr Whatsit who's just passing and thought he'd pop in to take the piss as well. Burning in a hot tunnel of dismay, my humiliation complete as I shake without reason and stumble over words and have nothing to say about my 'illness' which anyway amounts only to knowing that there's no point in anything because I'm going to die. And so I am deadlocked by that smooth psychiatric voice of reason which tells me there is an objective reality in which my body and mind are one. But I am not here and never have been. Dr This writes it down and Dr That attempts a sympathetic murmur. Watching me, judging me, smelling the crippling failure oozing from my skin, my desperation clawing and all-consuming panic drenching me as I gape in horror at the world and wonder why everyone is smiling and looking at me with secret knowledge of my aching shame. (Kane, 2000, p. 7)

There is a tension, made explicit here, over the reading of the patient's 'condition'. Whilst the patient can find no words to describe or explain his/her experience of meaninglessness, from the patient's perspective the doctors claim expertise by virtue of their possession of 'reason'. They watch and judge, and are understood to have the ability to divine and describe an 'objective reality'. A picture is painted of unequal and ulti-mately unhelpful interactions between patient and professionals. Such difficulties are explored further in a series of psychiatrist–patient conver-sations where imbalances of power are apparent.

The doctor–patient relationship

Parts of the play can be read in terms of how imbalances in relations of power can be problematic. There is an exchange during which the patient discusses suicide plans which is illustrative:

– Have you made any plans?
– Take an overdose, slash my wrists then hang myself.
– All those things together?
– It couldn't possibly be misconstrued as a cry for help.
  (*Silence.*) (Kane, 2000, p. 8)

Initially, there is a degree of force or strength in the patient's 'suicidal' position in relation to that of the doctor, for the doctor presumably wishes to stop this from happening, and therefore for the patient's saying they are going to kill themselves is both a challenge to the doctor to try and stop them and a test of the doctor's ability to do so. In the humour as well, in dismissing the notion of his/her actions being read as a 'cry for help', the patient gently mocks a possible 'psychiatric' interpretation of the act.

Medicine reasserts some authority by claiming a greater knowledge:

– It wouldn't work.
– Of course it would.
– It wouldn't work. You'd start to feel sleepy from the overdose and wouldn't
  have the energy to cut your wrists.
  (*Silence.*)
– I'd be standing on a chair with a noose around my neck.
  (*Silence.*) (pp. 8–9)

Again a dark humour is at work in the resistance to the doctor's authority, but also a determination to have the last word in the conversation. Given the nature of the discussion, the 'last word' may be of particular importance in determining any future actions.

– If you were alone do you think you might harm yourself?
– I'm scared I might.
– Could that be protective?
– Yes. It's fear that keeps me away from the rail tracks. I just hope to God that death
  is the fucking end. I feel like I'm eighty years old. I'm tired of life and my mind
  wants to die. (Kane, 2000, p. 9)

The doctor looks for evidence of any ambiguity about the patient's plans for suicide – a sense that s/he might not act because of fear. The conversation and positions of relative power shift again, though. The doctor seeks to assert 'reality' (a key function of psychiatry, according to Foucault's (2006, p. 133) analysis of psychiatric power) in the face of a 'metaphor', and in turn the patient questions the doctor's linguistic understanding – a challenge to medical authority as sole bearer of truth in interactions with the patient:

– That's a metaphor, not reality.
– It's a simile.
– That's not reality.
– It's not a metaphor, it's a simile, but even if it were, the defining feature of a
  metaphor is that it's real.
  (*A long silence.*) (Kane, 2000, p. 9)

Who gets to define reality comes to be the site of confrontation between patient and doctor. Foucault (2006) argued that it was the acceptance of the reality of the doctor by the patient that was taken to be the primary task of the asylum doctor and the prerequisite for 'cure', rather than a revelation of the truth of the patient's madness. Reality was to be imposed upon the patient through the force of the doctor's will. It is possible to see a similar dynamic at work in Kane's play, where the necessity of the patient accepting the reality of the doctor is insisted upon:

– You are not eighty years old.
  (*Silence.*)
  Are you?
  (*A silence.*)
  Are you?
  (*A silence.*)
  Or are you?
  (*A long silence.*) (Kane, 2000, pp. 9–10)

The doctor repeatedly insists the patient confirms the 'untruthfulness' of the simile. The patient resists so doing, and withdraws, for now, from the conversation. After another long silence, another challenge arises from the patient:

– Do you despise all unhappy people or is it me
  specifically? (p. 10)

The point of attack shifts from the accurateness, or otherwise, of the patient's speech to the intentions and feelings of the doctor. The doctor, placed under suspicion, responds by reasserting medical authority, and simultaneously disempowers the patient, by pronouncing her/him to be ill. In so doing any discontent of the patient is denied legitimacy or further enquiry:

– I don't despise you. Its not your fault. You're ill.
– I don't think so.
– No?
– No. I'm depressed. Depression is anger. It's what you did, who was there and who you're blaming.
– And who are you blaming?
– Myself. (p. 10)

The doctor has shifted the conversation onto stronger ground – the medical designation of illness – and the patient's challenges culminate in an admission that it is self-directed anger and self-blame that constitute their depression. It is the individual patient who comes to be read as the location of problems.

Another doctor–patient conversation follows later in the play. It is not clear if the doctor is the same person, but the patient probably is (if we assume there is a 'central character' in the play). Though the conversation is ostensibly about an episode of self-harm, the shifts in power as it proceeds can also be noted.

– Oh dear, what's happened to your arm?
– I cut it.

– That's a very immature, attention seeking thing to do.
   Did it give you relief?
– No. (p. 14)

The doctor again gets to name the behaviour, but also has a theory (commonly held) that 'cutting' can act to relieve or release tension in a person. This is pursued despite the patient's repeated denial, and again serves as a demonstration of the doctor's assumed right to define what is real and true, and the relative powerlessness of the patient in resisting:

– I thought you might do this. Lots of people do. It relieves the tension.
– Have you ever done it?
– … (Kane, 2000, p. 15)

Another shift, as the patient insists on the doctor relocating from the professional to some, potentially shared, personal ground. But the doctor refuses the personal, as the patient had refused the professional. This leads to another challenge:

– No. Far too fucking sane and sensible. I don't know where you read that, but it
   does not relieve the tension.
   (*Silence.*)
   Why don't you ask me *why*?
   Why did I cut my arm?
– Would you like to tell me?
– Yes.
– Then tell me.
– **ASK.**
   ME.
   WHY.
   (*A long silence.*)
– Why did you cut your arm?
– Because it feels fucking great. Because it feels fucking
   amazing.
– Can I look?
– You can look. But don't touch. (Kane, 2000, p. 15)

For a moment there is a possibility of *rapprochement*, but it doesn't last:

– (*Looks*) And you don't think you're ill? (Kane, 2000, p. 15)

The doctor reasserts the primacy of the professional, and the patient again is reduced to monosyllabic denial:

– No.
– I do. It's not your fault. But you have to take responsibility for your own actions.
   Please don't do it again. (Kane, 2000, p. 16)

These are somewhat paradoxical assertions – of the absence of fault (and hence responsibility) due to illness, followed by a demand that the patient take responsibility for his/her actions, and then a plea not to do it again – which positions the patient less as an autonomous actor (and thus fully accountable and responsible for his/her actions), but rather as someone who must follow doctor's orders.

In another conversation the desirability, or otherwise, of taking medication to treat the illness is negotiated, and the discussion concerning responsibility and blame is taken up again:

– Please. Don't switch off my mind by attempting to straighten me out. Listen and understand, and when you feel contempt don't express it, at least not verbally, at least not to me.
(Silence.)
– I don't feel contempt.
– No?
– No. It's not your fault.
– It's not your fault, that's all I ever hear, it's not your fault, it's an illness, it's not your fault, I know it's not my fault. You've told me that so often I'm beginning to think it *is* my fault.
– It's *not* your fault.
– **I KNOW**.
– But you allow it.
(Silence.)
Don't you? (p. 18)

Here is another paradoxical assertion of the simultaneous absence and presence of responsibility and blame in mental illness. The patient is excused blame for the illness, but is also, at the same time, held responsible for 'allowing it'. The patient's refusal of medication is interpreted as allowing the illness. The patient agrees to take medication, but this temporary 'victory' for the doctor is subverted somewhat a little later in the play, when the 'effects' of the psychiatric treatments on the patient are described, in the form of a set of case notes.

An ironic redescription of case notes regarding medical treatment

Symptoms: Not eating, not sleeping, not speaking, no sex drive, in despair, wants to die.
Diagnosis: Pathological grief.

The side-effects of the various medications are documented:

Sertraline, 50 mg. Insomnia worsened, severe anxiety, anorexia (weight loss 17 kgs), increase in suicidal thoughts, plans and intention. Discontinued following hospitalization.

Zopiclone, 7.5 mg. Slept. Discontinued following rash. Patient attempted to leave hospital against medical advice. Restrained by three male nurses twice her size. Patient threatening and uncooperative. Paranoid thoughts – believes hospital staff are attempting to poison her. (Kane, 2000, pp. 21–22)

There is again a dark humour at work, highlighting the injustice of being labelled 'threatening and uncooperative' while being forcibly restrained against your will, and 'paranoid' for believing you are being poisoned when your prescribed medication has indeed caused an 'adverse reaction'. One final self–treatment, though, is attempted, and documented in the form of medical notes:

100 aspirin and one bottle of Bulgarian Cabernet Sauvignon, 1986. Patient woke in a pool of vomit and said 'Sleep with a dog and rise full of fleas.' Severe stomach pain. No other reaction. (Kane, 2000, p. 23)

The examination of the relationship between the patient and doctor continues. The different roles of each, and their inequality, from the patient's perspective, are set out:

I came to you hoping to be healed

You are my doctor, my saviour, my omnipotent judge, my Priest, my god, the surgeon of my soul.

And I am your proselyte to sanity. (Kane, p. 31)

The patient looks for salvation from the doctor as healer, judge, priest and god. For the doctor (as seen by the patient), 'converting' the patient to sanity (in Foucault's (2006) analysis the principal aim and technique of psychiatric power) is the primary requirement. The patient resists, verbally and later by means of suicide.

4.48 Psychosis is, then, both citational and critical of psychiatric truths and practices with regard to suicide and the suicidal. The critique consists of highlighting the 'adverse effects' of the physical treatments outlined in the 'case notes' section, but also concerns the means by which the patient's identity is formed as deficient and pathological in relation to the doctor's truths. The patient experiences his/her position as humiliating, and the doctor retreats behind a professional façade when confronted by the force of the patient's need for hope and salvation.

4.48 Psychosis as subverting foundational psychiatric assumptions of the self and suicide

As discussed above, it is possible to understand the main character (indeed all the characters) in the play as formed in relation to authoritative discourse and practices – a 'suicidal subject' in part constituted from 'psy' truths of suicide. In creating an image of the self as contingent and constructed, lacking any 'essential' properties, *4.48 Psychosis* can be read as discarding the traditional Western notion of the self as transparent, autonomous and the source of meaning as well as pathology. Such an idea of the self tends to be embedded in Western psychiatric discourse. John Z. Sadler, Professor of Psychiatry at the University of Texas, Dallas, for instance, writes that '[i]n Western countries, the individual tends to view the self as governed by internal beliefs, desires, commitments, thoughts, and feelings. In many Asian cultures, for instance, the individual conceives himself or herself as interdependently governed by social relationships, duties and responsibilities, as well as by the thoughts, feelings, and beliefs of others' (2005, p. 271). Sadler then argues that an 'individualist' bias is embedded in the diagnostic systems most commonly drawn upon in the West – the *Diagnostic and Statistical Manual of Mental Disorders* of the American Psychiatric Association (DSM) and the International Classification of Disease developed by the World Health Organization (ICD) – and notes that 'core DSM-ICD cognitive symptoms of depression (feelings of guilt, self-deprecation, despair, and suicidal ideation) are relatively infrequent in Asian societies' (pp. 270–1).

In *4.48 Psychosis* the character 'presents' with symptoms similar to those mentioned by Sadler, but Kane's text offers the possibility of reading these not as evidence of an underlying, biological illness ('depression'), but as a cultural construction, formed from culturally available resources, namely psychiatric and psychological discourse. The idea of there being an 'essential' self, or of the individual as autonomous, separate, and in 'possession' of an interiority containing beliefs, ideas and desires, is subtly undermined. It is in this way that *4.48 Psychosis* can be read as subversive.

Even the form of the play, the absence of named characters, seems to undermine any notion of an inviolable, sovereign subject, and instead any sense of a separate individuality is created through performance and dialogue. Mostly what is produced in the text, though, is a sense of the person as fragmented. Within the play the 'suicidal' or 'patient' character is not depicted as a unified individual (a singular mind enclosed in a singular body), but rather mind and body are presented as separate. The first description of the character sets the scene for this ongoing ambiguous portrayal:

a consolidated consciousness resides in a dark banqueting hall near the ceiling of a mind whose floor shifts as ten thousand cockroaches when a shaft of light enters as all thoughts unite in an instant of accord body no longer expellent as the cockroaches comprise a truth which no one ever utters. (Kane, 2000, p. 3)

Here an interiority is suggested, but the image is unsettling for it involves both an unusual sense of space ('a dark banqueting hall near the ceiling of a mind') and description of contents ('ten thousand cockroaches').

The gender of the speaker is also ambiguously described:

the broken hermaphrodite who trusted hermself alone finds the room in reality teeming and begs never to wake from the nightmare. (Kane, 2000, p. 3)

Neither male nor female, but also residing neither within nor outside the body:

And I am deadlocked by that smooth psychiatric voice of reason which tells me there is an objective reality in which my body and mind are one. But I am not here and never have been (p. 7)
Do you think it's possible for a person to be born in the wrong body? (p. 13)
Here am I
and there is my body

       dancing on glass (p. 28)

It could, of course, be argued that the play represents a psychotic mind, and, consequently, the fragmentation evident should be understood as symptomatic of an underlying illness – Kane herself spoke of the play being 'about a psychotic breakdown and what happens to a person's mind when the barriers which distinguish between reality and different forms of imagination completely disappear, so that you no longer know the difference between your waking life and your dream life' (in Saunders, 2002, pp. 111–12). *4.48 Psychosis* can, however, also be read as challenging the dominant view of the sovereign, self-contained individual, and the idea that mental illness and suicide are primarily caused by (acultural and ahistorical) forces arising from within the interiority of the person. By highlighting the constituted nature of the self, and the ways in which pathological and suicidal identities are formed in relation to 'psy' practices and truths, mental illness and acts of self-destruction can be read not only as individual abnormalities, but also as historically and culturally situated and constructed discursive formations.

Witnessing a private act

As has been argued in this book, suicide is mostly conceptualised, and has to a large part become, in Western culture at least, an essentially private act. Another way in which *4.48 Psychosis* can be read as subvert-ing dominant assumptions of suicide is by the way the private/public distinction is undermined. The suicidal character in *4.48 Psychosis* makes numerous pleas to be seen and validated – to be witnessed. These originally arise in the context of wishing to find salvation in the presence of an Other:

> Find me
> Free me
>   from this
>   corrosive doubt
>   futile despair (Kane, 2000, p. 17)

Later, the idea of being saved by another gives way to despair. The Other remains absent, even when insistently called upon:

> this vital need for which I would die
>   to be loved
> I'm dying for one who doesn't care
> I'm dying for one who doesn't know
>   you're breaking me
> Speak
> Speak
> Speak
>   ten yard ring of failure
>   look away from me
> My final stand
>   No one speaks   (Kane, 2000, pp. 40–1)

No one speaks, and nobody appears as rescuer. The possible suicide asks again, though, to become fully present in the eyes of another:

> Validate me
> Witness me
> See me
> Love me (Kane, 2000, p. 41)

It becomes apparent that the person will end their life, and is asking that this be witnessed:

> watch me vanish
> watch me
>
>   vanish
>
> watch me
>
> watch me
>
>   watch (Kane, 2000, p. 42)

The suicide is a harrowing end to the play, made more so because the audience, or readers, are present and do not or cannot intervene. The play insists that we do not look away from suicide, but somehow bear witness to it, react to it, become involved and moved by the scene that unfolds before us. In this way, the play can be read as a challenge to the idea that, as suicide is an act of an 'unbalanced' individual, we always remain somehow outside it, implicated only incidentally, that we must look away and leave to the experts the jobs of interpretation, observation, assessment, containment and treatment that are taken to be necessities in the 'management' of the suicidal. The idea of a 'public' suicide, of a relational act, one witnessed not just by a direct 'seeing' but also a witnessing that suggests a recognising of a shared experience, one that has cultural meaning beyond the designation of the suicide as merely 'mentally unwell', is a concept largely alien to us. Media guidelines place limits on the portrayal and interpretation of suicide (see chapter 3). We are asked to look away, and if we do think about the subject, to do so in one way only (as an act arising from individual pathology). *4.48 Psychosis* challenges us to be present and not to look away, and in so doing to witness and validate the experience of the suicide.

Having proclaimed that:

It is myself that I have never met, whose face is pasted on the underside of my mind

reiterating the idea of a vital absence, the very last line reads:

please open the curtains (Kane, 2000, p. 43)

There is an ambiguity about this line. Saunders (2002) writes of how, in the first performance at the Royal Court Theatre, after the last line was spoken, the actors moved to the side of the stage, opened the shutters to the windows, and let in the light and sound of the London street outside. 'The experience was simple but profoundly moving,' he writes, '[a]s one reviewer put it, "the effect is strangely uplifting, like watching the final release of a turbulent spirit"' (p. 117). According to another playwright, Edward Bond, the play changes 'from a painful suicide note about death and loss and waste – into a sort of treatise about living consciously, and this is even more painful' (in Saunders, 2002, p. 116). This suggests that the curtains are opened in order to allow the audience to look away from the drama that has now come to an end and to begin to live again, but more consciously now. Yet it could also be read as inviting the outside world to look in, so that they too can bear witness and validate the events that have unfolded. Such a move – the invitation to witness a person's self-accomplished death – has echoes of the acts of Thrasea Paetus and Cato discussed in chapter 5. There, friends and family gathered to take their leave of the dying person, to listen to their final thoughts, and to attempt to dissuade or to provide comfort. With Sarah Kane's play, we are mute and unable to reach out either to prevent the unfolding death or to provide any support or comfort to the person in their dying. The act is watched from the outside, and passively endured – there can be no Demetrius to smooth the passage from life to death, the suicide is alone in his/her dying and we are encouraged to look away and then to move on with our own lives.

Conclusions

Within the 'regime of truth' identified in this book suicide is almost always in some way pathological. The patient is read as not responsible in relation to the responsible and accountable clinician, and practices of confinement, constant observation and restraint are deemed necessary. The events that followed Sarah Kane's own suicide after she completed *4.48 Psychosis* are illustrative of how such deaths can come to reinforce, rather than challenge, such ways of thinking and acting. A letter appeared in the *Guardian*, from another playwright, Anthony Neilson. Under the headline 'Insane thesis', it read:

It worries me when Sarah Kane's agent Mel Kenyon talks about 'existential despair' being 'what makes artists tick' (Playwright Kane kills herself, February 24). Nobody in despair 'ticks' – and for Sarah Kane the clock has stopped. Truth didn't kill her, lies did: the lies of worthlessness and futility whispered by an afflicted brain. They're lies told to artists and check-out girls alike, but we canonise one and stigmatise the other. They both battle the same banal forces: crazy and irregular tides of chemicals that crash through the brain. Far from enhancing talent, these neurological storms waste time, narrow vision and frequently lead, as here, to that most tragic, most selfish of actions.

Mental illness is pointless, undignified and ultimately, always physical. It deserves neither blind fear not romantic rumination. The various diseases should be attacked, the public comprehensively educated and the medical system overhauled. We stand on the verge of an epidemic of which this death is yet another indicator. Sarah Kane possessed the seeds of greatness, but did not live to reap them. She never found the 'truth' either, mental illness saw to that too. (Neilson, 1999)

At the inquest into Sarah Kane's death the coroner said she had killed herself while 'the balance of her mind was disturbed' (the *Guardian*,

23 September 1999), shorthand for something akin, perhaps, to Anthony Neilson's formulation of her death. Both in the media and in the coroner's court the compulsory ontology of pathology came to be reasserted. Further, the positioning of the suicide as victim of illness proceeded hand in hand with criticism of staff for failing to adequately protect the patient. The *Guardian* reported the findings of the inquest under the heading: 'Suicidal writer was free to kill herself: Sarah Kane unchecked by nurses despite risk, inquest hears'. Individual staff were criticised in court, but at the same time the necessity of practices of confinement and constant watching were reaffirmed; an internal hospital review recommended the introduction of more formal communication processes between staff in relation to the level of observations suicidal patients required on the ward.

Such responses to Sarah Kane's death are entirely legitimate and reasonable. For her family and friends her death was experienced as tragic, and many expressed bewilderment that she had not been monitored more closely in hospital given that it was known she wanted to kill herself. The analysis presented here is not intended to undermine the belief that she was mentally ill, or to argue that hospital was not the right place for her, or that the practices in place to manage suicidal patients are unethical or ineffective. Rather, her death and the statements made in its wake have been set out as illustrative of how a particular 'regime of truth' can come to be reinforced even by an act that on another reading could be said to challenge the legitimacy and reasonableness of such a 'regime'.

Such an argument relies on a degree of conflation between Sarah Kane's own life and death and her work. However, the analysis presented above relating to *4.48 Psychosis*, it is argued, warrants such a position, for in the play Sarah Kane highlights elements of the difficulties and complexities involved in relations between suicidal patient and clinical staff that do not normally surface.

Within the play suicide is both a determined act and an act of resistance, and the suicidal 'subject' of the text could be read as largely formed within the terms of a dominant, pathologising 'regime of truth' but, at the same time, containing elements that subvert and resist dominance. Unfortunately, these forces, although apparently contradictory, can come together in suicide. Self-destruction can be both determined (as where the imposition of a pathologised identity contributes to the experience of an intolerable, unlivable life), yet also read as an act of resistance to those same determining forces (the rejection of such an identity through an act of suicide).

Analysis of Sarah Kane's play in terms of relations of power can also help to throw into question the clear separation of forces usually posited to be involved in any encounter between suicidal individuals and those agencies charged with preventing suicide – mostly, in practice, mental health services. Such encounters are usually read as involving, on the one hand, a malign destructive force located within the mentally ill individual and, on the other, those services that are charged with identifying, confining, containing or restraining such a force. Rather than an unambiguous separation, *4.48 Psychosis* points to a more complex arrangement – something perhaps more akin to Deleuze's notion of different forms (objects, concepts and subjects) arising out of a 'compound of relations between forces' within a 'given historical formation' (2006, p. 102). Within the play the suicidal patient is taken as formed by the actions of many disparate forces, many of them apparently only partially known to the subject her/himself, and some originating from interactions with psychiatric services themselves. The act of suicide itself within the play is in part constituted by reference to medical/psychiatric notions, as is the suicidal subject. So rather than services standing 'outside' suicide, reacting when confronted with the possibility of such an act, it could be said that in actuality psychiatry/medicine is always already present prior to any contact with the suicidal individual, has in part already formed the act considered by the patient, and has also in part already constituted the person her/himself in relation to the truths of pathology and suicide produced and circulated within a culture. Thus the relationship between suicidal patient and preventative services is shown to be tangled and complex – each constituting, as well as reacting to, the other to varying degrees.

Such a position – that services are not simply engaged in managing destructive forces that have arisen solely within the mentally ill individual, and that the suicidal patient, as well as current notions of the nature of suicide itself, are historical and cultural products formed in relation to medical/psychiatric/scientific truths – can be contrasted with more mainstream thinking on the subject. In the majority of journal articles, books and conference papers that relate to the prevention of suicide, professional practices are read as essentially reactive rather than in any way formative of the object of study. This is not to suggest that preventative agencies intend to be anything other than helpful to people who present in distress, or that it is somehow not the case that many suicides are prevented by the actions of such services. Rather, the reading of *4.48 Psychosis* above is set out as a way of understanding the various lines of force that may be present in any encounter between suicidal patient and mental health, or other, professional – a different form of knowledge, perhaps, than is generally sought, but nonetheless one that may have a certain utility in relation to the problems presented by self-accomplished deaths. As a form of 'subjugated' knowledge (Foucault, 1980, 2003) Sarah Kane's *4.48 Psychosis* stands out as revelatory of certain ways by which suicide and the suicidal patient can be constituted in relation to those medical/psychiatric/scientific notions and practices seen as possessing the 'currency' and necessity of truth, and at the same time offering a critique of those very same ideas and ways of working usually read as benign and merely reactive.

Part IV

Summary and conclusions

My intention was not to deal with the problem of truth, but with the problem of the truth-teller, or of truth-telling as an activity ... who is able to tell the truth, about what, with what consequences, and with what relations to power...   Michel Foucault (2001)

In order to exercise a relation of power, there must be on both sides at least a certain form of liberty. Even though the relation of power may be completely unbalanced or when one can truly say that he has 'all power' over the other, a power can only be exercised over another to the extent that the latter still has the possibility of committing suicide, of jumping out of the window or of killing the other. That means that in the relations of power, there is necessarily the possibility of resistance.   Michel Foucault (in Bernauer and Rasmussen, 1987, p. 12)

12   Summary and conclusions

Summary of arguments and findings

This book has analysed the formation of a particular 'regime of truth' in relation to suicide, one centring on the production and maintenance of a compulsory ontology of pathology. Such a 'regime' (functioning through circular relations of power-to-knowledge and knowledge-to-power) has opened up many possibilities for understanding and managing self-destructive thoughts, desires and acts, but equally it could also be said to be problematic. It has been argued that an individualised, 'internal-ised', pathologised, depoliticised and ultimately tragic form of suicide has come to be produced, with alternative interpretations of acts of self-accomplished death marginalised or foreclosed.

One way to unsettle these truths in order to open up possibilities for thinking and acting in potentially more helpful ways with regard to self-accomplished deaths is to highlight the contingency of contemporary thought and practices. To this end descriptions of different acts that would now be subsumed under the singular term 'suicide' and under-stood primarily by reference to notions of individual pathology were set out. The death of Thrasea Paetus in Rome in AD 66, which could be described as relational, political and philosophical, and that of Amy Stokes in London in 1590, a death constituted in relation to notions of sin and crime, transgression and punishment, were described in order to illustrate the argument that all 'games of truth' in relation to self-accomplished deaths are products of particular times and places.

The constructing of a history of the emergence of contemporary truths by reference to specific historical and cultural practices and events, as well as to particular relations of power and power-knowledge, was another strategy pursued in order to call into question the universality of the claims made. New medical truths of suicide came to be formulated in the early nineteenth century and certain conditions of possibility for their emer-gence were identified – the 'coinage' and uptake of suicide as a unitary descriptor for particular acts of self-accomplished death; changing conceptions of knowledge and the subject from the seventeenth century on; the 'secularisation' of suicide; and the creation of lunatic asylums under medical management. The asylums acted as laboratories for the production of medical truths of insanity and, later, of suicide by means of a variety of technologies – the importation of techniques such as medical examinations, the questioning of patients to elicit symptoms, hierarchical surveillance, diagnostic practices and other forms of classification, the prescribing of treatments, the recording of information in individual case files, and the dispersal of patients to designated spaces within the asylum all allowed the 'suicidal patient' to be formed in relation to medical authority. Circular and productive relations of power-knowledge within the asylum (that is, the knowledge produced from such sites acting to justify practices of confinement, containment, constant watching and restraint, leading in turn to the creation of more knowledge) enabled the establishment to strengthen and extend psychiatric power with regard to suicide and the suicidal.

Such a 'medicalisation' of suicide can be understood by reference to shifting 'economies' of power. Whereas sovereign power had constituted self-killing as a negation of the right of the king, or God, to take life or let live, now numerous techniques that sought 'no longer to kill, but to invest life through and through' (Foucault, 1998, p. 139) emerge in the eighteenth century. Understood in terms of a history of problems (Osborne, 2003) suicide now came to represent less a transgression – a challenge to the authority of the king and God as it had in the Middle Ages – that necessitated punishment, more an act of provocation to a bio-power that sought to foster life and manage, maintain and maximise all aspects of life at both individual and population level. In the face of such an incitement, the investing of authority in medicine, and the imposition of numerous technologies that sought to manage and control the suicidal patient's body and actions, as well as the development of preventative measures aimed at the level of the population, represented solutions to this newly problematised form of death.

In order to illustrate the formulation of medical truths of suicide in relation to asylum practices, *aliéniste* Jean-Etienne Esquirol's contribution to the 1821 *Dictionnaire des sciences médicales* was analysed in detail. Here particular relations of power, productive configurations of power-knowledge and certain problematic aspects of constituting acts of self-accomplished death by reference to the discourse and practices of medicine were identified. In particular, through the deployment of the passions as the prime causative factor in suicide, and by focusing attention on the pathologising effects the passions were said to have on the body rather than on the social/interpersonal/political context of their arising, it became possible to constitute suicide as an individual, somatic and thus medical issue. Such a move opened up many possibilities for thought and action in relation to the threat of suicide, but also restricted others. A propensity to suicide came to be constituted as a symptom of insanity, caused by the effects of an excess of passion on the body, and thus requiring treatment in the form of confinement and isolation away from friends and family. The 'external' context of the emergence of a desire to die could now be noted, but came to be considered as for the most part superfluous to the medical management and treatment of the suicidal condition. Suicide thus came to be formed as primarily an individual act of pathology, and the social and political context of its arising was taken to be of secondary importance. Such a move justified the function and practices of the asylum and consolidated medical authority with respect to suicide and the suicidal.

The proliferation of medical discourse and practices regarding suicide was then mapped across the nineteenth century. It was argued that medical discourses on insanity and suicide emerged in relation to each other, as suicide came to be defined by reference to insanity and, reciprocally, insanity by reference to suicide.

In terms of defining suicide by reference to insanity it was noted that physicians initially theorised on the existence of diseased organs (in the viscera) that were said to account for a propensity to suicide. In the absence of validating anatomical evidence in autopsy, speculation focused instead on the brain as the 'seat' of suicide, but no consistent findings of abnormality could be found. Talk of diseased and perverted impulses and instincts came to the fore around mid-century, but again, as unobservable phenomena, evidence remained elusive as to their exact location and nature. The constituting of suicide through a discourse on insanity also had a reciprocal effect in that notions of insanity came to be, in part, defined by reference to medically formulated truths of suicide. Insanity could be shown to be dangerous, as well as essentially an individual, private and internal phenomenon.

Subjects came to be formed in relation to such truths. The notion of the 'suicidal patient' and the 'responsible, accountable and culpable clinician' as a 'truth-effect' was proposed, and an account of this process of subject formation, drawn mostly from Foucault's writings on the relationship between processes of subjectivation and objectification, was set out alongside examples drawn from medical texts as well as other sources such as popular magazines and published biographies and diaries. As noted, suicide was generally constructed as arising due to some form of internal pathology or abnormality, and subject positions were formed in relation to authoritative medical/psychiatric knowledge. The 'suicidal patient' was constituted in medical/psychiatric discourse as dangerous and driven to self-destruction, and measures for the prevention of such acts came to focus on the identification and containment of an unseen, dangerous internal force. Practices such as confinement in locked wards and dormitories, constant watching and physical restraint were employed as preventative measures, with staff deemed accountable and potentially culpable in relation to the self-accomplished deaths of their patients.

It was argued that the prevention of suicide acted as a rationale for the practices of the emerging psychiatric profession. Interestingly, high numbers of suicidal patients in the asylums were reported throughout the century, alongside very few actual deaths by such means. One interpretation, put forward by the doctors themselves, was that the medical management of suicide was successful in preventing such deaths. Another would be that alienism, and later psychiatry, made tactical use of the notion of an internal destructive drive in order to justify their practices; the notion of the inherent dangerousness of the insane patient was deployed to such ends, and the suicidal patient was constituted as exemplary of such dangers. The social functions of mental medicine – in terms of the control of the dangerous individual, the imposition of medical restraint in the absence of internal restraint, and the idea of psychiatry as a form of public hygiene – were explored in chapter 8.

By the end of the nineteenth century the identification, containment and management of the suicidal, centring on the asylum and based on notions of individual, 'internal' pathology as the primary cause of self-destructive acts, had come to dominate. Challenges to the authority of psychiatric theory and practice with regard to suicide did emerge, though, during the twentieth century, both from 'outside' in the shape of sociological explanations of such acts, and from 'within' in the form of the criticisms of Thomas Szasz based on the restrictions of individual liberty inherent in psychiatric management of the suicidal. The twentieth century also saw an extension in the possibilities for suicide to be formed as a pathological phenomenon. Psychoanalytic theories constituted suicide in relation to innate destructive drives, the sexual nature and history of the patient as well as their dreams, phantasies and childhood memories, and, later in the century, psychological autopsy studies enabled signs of a propensity to suicide to be found in numerous everyday gestures, attitudes and actions. There was thus a deepening as well as a broadening of the ground upon which truths of suicide could be formed, and through such means the truth of the pathology of suicide could be maintained and reaffirmed.

Suicide is now mostly constituted as the tragic act of a mentally unwell individual and other ways of conceiving self-accomplished death possess relatively limited currency. The 'regime of truth' centring on a compulsory ontology of pathology asserts itself across a range of sites and in numerous situations. It remains the case, though, that mental health services, particularly in-patient services, are still central to suicide prevention measures. Of particular interest to this study has been the idea that on occasion a death by suicide may arise as an act of defiance or resistance to psychiatric power. Most usually the relationship between mental health staff and suicidal patient is taken to be a confrontation between the internal destructive force present in the patient – existing somehow prior to psychiatric knowledge and practices – and the identification, containment and restraint of such a force on the part of the professional. But much more can be involved; if such an encounter is read as an historical and cultural formation, many lines of force could be said to constitute it: authoritative knowledge, centred on the individual body, in relation to the causation and prevention of suicide; the identification, often by a process of self-examination and confession, of a propensity to suicide or desire to harm oneself; fears about involuntary confinement and treatment; the necessity of recording information in case notes that may be drawn upon if an enquiry is instituted in the event of the patient's death; fear of blame or censure from colleagues; concerns about the possible effects on others of such a death; and knowledge of the relations of power, often formed in terms of a confrontation despite the benign intent of the staff involved. Each of these elements may be present in clinical encounters between staff and patients. Sarah Kane's play *4.48 Psychosis* (2000) was used to illustrate how suicidal patients can come to be formed in relation to authoritative knowledge and practices, and how suicide arises in the context of relations of power inherent in the contemporary psychiatric 'regime of truth', through processes of subjection whereby they are constituted as a 'suicidal patient' and/or through resistance to being so constituted. Finally, the aftermath of Sarah Kane's own death by suicide was discussed. Here, although individual staff were publicly criticised, the overall 'regime of truth' was strengthened – suicide was reaffirmed as pathological, and the necessity of psychiatric practices reasserted. Such are the dynamics of modern suicide that even an act that could be read as challenging the utility of such a 'regime' comes to reinforce it.

Conclusions

An attempt to apply a historicist, nominalist, broadly Foucauldian analytic strategy to the subject of suicide has been the overarching purpose of this book. This final section looks at what such an approach might have to offer the study of this difficult issue and also considers some of the possible limitations.

The main principles that guided and shaped the analytic strategy could be summarised as:

- a scepticism towards all 'anthropological universals' (Foucault, 2000, p. 461), indeed, to all universals. Such ways of understanding suicide – by appealing to ahistorical or acultural elements of suicide or unchanging features of human nature – were not rejected outright, but rather called into question. In practice this amounted to an attempt to avoid grounding any analysis in either an invariant object (that is, the assumption of 'essential' or universal features of suicide) or subject (the idea that certain attributes or characteristics are to be found in all suicides and suicidal individuals) of study;
- the establishment of the idea of suicide as an historical and cultural formation, rather than an unchanging object of study; similarly, the rejection of the idea of the 'constituting' subject in favour of one taken to be 'constituted', or formed in relation to certain historically and culturally specific 'regimes of truth';
- finally, the understanding of practices and power relations as central to the production of such 'regimes of truth', and as accounting for the formation of subjects and objects at particular times and places.

Through adherence to these principles it has been possible to explore the processes involved in the formation and maintenance of a contemporary 'regime of truth' centring on suicide constituted as an act of pathology. Here, the production and circulation of truths were analysed by reference to particular relations of power-to-knowledge and knowledge-to-power, and certain 'truth effects' in terms of the constitution of objects and subjects of knowledge were examined. Finally, the possibilities opened up by such a 'regime of truth' were explored, alongside a consideration of areas where such dominant forms of knowledge and practices could be said to be problematic.

By such means it was possible to analyse certain aspects of suicide relatively underexamined in other studies:

- understanding the move from constituting suicide by reference to sin and crime (a transgression to be punished) to notions of pathology and abnormality (and thus a defect to be diagnosed, managed, treated or corrected) in terms of changing 'economies' of power between the seventeenth and eighteenth centuries and the nineteenth;
- the strategic utility of constituting suicide as pathological for the consolidation and extension of psychiatric (and later 'psy') power. By positing that truth is not outside power (Foucault, 2002a, p. 131), analysis could be conducted in terms of the strategic deployment of

authoritative knowledge in the service of power; thus, the means by which suicide came to be formed as an act of insanity and, concurrently, insanity came to be read as by its nature dangerous were analysed as tactical moves which acted to justify asylum practices of confinement, surveillance and restraint, as well as providing the emerging psychiatric profession with a rationale; namely, the protection of individuals and the public from the dangers inherent in madness;

- the circular relations of power-to-knowledge and knowledge-to-power immanent in the formation of suicide as pathological and primarily a concern of medicine. As noted, asylum practices of confinement, constant watching and restraint were justified by reference to the truths of insanity – that is, the madman was taken to be inherently dangerous and thus needed to be contained, watched and restrained for fear of an explosion of destructive force that would lead to suicide or homicide. Equally, the confinement, control and watching of patients deemed insane and suicidal enabled the production of more and more knowledge of suicide and insanity (alongside other practices such as the medical examination and the keeping of case files) that in turn justified such practices. Power could thus be analysed as productive and not merely repressive in its effects.

- the constitution of subjects in relation to the production of truths of suicide. By positing a constituted rather than constituting subject it was possible to map the effects of the production and circulation of authoritative knowledge on the formation of subjects – in Foucault's terms, the connected processes of objectivation and subjectivation. Thus, the production of truths of suicide have been read within this book as formative rather than merely representative of reality, particularly in relation to the constitution of certain subjects such as the 'suicidal patient' and the 'responsible, accountable and culpable clinician';

- relations of power in the clinical encounter between suicidal patient and clinician. Imbalances of power in practices of identifying and assessing suicide risk and preventing such acts, as well as in the production of authoritative knowledge of suicide and the suicidal patient, were explored;

- understanding acts of suicide as arising in relation to a 'regime of truth'. Through analysis of the productive effects of dominant configurations of power-knowledge it was argued that acts of suicide have come to be formed in relation to a 'regime of truth' centring on the constitution of suicide as pathological. Particularly in suicides that arise in the context of mental health services, such acts can be understood as formed in part in relation to certain truths and practices and/or as resistance to such truths and practices;

- the relationship of resistance to power with regard to suicide. Following on from the previous point, and linking back to an earlier one concerning the analysis of strategies and tactics in relation to the deployment of the threat of suicide, a Foucauldian analytics of the workings of power in relation to suicide allows connections to be made between power and resistance to power with regard to acts of self-accomplished death. Foucault (1981) insisted that 'where there is power, there is resistance' (p. 95), and talked of the ways in which power needed resistance in order to function; in David Hoy's phrase, '[p]ower depends on points of resistance to spread itself more extensively through the social network' (2005, p. 82). It becomes possible to conceive of suicidal acts as in part a form of resistance to power (e.g. as revolt against disciplinary practices that subjugate, or against the burden of a bio-power that demands health, happiness and vitality at all times and is intolerant of the obverse), but a resistance that also serves power in that, as noted, such deaths provide a justification for disciplinary and bio-political practices and a rationale for the extension of power into ever more sites. The circularity between relations of power and particular forms of resistance can thus be mapped through the application of an analytic strategy open to such possibilities, and original insights can be gained into certain ambiguities inherent in contemporary suicide prevention measures.

With respect to the possible utility of approaching the subject in this way, analysis of the truths of suicide in terms of their production and circulation, their history and their effects, opens up new lines of enquiry in relation to such acts. What may emerge from such a process are new ways of thinking and acting; when suicide is no longer read as determined by forces taken to be outside historical formations of power and knowledge or unaffected by specific relations of power, self-destructive thoughts, desires and acts can be understood differently by those engaged in prevention and in caring for suicidal people, as well as those who experience such thoughts and desires themselves.

Clinical staff may come to understand more clearly the ways in which they are positioned as responsible and accountable in relation to the suicidal patients entrusted to their care and protection. Similarly, the processes by which the self-accomplished death of such a patient can leave them open to criticism and blame, yet simultaneously reaffirm the necessity of certain practices and relations of power, can be more readily understood and can come to be questioned.

Giving clinicians the resources to critique existing practices and assumptions can be liberating for the staff involved. As Foucault said '[p]eople know what they do; they frequently know why they do what they do; but what they don't know is what what they do does' (in Dreyfus and Rabinow, 1982, p. 187). The opening up of everyday clinical practices of identifying, assessing and managing suicidal patients to new forms of analysis, and the examination of elements of such practices not normally interrogated (relations of power; productive configurations of power-knowledge; the constitution of subjects in relation to authoritative knowledge) may go some way towards staff being able to formulate what it is that what they do does. No prescription for action is suggested here, except for asserting the utility of engaging clinical staff in critiquing the 'regime of truth' that in part both constitutes and is constituted by their actions.

Another aim of critique, although a more controversial one with regards to the prevention of suicide, can be the desubjectivation of those constituted as patients in relation to their desire to die. Here, as David Hoy (2005) notes with regard to such a process, 'critique functions not by providing an alternative account of who you are and what you ought to do, but by dissolving your sense of who you are and disrupting your sense of what the right thing to do is' (p. 89). Instead of reifying a desire to die by positing some form of internal destructive impulse or instinct, or reinforcing beliefs in this essential or innate dangerousness of mental illnesses, what is suggested is more a *refusal* of what is taken to be, of domination, and part of that may involve a 'dissolving' of oneself, a 'déprendre de soi-même' in Foucault's idiomatic phrase. As discussed, some suicides can be read as resistance to domination, to being constituted solely in terms of deficit and pathology and subject to practices of control experienced as intolerable. However, for those seeking to resist the imposition of a pathologised identity, who wish to reconfigure relations of power between themselves and mental health services, who find the practices of confinement and constant watching intrusive and dehumanising (Cutcliffe and Stevenson, 2007, pp. 29–34), a refusal to be what you are taken to be through a process of desubjectivation offers other possibilities for resistance than suicide. Here, the work of mental health service 'users' and 'survivors' such as the 'successful schizophrenia' group in the UK are exemplary of such resistance, as are the writings and workshops of 'retired' schizophrenic Ron Coleman (e.g. 2000). It may well be that for many people contemporary assumptions and practices in relation to the prevention of suicide are experienced as useful, and in such cases there is little need for critique, but for others the formulation of non-lethal strategies of resistance may prove to be of help.

In more general terms it is argued that to understand what suicide has come to be for us today – what is involved in such acts in terms of relations of power and of power-knowledge, of the constitution of subjects in relation to the production and circulation of authoritative knowledge and practices – it is necessary to have recourse to a form of analysis able to grasp the formative/constitutive capabilities of such elements. In the absence of such an analytic strategy, understanding of acts of self-accomplished death will remain partial, and the field of study will be constituted by forms of knowledge uncritical in their approach, and unaware of their, at times, quite substantial effects.

As has been noted throughout this book, the 'regime of truth' mapped in this study has opened up many possibilities for thought and action with respect to the problem of suicide – the sheer amount written on the subject from the point of view of its being a pathological phenomenon testifies to the productivity of the relations of power-knowledge that have come to be formed. Effective treatments have not always followed on from the claims made of them, but the hope for interventions that could ameliorate or extinguish suicidal states has not itself gone away. It may be that advances in imaging technologies will enable researchers to identify brain abnormalities in the suicidal that are of clinical use, or that one of the various chemical compounds developed and manufactured as psychotropic medication by the pharmaceutical industry is found to be effective in reducing the risk of suicide in individual patients. In terms of everyday practices, new ways of working with suicidal people on in-patient wards (Bowles, 2004; Cutcliffe and Stevenson, 2007) and in the community with crisis resolution and home treatment teams (Johnson *et al.*, 2005) are being championed that challenge the 'confinement/constant observation/ restraint' model of working that has been the mainstay of prevention strategies for the last 200 years or so. Each of these could turn out to be effective in the prevention of suicide. Where does a Foucauldian approach leave one in relation to the possibilities offered by medicine, psychiatry and other therapeutic disciplines? It could well be assumed that such an approach necessarily entails calls for the dismantling of all 'oppressive' regimes, the resistance to unequal relations of power wherever they are found, the overthrowing of established ways of working in the name of 'liberation'. Such would be a misreading of Foucault's project. Foucault did not advocate blind resistance to 'power', certainly not on the grounds of a naive 'liberation'. His theoretical position was antithetical to such calls. What a Foucauldian approach can lead to is more a questioning of the utility of the dominance of particular 'regimes of truth'. With regards to this book, such a move has entailed the problematising of the assumption that suicide should always be read as pathological, that psychiatric (and more broadly 'psy') approaches provide us with sufficient resources for thought and action in relation to self-accomplished deaths. It has also been suggested that certain effects of the production and circulation of truths should be made more visible, as should the complex relations of power immanent in certain clinical encounters between staff and suicidal patient.

It is these areas that have been subject to critique in this book. What tend not to emerge out of a Foucauldian analytic approach are prescriptions for change. The questioning of certainties and the problematising of particular practices do not lead inevitably to answers as to what should be done. Foucault's own studies relating to madness (1965), prisons (1977) and sexuality (1981) do not end with calls for change, and were subsequently criticised for providing insufficient grounds for challenging identified injustices and forms of oppression (e.g. Taylor, 1986; Fraser, 1989). The lack of normative grounds for mounting effective resistance in Foucault's work can thus be read as a weakness of such an approach. It has not been possible here to offer new certainties, or to prescribe new ways of thinking and acting in place of older ones. Instead, Foucauldian critique offers more of a constant contestation of meaning and practices through which may emerge new ways of constituting particular problems, and the asking of a different set of questions from those habitually formulated. However, for those wishing to know 'what is to be done' in relation to problems such as suicide, Foucauldian analytics can provide much frustration and too little enlightenment.

Given the sensitivity of the subject matter, such an approach may also not be welcome. There are many who insist on the truth of their understanding of what suicide is, and how such deaths, or the threat of such deaths, should be responded to, and who become unsettled, irritable or downright angry when faced with a form of analysis that calls into question these certainties. A Foucauldian critical analysis has perhaps too little to offer by way of reassurance, but then, as Butler notes, for critique to 'do its job' it must risk the censure and denunciation of those who 'naturalize and render hegemonic' the very ground 'put into question by critique itself' (in Salih, 2004, pp. 313–14). This book has addressed certain themes not usually associated with the study of suicide – issues of relations of power, of power-knowledge, and the formation of objects and subjects of knowledge in relation to production and maintenance of particular 'regimes of truth' – and the benefits of such analysis argued for above. It is acknowledged, however, that not all will welcome the introduction of such a form of analysis into the 'field of study'.

With regard to this book specifically, certain weaknesses are also apparent. The most problematic area of analysis, an area where a Foucauldian approach has perhaps least to offer (or was applied in the least effective way), is in the identification of strategies and tactics of power in contemporary thought and practices. With the historical sections it has been possible to trace emerging and changing relations of power, the outcomes of strategic moves and tactics (for example, in the deployment of the threat of suicide to justify asylum practices in the early nineteenth century, or the use of psychological autopsy studies in the 1950s to demonstrate the ubiquity of psychopathology in suicide and thus the necessity of wider community psychiatric involvement), and the productivity of power-knowledge relations. Contemporary strategies of power and the effects of present-day formations of power-knowledge are much harder to analyse given that such effects have sometimes yet to reveal themselves, and power often necessarily conceals its workings in order to ensure its effectiveness and continuation (Foucault, 1981, p. 86). Because of this, the sections on the contemporary formation of a 'regime of truth' based on suicide as a form of pathology (chapters 3 and 4) could mostly map the production and circulation of truths, and comment on 'truth effects', but was more limited in terms of effective analysis of relations of power.

Another possible limitation has been an occasional overemphasis on discourse as text at the expense of analyses of discursive *practices*. Initially, the book was conceived as a form of discourse analysis, and the linguistic elements of particular texts were taken to be the data for examination. The utility of analysing relations of power, the circularity of power-to-knowledge and knowledge-to-power relations, as well as those practices that enabled, or were enabled by, the production of authoritative knowledge, in order to more fully grasp how suicide has come to be formed and with what effects, dawned on me rather slowly. As a defence, Foucault traced a somewhat similar path in the 1970s, moving away from a 'structuralist' emphasis on discourse (e.g. *The Archaeology of Knowledge* (2002b)) to an analytics of power in his 'genealogical' studies, and was not himself averse to drawing on quite extensive textual sources for some of his studies (e.g. *I, Pierre Riviere* (1987) or *Hercule Barbin* (1998)).

Despite these limitations I believe that the work of Michel Foucault (or at least the appropriation of certain of his analytic tools underpinned by the principles outlined above) has a great deal to offer to the study of suicide. Such an approach can, in Nikolas Rose's phrase, help us to 'think *against* the present' (1998, p. 18), so that which has come to seem most necessary, true and real can be called into question, and the forces and contingencies involved in the formation of our taken-for-granted ways of thinking and acting can be uncovered. Perhaps most usefully, though, a Foucauldian analytic approach can expose a whole field of enquiry to new (albeit challenging) questions. Easy answers may not be forthcoming but, at the least, we might be *provoked* into considering the different possibilities for thought, action and experience that exist.

References

Unpublished archival material

The following are records from St Augustine's Hospital, Chartham, 1854–1993, held in the East Kent Archives Centre, Whitfield.

East Kent Archives: EK/MH/T3/Aa2 Annual report of the medical superintendent. 1876–1890.

East Kent Archives: EK/MH/T3/Aa3–38 Annual reports 1890–1953.

East Kent Archives: EK/MH/T3/Ab Records of the Commissioners in Lunacy. 1875–1928.

East Kent Archives: EK/MH/T3/Ab1–2 Report book 1875–1960.

East Kent Archives: EK/MH/T3/Ar19 Article: A brief history of St Augustine's Hospital. c. 1993.

East Kent Archives: EK/MH/T3/Ca1–4 Journal of the Medical Superintendent, 1875–1909.

East Kent Archives: EK/MH/T3/Ka1–8 Register of pauper admissions: male and female patients. 1875–1906.

East Kent Archives: EK/MH/T3/Ka16–17 Register of private admissions; Male and female patients. 1881–1906.

East Kent Archives: EK/MH/T3/Kr2–5 Register of removals, discharges and deaths; Male and female patients. 1875–1906.

East Kent Archives: EK/MH/T3/Kr14–17 Register of removals, discharges and deaths; Private patients 1890–1930.

East Kent Archives: EK/MH/T3/Ks1–4 Register of deaths; Male and female private patients 1907–1930.

East Kent Archives: EK/MH/T3/Ks5 Register of deaths; Voluntary, temporary and certified male patients 1931–1947.

East Kent Archives: EK/MH/T3/Ks8–11 Register of deaths; Female paupers. 1907–1930.

East Kent Archives: EK/MH/T3/Ks12 Register of deaths; Voluntary, temporary and certified female patients 1931–1947.

East Kent Archives: EK/MH/T3/Kz2–3 Register of burials (Chartham Asylum burial ground) 1875–1972.

East Kent Archives: EK/MH/T3/Mc Medical Case Books 1877–1949.

East Kent Archives: EK/MH/T3/Md Medical Case Papers 1925–1948.

East Kent Archives: EK/MH/T3/Mj Medical Journals 1875–1925.

East Kent Archives: EK/MH/T3/Mk Medical Registers 1907–1949.
East Kent Archives: EK/MH/T3/Mp Post-Mortem/Necropsy Books 1875–1943.

Published works

Alvarez, A. (1971). *The Savage God: A Study of Suicide*. London: Weidenfeld and Nicolson.

American Psychiatric Association (2000). *Diagnostic and Statistical Manual of Mental Disorders* (DSM-IV-TR). 4th edn. Washington, DC: American Psychiatric Association.

Améry, J. (1999). *On Suicide: A Discourse on Voluntary Death*. Bloomington: Indiana University Press.

Andersen, N. Å. (2003). *Discursive Analytical Strategies: Understanding Foucault, Koselleck*. Bristol: The Policy Press.

Anderson, M. and Jenkins, R. (2006). The National Suicide Prevention Strategy for England: the reality of a national strategy for the nursing profession. *Journal of Psychiatric and Mental Health Nursing*, 13: 641–50.

Anderson, O. (1987). *Suicide in Victorian and Edwardian England*. Oxford University Press.

Andrew, D. (1988). The secularization of suicide in England, 1660–1800. *Past and Present* 119, May: 158–65.

Angst, J., Angst, F. and Stassen, H. H. (1999). Suicide risk in patients with major depressive disorder. *Journal of Clinical Psychiatry*, 60 (supp. 2): 57–62.

Annual Register, The (1847). edited by H. V. Hodson. London: Longmans.

Anon. (1853). Haydon: – a psychological study. *Journal of Psychological Medicine*, 6: 501–27.

Appleby, L., Shaw, J., Amos, T., McDonnell, R., Kiernan, K., Davies, S. *et al.* (1999). *Safer Services. Report of the National Confidential Inquiry into Suicide and Homicide by People with Mental Illness*. London: The Stationery Office.

Appleby, L., Shaw, J., Sherratt, J., Amos, T., Robinson, J., McDonnell, R. *et al.* (2001). *Safety First. Report of the National Confidential Inquiry into Suicide and Homicide by People with Mental Illness*. London: The Stationery Office.

Appleby, L., Shaw, J., Kapur, N., Windfuhr, K., Ashton, A. Swinson, N. *et al.* (2006). *Avoidable Deaths: Five Year Report by the National Confidential Inquiry into Suicide and Homicide by People with Mental Illness*. Available online: www.medicine.man chester.ac.uk/suicideprevention/nci/Useful/avoidable_deaths_full_report.pdf

Arango, V. and, Mann, J. J. (1992). Relevance of serotonergic postmortem studies to suicidal behavior. *International Review of Psychiatry*, 4: 131–140.

Arango, V., Underwood, M. D. and Mann, J. J. (1997). Postmortem findings in suicide victims. Implications for *in vivo* imaging studies. *Annals of the New York Academy of Science*, 836: 269–87.

Asberg, M., Traskman, L. and Thoren, P. (1976). 5-HIAA in the cerebrospinal fluid: a biochemical suicide predictor? *Archives of General Psychiatry*, 33: 1193–17.

Atkinson, J. M. (1978). *Discovering Suicide: Studies in the Social Organization of Sudden Death*. London: Macmillan Press.

Baller, R. D. and Richardson, K. K. (2002). Social integration, imitation, and the geographical pattern of suicide, *American Sociological Review*, 67(6): 873–88.

Barraclough, B., Bunch, J., Nelson, B. and Sainsbury, P. (1974). A hundred cases of suicide: clinical aspects. *British Journal of Psychiatry*, 125: 355–73.

Battin, M. P. (1982). *Ethical Issues in Suicide*. Prentice-Hall Series in the Philosophy of Medicine. Englewood Cliffs, NJ: Prentice-Hall.

(2005). *Ending Life: Ethics and the Way We Die*. Oxford University Press.

Beck, A. T., Ward, C. H., Mendelson, M., Mock, J. and Erbaugh, J. (1961). An inventory for measuring depression. *Archives of General Psychiatry*, 4: 561–71.

Beck, A. T., Steer, R. A. and Garbin, M. G. (1988). Psychometric properties of the Beck Depression Inventory: Twenty-five years of evaluation. *Clinical Psychology Review*, 8(1): 77–100.

Benham, H. A. (1903). Some remarks on suicide in public asylums. *Journal of Mental Science*, 49: 447–53.

Bennett, S., Coggan, C. and Adams, P. (2003). Problematising depression: young people, mental health and suicidal behaviours. *Social Science and Medicine*, 57(2): 289–99.

Bentley's Miscellany, vol. XX (1846). London: Richard Bentley.

Bernauer, J. and Rasmussen, D. (eds) (1987). *The Final Foucault*. Cambridge, MA: MIT Press.

Berrios, G. E. and Mohanna, M. (1995). Suicide and self-harm, in G. E. Berrios and R. Porter (eds), *A History of Clinical Psychiatry: The Origin and History of Psychiatric Disorders*, pp. 612–24. London: Athlone.

Bertolote, J. M., Fleischmann, A., De Leo, D. and Wasserman, D. (2004). Psychiatric diagnoses and suicide: revisiting the evidence. *Crisis: Journal of Crisis Intervention and Suicide*, 25(4): 147–55.

Beskow, J. (1979). Suicide and mental disorder in Swedish men. *Acta Psychiatrica Scandinavica*, 177 (suppl.): 1–138.

Bevan Lewis, W. (1889). *A Text-Book of Mental Disease with Special References to the Pathological Aspects of Insanity*. London: Griffin & Co.

Black, S. T. (1989). Gender differences in the content of genuine and simulated suicide notes, in D. Lester (ed.), *Suicide '89*. Denver, CO: American Association of Suicidology.

Blauner, S. R. (2002). *How I Stayed Alive When My Brain Was Trying to Kill Me: One Person's Guide to Suicide Prevention*. New York: William Morrow.

Bloor, D. (1976). *Knowledge and Social Imagery*. London: Routledge & Kegan Paul.

Boothroyd, L. J., Kirmayer, L. J., Spreng, S., Malus, M. and Hodgins, S. (2001). Completed suicides among the Inuit of northern Quebec, 1982–1996: a case–control study. *Canadian Medical Association Journal*, 165: 749–55.

Borch-Jacobsen, M. (2001). Making psychiatric history: madness as *folie à plusieurs*. *History of the Human Sciences* 14: 19–38.

Bowles, N. (2004). Mental health in-patient settings, in D. Duffy and T. Ryan (eds), *New Approaches to Preventing Suicide: A Manual for Practitioners*, pp. 69–82. London: Jessica Kingsley.

Brierre de Boismont, A. J. F. (1856). *Du suicide et de la folie suicide considérés dans leurs rapports avec la statistique, la médecine et la philosophie*. Paris: Germer Baillière.

Brown, R. M. (2001). *The Art of Suicide*. London: Reaktion Books.

Bucknill, J. C. and Tuke, D. H. (1858). *A Manual of Psychological Medicine: Containing the History, Nosology, Description, Statistics, Diagnosis, Pathology, and Treatment of Insanity*. London: John Churchill.

Burgess, S. A. and Hawton, K. (1998). Suicide, euthanasia, and the psychiatrist. *Philosophy, Psychiatry, and Psychology*, 5(2): 113–26.

Burrows, G. M. (1828). *Commentaries on the Causes, Forms, Symptoms, and Treatment, Moral and Medical, of Insanity*. London: Thomas and George Underwood.

Butler, J. (1990). *Gender Trouble: Feminism and the Subversion of Identity*. London and New York: Routledge.

    (1997). *The Psychic Life of Power: Theories of Subjection*. Stanford, CA: Stanford University Press.

    (2004). What is critique? in S. Salih (ed.), *The Judith Butler Reader*, pp. 302–22, Oxford: Blackwell.

Castel, R. (1988). *The Regulation of Madness*. Cambridge: Polity Press.

    (1994) 'Problematization' as a mode of reading history, in J. Goldstein (ed.), *Foucault and the Writing of History*, pp. 237–54. Oxford: Blackwell.

Castle, K., Duberstein, P. R., Meldrum, S., Conner, K. R. and Conwell, Y. (2004). Risk factors for suicide in blacks and whites: an analysis of data from the 1993 National Mortality Followback Survey. *American Journal of Psychiatry*, 161(3): 452–8.

Catechism of the Catholic Church. (1997), 2nd edn. Washington, DC: United States Catholic Conference: #2280–3. Available online: www.usccb.org/catechism/text/pt3sect2chpt2art5.shtml

Cavanagh, J. T. O., Owens, D. G. C. and Johnstone, E. C. (1999). Suicide and undetermined death in south east Scotland. A case-control study using the psychological autopsy method. *Psychological Medicine*, 29: 1141–9.

Cavanagh, J. T., Carson, A. J., Sharpe, M. and Lawrie, S. M. (2003). Psychological autopsy studies of suicide: a systematic review. *Psychological Medicine*; 33(3): 395–405.

Cazauvieilh, J. B. (1840). *Du suicide, de l'aliénation mentale et des crimes contre les personnes, comparés dans leurs rapports réciproques*. Paris: Baillière.

Cheng, A. T. A. (1995). Mental illness and suicide: a case-control study in East Taiwan. *Archives of General Psychiatry*, 52: 594–603.

    (2001). Case definition and culture: are people all the same? (Editorial) *British Journal of Psychiatry*, 179: 1–3.

Cheng, A. T. A. and Lee, C. H. (2000). Suicide in Asia and the Far East, in K. Hawton and K. van Heeringen (eds), *International Handbook of Suicide and Attempted Suicide*, pp. 29–48. Chichester: Wiley.

Chevalier, T. (1824). Remarks on suicide. *The Pamphleteer*, 23: 365–73.

Chynoweth, R., Tonge, J. I. and Armstrong, J. (1980). Suicide in Brisbane: a retrospective psychosocial study. *Australian and New Zealand Journal of Psychiatry*, 14: 37–45.

Coleman, R. (2000). The politics of the illness, in P. Barker and C. Stevenson (eds), *The Construction of Power and Authority in Psychiatry*, pp. 59–66. Oxford: Butterworth Heinemann.

Colt, G. H. (2006). *November of the Soul: The Enigma of Suicide* (ebook). New York: Scribner.

Conwell, Y., Duberstein, P. R., Cox, C., Herrmann, J. H., Forbes, N. T. and Caine, E. D. (1996). Relationships of age and axis I diagnoses in victims of completed suicide: A psychological autopsy study. *American Journal of Psychiatry*, 153: 1001–8.

Copland, J. (1858), *A Dictionary of Practical Medicine*, vol. II. London: Longman, Brown, Green, Longmans & Roberts.

Cornelius, J. R., Salloum, I. M., Lynch, K., Clark, D. B. and Mann, J. J. (2001). Treating the substance-abusing suicidal patient. *Annals of the New York Academy of Sciences*, 932: 78–93.

Cutcliffe, J. and Stevenson, C. (2007). *Care of the Suicidal Person*. Oxford: Elsevier.

Daily Telegraph (2001). Sarah Kane's howl of pain is an act of artistic heroism. 14 May. Available online: www.telegraph.co.uk/arts/main.jhtml?xml=/arts/2001/05/14/btkane14.xml

Daube, D. (1977). The linguistics of suicide. *Suicide and Life Threatening Behavior*, 7(3): 132–82.

Davey, J. (1878). On suicide, in its social relations. *Journal of Psychological Medicine*, n.s. 4: 230–55

Davidson, A. (1997). Structures and strategies of discourse, in A. Davidson (ed.), *Foucault and His Interlocutors*, pp. 1–17. University of Chicago Press.
    (2001). *The Emergence of Sexuality: Historical Epistemology and the Formation of Concepts*. Cambridge, MA: Harvard University Press.

Deleuze, G. (1999). *Foucault*, trans. Sean Hand, London: Athlone Press.
    (2006). What is a dispositif? in *Two Regimes of Madness. Texts and Interviews, 1975–1995*, pp. 338–48. New York: Semiotext(e).

Department of Health (2000). *An Organisation with a Memory. Report of an Expert Group on Learning from Adverse Events in the NHS*. London: The Stationery Office.

Department of Health (2002). *National Suicide Prevention Strategy for England*. London: Department of Health.

Department of Health (2006). *Help is at Hand: A Resource for People Bereaved by Suicide and Other Sudden, Traumatic Death*. London: Department of Health.

Dorpat, T. L. and Ripley, H. S. (1960). A study of suicide in the Seattle area. *Comprehensive Psychiatry*, 1: 349–59.

Douglas, J. D. (1967). *The Social Meanings of Suicide*. Princeton University Press.

Dreyfus, H. L. and Rabinow, P. (1982). *Michel Foucault: Beyond Structuralism and Hermeneutics*. University of Chicago Press.

Duffy, D. and Ryan, T. (eds) (2004). *New Approaches to Preventing Suicide: A Manual for Practitioners*. London: Jessica Kingsley.

Duncan, J. F. (1853). *Popular Errors on the Subject of Insanity Examined and Exposed*. Dublin: McGlashan.

Durkheim, E. (1897). *Le suicide: étude de sociologie*. Paris: Presses Universitaires de France.
    (1951). *Suicide, a Study in Sociology*. Glencoe, IL: Free Press.

Eagles, J. M., Klein, S., Gray, N. M., Dewar, I. G. and Alexander, D. A. (2001). Role of the psychiatrist in the prediction and prevention of suicide: a perspective from north-east Scotland. *British Journal of Psychiatry*, 178: 494–6.

East Kent Community NHS Trust, NHS Performance Ratings, July 2002. Available online: www.performance.doh.gov.uk/performanceratings/2002/rtm154ij.html

Edwards, C. (2005). Modelling Roman suicide? The afterlife of Cato. *Economy and Society*, 34(2): 200–22.

Ellis, W. C. (1838). *A Treatise on the Nature, Symptoms, Causes, and Treatment of Insanity*. London: S. Holdsworth.

Engstrom, G., Alling, C., Blennow, K., Regnell, G. and Traskman-Bendz, L. (1999). Reduced cerebrospinal HVA concentrations and HVA/5-HIAA ratios in suicide attempters. Monoamine metabolites in 120 suicide attempters and 47 controls. *European Neuropsychopharmacology*, 9: 399–405.

Esquirol, J.-E. D. (1805). Des passions considerées comme causes, symptômes, et moyens curatifs de l'aliénation mentale. Doctoral thesis. Université de Paris.

(1821). Suicide, in *Dictionnaire des sciences médicales: par une société de médecins et de chirurgiens*, vol. LIII. Paris: Panckouke.

(1838). *Des maladies mentales, considerées sous les rapports medicaux, hygiéniques, et medico-legaux*. Paris: Baillière.

(1845). *Mental Maladies. A Treatise on Insanity*, trans. E. K. Hunt. Philadelphia, PA: Lea & Blanchard.

Fairburn, G. (1995). *Contemplating Suicide: Language of Ethics and Self-harm*. London: Routledge.

Falret, J.-P. (1822). *De L'hypochondrie et du suicide: considérations sur les causes, sur le siège et le traitement de ces maladies, sur les moyens d'en arrêter les progrès et d'en prévenir le développement*. Paris: Croullebois.

Fawcett, J., Busch, K. A., Jacobs, D., Kravitz, H. M. and Fogg, L. (1997). Suicide: a four-pathway clinical-biochemical model. *Annals of the New York Academy of Sciences*, 836: 288–301.

Fielding Blandford, G. (1871/1976). *Insanity and Its Treatment: Lectures on the Treatment, Medical and Legal, of Insane Patients*. New York: Arno Press.

Fleck, L. (1981). *Genesis and Development of a Scientific Fact*. University of Chicago Press.

Flemming, R. (2005). Suicide, euthanasia and medicine: reflections ancient and modern. *Economy and Society*, 34(2): 295–321.

Forbes, T. R. (1971). *Chronicle from Aldgate*. London: Yale University Press.

Foster, T., Gillespie, K. and McClelland, R. (1997). Mental disorders and suicide in Northern Ireland. *British Journal of Psychiatry*, 170: 447–52.

Foucault, M. (1965). *Madness and Civilization: A History of Insanity in the Age of Reason*, trans. R. Howard. London: Tavistock.

(1970). *The Order of Things: An Archaeology of the Human Sciences*. New York: Pantheon, and London: Tavistock,

(1973). *The Birth of the Clinic: An Archaeology of Medical Perception*, trans. A. M. Sheridan-Smith. London: Tavistock.

(1977). *Discipline and Punish: The Birth of the Prison*, trans. A. M. Sheridan-Smith. Harmondsworth: Penguin.

(1980). *Power/Knowledge: Selected Interviews and Other Writings, 1972–1977* C. Gordon (ed.). New York: Pantheon Books.

(1981). *The History of Sexuality*, vol. I: *An Introduction*, trans. R. Hurley. Harmondsworth: Penguin.

(1985). *The Use of Pleasure*, vol. II of *The History of Sexuality*, trans. R. Hurley. Harmondsworth: Penguin.

(1986). *The Care of the Self*, vol. III of *The History of Sexuality*, trans. R. Hurley. Harmondsworth: Penguin.

(1987). *I, Pierre Riviere, having slaughtered my mother, my sister, and my brother: A Case of Parricide in the 19th Century.* Lincoln: University of Nebraska Press.

(1988a). *Politics, Philosophy, Culture: Interviews and Other Writings, 1977–1984,* ed. L. Kritzman. London: Routledge.

(1988b). Truth, power, self: an interview with Michel Foucault, in L. H. Martin, H. Gutman and P. Hutton (eds), *Technologies of the Self: A Seminar with Michel Foucault,* pp. 9–15. Amherst: University of Massachusetts Press.

Foucault, M. (ed.) (1998). *Hercule Barbin: Being the Recently Discovered Memoirs of a Nineteenth-Century French Hermaphrodite,* trans. Richard McDougall. New York: Pantheon Books.

(2000a). *The Essential Works of Foucault 1954–1984,* vol. I: *Ethics: Subjectivity and Truth,* ed. P. Rabinow. London: Penguin.

(2000b). *The Essential Works of Foucault 1954–1984,* vol. II: *Aesthetics, Method, Epistemology,* ed. J. D. Faubion. London: Penguin.

(2001). *Fearless Speech,* ed. J. Pearson. Los Angeles: Semiotext(e).

(2002a). *The Essential Works of Foucault 1954–1984,* vol. III: *Power,* ed. J. D. Faubion. London: Penguin.

(2002b). *The Archaeology of Knowledge,* trans. A. M. Sheridan-Smith. London: Routledge.

(2003). *Society Must be Defended: Lectures at the College of France 1975–1976.* New York: Picador.

(2004). *The Hermeneutics of the Subject: Lectures at the Collège de France 1981–1982,* ed. F. Gros, trans. Graham Burchell. New York: Palgrave Macmillan.

(2005). *History of Madness.* London: Routledge.

(2006). *Psychiatric Power. Lectures at the Collège de France, 1973–74.* New York: Palgrave Macmillan.

Fowler, R. C., Rich, C. L. and Young, D. (1986). San Diego suicide study, II: substance abuse in young cases, *Archives of General Psychiatry,* 43: 962–5.

Fraser, N. (1989). *Unruly Practices: Power, Discourse, and Gender in Contemporary Social Theory.* Minneapolis: University of Minnesota Press.

Freeman, A. and Reinecke, M. (1993). *Cognitive Therapy of Suicidal Behavior.* New York: Springer.

Freud, S. (1914). *The psychopathology of everyday life,* trans. A. A. Brill. London: T. Fisher Unwin. (Original work published 1901).

(1917). Mourning and melancholia in *The Standard Edition of the Complete Works of Sigmund Freud,* vol. XIV: *On the History of the Psycho-Analytic Movement: Papers on Metapsychology and Other Works,* trans. James Strachey, pp. 237–58. London: The Hogarth Press.

Gale, C. and Howard, R. (2003). *Presumed Curable: An Illustrated Casebook of Victorian Psychiatric Patients in Bethlem Hospital.* Petersfield: Wrightson Biomedical Publishing Ltd.

Gane, M. (2005). Durkheim's scenography of suicide. *Economy and Society,* 34(2): 223–40.

Gangat, A. E., Naidoo, L. R. and Wessels, W. H. (1987). Suicide in South African Indians, *South African Medical Journal,* 71: 169–171.

Gates, B. (1980). Suicide and the Victorian physicians, *Journal of the History of the Behavioral Sciences,* 16(2): 164–74.

(1989). *Victorian Suicide: Mad Crimes and Sad Histories*. Princeton University Press.

Gauchet, M. and Swain, G. (1999). *Madness and Democracy: The Modern Psychiatric Universe*, trans. Catherine Porter. Princeton University Press.

Geddes, J. (1999). Suicide and homicide by people with mental illness. We still don't know how to prevent most of these deaths. *British Medical Journal*, 318: 1225–6.

Gentleman's Magazine and Historical Review (1853). August.

Gergen, K. J. (1994). *Realities and Relationships: Soundings in Social Construction*. Cambridge, MA: Harvard University Press.

(1999). *An Invitation to Social Construction*. Thousand Oaks, CA: Sage.

Gilbert, N. and Mulkay, M. (1984). *Opening Pandora's Box: A Sociological Analysis of Scientists' Discourse*. Cambridge University Press. Available online: www.soc.surrey.ac.uk/books/OPB/contents.html

Goldney, R. D. (2005). Suicide prevention: a pragmatic review of recent studies. *Crisis*, 26(3): 128–40.

Goldney, R. D. and Schioldann, J. A. (2000). Pre-Durkheim suicidology. *Crisis*, 21: 181–6.

(2002). *Pre-Durkheim Suicidology: The 1892 Reviews of Tuke and Savage*. Burnside: Adelaide Academic Press.

Goldstein, J. (1987). *Console and Classify: The French Psychiatric Profession in the Nineteenth Century*. Cambridge University Press.

Greig, D. (2001). Introduction, in *Complete Plays* by Sarah Kane, pp. ix–xviii. London: Methuen.

Griffin, M. (1986) Philosophy, Cato and Roman suicide, *Greece and Rome* 33(1): 64–77, 33(2): 330–7.

Guardian, The (1999). Suicidal writer was free to kill herself. 23 September. Available online: www.guardian.co.uk/uk_news/story/0,,271851,00.html

Guardian, The. (2005). Gifted student with place at Oxford decided 'life is not for me'. 3 August. Available online: www.education.guardian.co.uk/higher/news/story/0,,1541564,00.html

Gurnhill, Rev. J. (1900). *The Morals of Suicide*. London: Longmans, Green and Co.

Gutman, S. A. (2005). Understanding suicide: What therapists should know. *Occupational Therapy in Mental Health*, 21(2): 55–77.

Hacking, I. (1986). Making up people,' in T. C. Heller (ed.), *Reconstructing Individualism: Autonomy, Individuality and the Self in Western Thought*, pp. 222–36. Stanford University Press.

(1990). *The Taming of Chance*. Cambridge University Press.

(1995a) *Rewriting the Soul: Multiple Personality and the Science of Memory*. Princeton University Press.

(1995b) The looping effect of human kinds, in D. Sperber, D. Premack and A. J. Premack (eds), *Causal Cognition: An Interdisciplinary Approach*, pp. 351–83. Oxford University Press.

(1998). *Mad Travellers: Reflections on the Reality of Transient Mental Illness*. Cambridge, MA: Harvard University Press.

(1999). *The Social Construction of What?* Cambridge, MA: Harvard University Press.

(2002). *Historical Ontology*. Cambridge, MA: Harvard University Press.

Hagnell, O. and Rorsman, B. (1978). Suicide and endogenous depression with somatic symptoms in the Lundby study. *Neuropsychobiology*, 4: 180–7.
    (1979). Suicide in the Lundby study: a comparative investigation of clinical aspects. *Neuropsychobiology*, 5(2): 61–73.
Halbwachs, M. (1978). *The Causes of Suicide*. New York: Free Press.
Halperin, D. M. (1995). *Saint Foucault: Towards a Gay Hagiography*. New York and Oxford: Oxford University Press.
Harding, W. (1894). *Mental Nursing, or Lectures for Asylum Attendants*. 2nd edn. London: The Scientific Press.
Hawton, K. (ed.) (2005). *Prevention and Treatment of Suicidal Behaviour: From Science to Practice*. Oxford University Press.
Hawton, K. and Van Heeringen, K. (eds) (2000). *The International Handbook of Suicide and Attempted Suicide*. Chichester: Wiley.
Hawton, K., Appleby, L., Platt, S., Foster, T., Cooper, J., Malmberg, A. *et al.* (1998). The psychological autopsy approach to studying suicide: a review of methodological issues. *Journal of Affective Disorders*, 50: 269–76.
Hawton, K., Houston, K., Haw, C., Townsend, E. and Harriss, L. (2003). Comorbidity of axis i and axis ii disorders in patients who attempted suicide. *American Journal of Psychiatry*, 160(8): 1494–500.
Healy, D. (1994). The fluoxetine and suicide controversy. *CNS Drugs*, 1: 223–31.
    (2000). Emergence of antidepressant induced suicidality. *Primary Care Psychiatry*, 6: 23–8.
Healy, D., Harris, M., Tranter, R., Gutting, P., Austin, R., Jones-Edwards, G. *et al.* (2006). Lifetime suicide rates in treated schizophrenia: 1875–1924 and 1994–1998 cohorts compared. *British Journal of Psychiatry*, 188: 223–8.
Healy, R. (2006). Suicide in early modern and modern Europe. *Historical Journal*, 49: 903–19.
Heckler, R. A. (1996). *Waking up Alive: The Decent, the Suicide Attempt, and the Return to Life*. New York: Ballantine.
Hendin, H. (1964): *Suicide in Scandinavia*. New York: Grune & Stratton.
Henry, A. and Short, J. (1954). *Suicide and Homicide*. New York: McGraw-Hill.
Henson, H. H. (1897). *Suicide*. London: Oxford House.
Hill, T. (2004). *Ambitiosa Mors. Suicide and Self in Roman Thought and Literature*. London: Routledge.
Hoy, D. C. (2005). *Critical Resistance: From Poststructuralism to Post-Critique*. Cambridge, MA: MIT Press.
Huneman, P. (2003) 'Animal economy' and the rise of psychiatry. Paper presented at ISECS International conference/Congrès des Lumières, round-table 'Anthropology of the Enlightenment', UCLA (Los Angeles), August 2003.
Jamison, K. R. (1999). *Night Falls Fast: Understanding Suicide*. New York: Vintage Books.
Jamison, K. R. and Hawton, K. (2005). The burden of suicide and clinical suggestions for prevention, in K. Hawton (ed.), *Prevention and Treatment of Suicidal Behaviour: From Science to Practice*. Oxford University Press.
Jobes, D. A. (2006). *Managing Suicide Risk: A Collaborative Approach*. New York: Guilford Press.

Jobes, D. A., Luoma, J. B., Hustead, L. A. T., and Mann, R. (2000). In the wake of suicide: survivorship and postvention, in R. Maris (ed.), *Textbook of Suicidology and Suicide Prevention*, pp. 536–61. New York: Guilford Press.

Johnson, S., Nolan, F., Hoult, J., White, I., Bebbington, P., Sandor, A. *et al.* (2005). Outcomes of crises before and after introduction of a crisis resolution team. *British Journal of Psychiatry*, 187: 68–75.

Kane, S. (2000). *4.48 Psychosis*. London: Methuen Drama.

(2001). *Complete Plays*. London: Methuen Drama.

Khan, M. M. (2005). Suicide prevention and developing countries. *Journal of the Royal Society of Medicine*, 98: 459–63.

Kleespies, P. M., Smith, M. R. and Becker, B. R. (1990). Psychology interns as patient-suicide survivors: incidence, impact, and recovery. *Professional Psychology: Research and Practice*, 21: 257–63.

Kleespies, P. M., Penk, W. and Forsyth, J. (1993). The stress of patient suicidal behavior during clinical training: incidence, impact, and recovery. *Professional Psychology: Research and Practice*, 24: 293–303.

Knighton, W. (1881). Suicidal mania. *Contemporary Review*, 39, reprinted in *Littel's Living Age*, 148 (5 February 1881): 376–81.

Knox, K. L., Conwell, Y. and Caine, E. D. (2004). If suicide is a public health problem, what are we doing to prevent it? *American Journal of Public Health*,. 94(1): 37–45.

Koivumaa-Honkanen, H., Honkanen, R., Viinamäki, H., Heikkilä, K., Kaprio, J. and Koskenvuo, M. (2001). Life satisfaction and suicide: a 20-year follow-up study. *American Journal of Psychiatry*, 158: 433–9.

Kunugi, H., Takei, N., Aoki, H. and Nanko, S. (1997). Low serum cholesterol in suicide attempts. *Biological Psychiatry*, 41: 196–200.

Latour, B. and Woolgar, S. (1979). *Laboratory Life: The Social Construction of Scientific Facts*. London: Sage.

Leenaars, A. (2004). *Psychotherapy with Suicidal People: A Person-Centered Approach*. New York: John Wiley & Sons.

Leonard, B. E. (2005). The biochemistry of suicide. *Crisis*, 26(4): 153–5.

Lieberman, L. J. (2003). *Leaving You: The Cultural Meaning of Suicide*. Chicago: Ivan R. Dee.

Litman, R. E. (1996). Sigmund Freud on suicide, in J. T. Maltsbeger and M. J. Goldblatt (eds), *Essential Papers on Suicide*, pp. 200–20. New York University Press.

Locke, J. (1690/1959) *An Essay Concerning Human Understanding*, 2 vols, ed. A. C. Fraser. Oxford: Clarendon Press. Reprinted 1959, New York: Dover.

MacDonald, M. (1986). The secularization of suicide in England, 1660–1800. *Past and Present*, 111: 50–110.

(1995). Suicidal behaviour – social section, in G. E. Berrios and R. Porter (eds), *A History of Clinical Psychiatry*, pp. 625–32. London: Athlone Press.

(1997). The medicalization of suicide in England: laymen, physicians, and cultural change, 1500–1870, in C. Rosenberg and J. Golden (eds), *Framing Disease: Studies in Cultural History*, pp. 85–103. New Brunswick, NJ: Rutgers University Press.

MacDonald, M. and Murphy, T. R. (1990). *Sleepless Souls: Suicide in Early Modern England*. Oxford University Press.

Maltsberger, J. T. (2004). The descent into suicide. *International Journal of Psychoanalysis*, 85(3): 653–67.

Maltsberger, J. T. and Goldblatt, M. J. (eds) (1996). *Essential Papers on Suicide*. New York University Press.

Mann, J. J., Huang, Y. Y., Underwood, M. D., Kassir, S. A., Oppenheim, S., Kelly, T. M. *et al.* (2000). A serotonin transporter gene promoter polymorphism (5-HTTLPR) and prefrontal cortical binding in major depression and suicide. *Archives of General Psychiatry*, 57: 729–38.

Mann, J. J., Brent, D. A. and Arango, V. (2001). The neurobiology and genetics of suicide and attempted suicide: a focus on the serotonergic system. *Neuropsychopharmacology*, 24: 467–77.

Mansfield, N. (2000). *Subjectivity: Theories of the Self from Freud to Haraway*. New York University Press.

Maris, R. W., Berman, A. and Silverman, M. (2000). *Textbook of Suicidology*. New York: Guilford Press.

Martin, R. and Barresi, J. (2006). *Rise and Fall of Soul and Self: An Intellectual History of Personal Identity*. New York: Columbia University Press.

Maudsley, H. (1861). The love of life. *Journal of Mental Science*, 7: 191–209.

(1892a) *Responsibility in Mental Disease*. London: Kegan Paul.

(1892b). Suicide in simple melancholy. *Medical Magazine of London*, 1: 45–56.

(1895). *The Pathology of Mind. A Study of Its Distempers, Deformities, and Disorders*. London: Macmillan & Co.

Mayo, T. (1838). *Elements of the Pathology of the Human Mind*. London: John Murray.

Medical Times and Gazette, The. (1858). Suicide Melancholy. 37(January–June): Plate 2 opposite p. 64.

Menninger, K. A. (1938). *Man Against Himself*. New York: Harcourt, Brace & Co.

(1933/1996). Psychoanalytic aspects of suicide, in J. T. Maltsberger and M. J. Goldblatt (eds), *Essential Papers on Suicide*, pp. 20–35. New York University Press.

Mercier, C. A. (1890). *Sanity and Insanity*. London: Walter Scott.

Miller, A. L., Rathus, J. H. and Linehan, M. M. (2006). *Dialectical Behavior Therapy for Suicidal Adolescents*. New York: Guilford Press.

Millingen, J. G. (1839). *Curiosities of Medical Experience*, 2nd edn. London: Richard Bentley.

Minois, G. (1999). *History of Suicide: Voluntary Death in Western Culture*. Baltimore, MD: Johns Hopkins University Press.

Monthly Gazette of Health. (1822). Suicide and hypochondriacism. September: 253–6.

Moore, C. (1790). *A Full Inquiry into the Subject of Suicide*. London: J. F. & C. Rivington.

Morison, A. (1828). *Cases of Mental Diseases with Practical Observations on the Medical Treatment*. London and Edinburgh: Longman & Co and S. Highley.

(1840). *The Physiognomy of Mental Diseases*, London: Longman.

(1848). *Outlines of Lectures on the Nature, Causes and Treatment of Insanity*. London: Longman, Brown, Green & Longmans.

Morselli, E. A. (1882). *Suicide: An Essay on Comparative Moral Statistics*. New York: Appleton.

Murray, A. (1998). *Suicide in the Middle Ages*, vol. I: *The Violent Against Themselves*. Oxford University Press.

(2000). *Suicide in the Middle Ages*, vol. II: *The Curse on Self-Murder*. Oxford University Press.

Murray, H. (1938). *Explorations in Personality*. New York: Oxford University Press.

Neilson, A. (1999). Insane thesis, letter to *The Guardian*, 25 February. Available online: www.guardian.co.uk/comment/story/0,,311080,00.html

Nielsen, D. A., Virkkunen, M., Lappalainen, J., Eggert, M., Brown, G. L., Long, J. C., *et al.* (1998). A tryptophan hydroxylase gene marker for suicidality and alcoholism. *Archives of General Psychiatry*, 55: 593–602.

Noble, D. (1853). *Elements of Psychological Medicine, An Introduction to the Practical Study of Insanity*. London: John Churchill.

O'Connor, R. and Sheehy, N. (2000). *Understanding Suicidal Behaviour*. Leicester: BPS Books.

O'Connor, R., Sheehy, N. and O'Connor, D. B. (2000). Fifty cases of general hospital parasuicide. *British Journal of Health Psychology*, 15: 83–95.

O'Farrell, C. D. (2005). *Michel Foucault*. London: Sage.

Ordway, G. A., Smith, K. S. and Haycock, J. W. (1994). Elevated tyrosine hydroxylase in the locus coeruleus of suicide victims. *Journal of Neurochemistry*, 62: 680–5.

Osborne, T. (1998). *Aspects of Enlightenment*. London: University College London Press.

(2003). What is a problem? *History of the Human Sciences*, 16(4): 1–17.

(2005). 'Fascinated dispossession': suicide and the aesthetics of freedom. *Economy and Society*, 34(2): 280–94

Oyebode, F. (2005). Suicide, national inquiries and professional judgement. *Advances in Psychiatric Treatment*, 11: 81–3.

(2006). Clinical errors and medical negligence. *Advances in Psychiatric Treatment*, 12: 221–7.

Pahor, A. (2006). Did the ancient Egyptians know about the psychopathology of suicide? Paper delivered at the 40th International Congress on the History of Medicine, 27 August.

Pandey, G. N., Pandey, S. C., Dwivedi, Y., Sharma, R. P., Janicak, P. G. and Davis, J. M. (1995). Platelet serotonin-2A receptors: a potential biological marker for suicidal behavior. *American Journal of Psychiatry*, 152(6): 850–5.

Patel, S. P. and Gaw, A. C. (1996). Suicide among immigrants from the Indian subcontinent: a review. *Psychiatric Services*, 47: 517–21.

Perlin, S. (ed.) (1975). *A Handbook for the Study of Suicide*. London: Oxford University Press.

Phillips, M. R., Li, X. and Zhang, Y. (2002). Suicide rates in China, 1995–99. *Lancet*; 359: 835–40.

Pinel, P. (1806/1962). *A Treatise on Insanity*. London: Facsimile edn. New York: Hafner.

Plass, Paul (1995). *The Game of Death in Ancient Rome*. Madison: University of Wisconsin Press.

Pokorny, A. D. (1983). Prediction of suicide in psychiatric patients. Report of a prospective study. *Archives of General Psychiatry*, 40: 249–57.

(1993). Suicide prediction revisited. *Suicide and Life Threatening Behavior*, 23: 1–10.

Pollock, L. and Williams, M. (2004). Problem solving in suicide attempters. *Psychological Medicine*, 34: 163–7.

Porter, R. (1987). *Mind-Forg'd Manacles: A History of Madness in England from the Restoration to the Regency*. London: Athlone.

(2000). *Enlightenment: Britain and the Making of the Modern World*. London: Allen Lane.

Potter, J. (1996). *Representing Reality: Discourse, Rhetoric and Social Construction*. London: Sage.

(2003). Discourse analysis, in M. Hardy and A. Bryman (eds), *Handbook of Data Analysis*, pp. 607–24. London: Sage.

Prado, C. G. (2000). *Starting with Foucault: An Introduction to Genealogy*. Boulder, CO: Westview.

(2006). *Searle and Foucault on Truth*. Ontario: Queen's University.

Prichard, J. C. (1835). *A Treatise on Insanity and Other Disorders Affecting the Mind*. London: Sherwood, Gilbert & Piper.

(1840). Suicide, in *A System of Practical Medicine, Comprised in a Series of Original Dissertations, Arranged and Edited by Alexander Tweedie*, pp. 120–3. London: Whittaker & Co.

Qin, P. and Nordentoft, M. (2005). Suicide risk in relation to psychiatric hospitalization: evidence based on longitudinal registers. *Archives of General Psychiatry*, 62: 427–32.

Quarterly Review, 93 (1853). Article VII: 295–318.

Rabinow, P. and Rose, N. (2003). *The Essential Foucault*. New York: The New Press.

Radcliffe, J. N. (1859). The method and statistics of suicide, *Journal of Psychological Medicine*, 12: 209–23.

(1862). The English suicide-fields, and the restraint of suicide, *Medical Critic and Psychological Journal*, 2: 701–10.

Rimke, H. (2003). Constituting transgressive interiorities: Nineteenth-century psychiatric readings of morally mad bodies, in A. Arturo (ed.), *Violence and the Body: Race, Gender and the State*, pp. 403–28. Bloomington: Indiana University Press.

(2005). Ungovernable subjects: a radical genealogy of moral insanity. Unpublished dissertation, Department of Sociology and Anthropology, Carleton University, Ottawa.

Robins, E. (1981). *The Final Months: A Study of the Lives of 134 Persons*. New York: Oxford University Press.

Robins, E., Murphy, G. E., Wilkinson, R. H., Gassner, S. and Kayes, J. (1959/ 1996). Some clinical considerations in the prevention of suicide based on a study of 134 successful suicides. *American Journal of Public Health*, 49: 888–99. Reprinted in J. T. Maltsberger and M. J. Goldblatt (eds), *Essential Papers on Suicide*, pp. 142–59. New York University Press.

Robinson, G. (1859). *On the Prevention and Treatment of Mental Disorders*. London: Longman, Brown, Green, Longmans & Roberts.

Rorsman, B. (1973). Suicide in psychiatric patients: a comparative study. *Social Psychiatry*, 8: 45–66.

Rose, N. (1986). *Psychiatry: the discipline of mental health*, in P. Miller and N. Rose (eds), *The Power of Psychiatry*, pp. 43–84. Cambridge: Polity Press.

(1996). Psychiatry as a political science: advanced liberalism and the administration of risk. *History of the Human Sciences*, 9: 1–23.

(1998). *Inventing Our Selves: Psychology, Power and Personhood*. Cambridge University Press.

(2000). Biological psychiatry as a style of thought. Paper presented to a symposium on models and cases in scientific thought at Princeton University.

(2003). The neurochemical self and its anomalies, in R. Ericson (ed.), *Risk and Morality*, pp. 407–37. University of Toronto Press.

(2007). *The Politics of Life Itself: Biomedicine, Power, and Subjectivity in the Twenty-First Century*. Princeton University Press.

Rosen, G. (1971). History in the study of suicide. *Psychological Medicine*, 1: 267–85.

(1975). History, in S. Perlin (ed.), *A Handbook for the Study of Suicide*, pp. 3–29. London: Oxford University Press.

Royal College of Psychiatrists. (2006). Ancient Egyptian poem could be oldest description of suicidal thoughts. Press release. Available online: www.rcpsych.ac.uk/pressparliament/pressreleases2006/pr805.aspx

Sadler, J. Z. (2005). *Values and Psychiatric Diagnosis*. Oxford University Press.

Salih, S. (ed.) (2004). *The Judith Butler Reader*. Oxford: Blackwell.

Samaritans. (2002). *Media Guidelines: Portrayals of Suicide*. Ewell: The Samaritans.

Saunders, G. (2002). *Love Me or Kill Me: Sarah Kane and the Theatre of Extremes*. Manchester University Press.

(2003). 'Just a word on a page and there is the drama.' Sarah Kane's theatrical legacy. Available online: www.serieslitteraires.org/publication/article.php3?id_article=233

Savage, G. H. (1884). Constant watching in suicidal cases. *Journal of Mental Science*, 129: 17–20.

(1893). *Insanity and Allied Neuroses: Practical and Clinical*. London: Cassell and Co.

Scull, A. T. (ed.) (1981). *Madhouses, Mad-Doctors and Madmen: The Social History of Psychiatry in the Victorian Era*. London: Athlone.

(1993). *The Most Solitary of Afflictions: Madness and Society in Britain*. New Haven, CT: Yale University Press.

Seigel, J. (2005). *The Idea of the Self: Thought and Experience in Western Europe since the Seventeenth Century*. Cambridge University Press.

Seymour, E. J. (1832). *Observations on the Medical Treatment of Insanity*. London: Longman, Rees, Orme, Brown & Co.

Shepherd, A. and Wright, D. (2002). Madness, suicide and the Victorian asylum: attempted self-murder in the age of non-restraint. *Medical History*, 46: 175–96.

Shergill, S. and Szmukler, G. (1998). How predictable is violence and suicide in psychiatric practice? *Journal of Mental Health*, 7: 393–401.

Shneidman, E. S. (1973). Suicide notes reconsidered. *Psychiatry*, 36: 379–94.

(1985). *Definition of Suicide*. New York: John Wiley and Sons.

(1993). *Suicide as Psychache: A Clinical Approach to Self-Destructive Behavior*. Northvale, NJ: Aronson.

(1996). *The Suicidal Mind*. New York: Oxford University Press.

(2004). *Autopsy of a Suicidal Mind*. New York: Oxford University Press.

Shorter, E. (1997). *A History of Psychiatry: From the Era of the Asylum to the Age of Prozac*. New York: John Wiley & Sons.

Sierz, A. (2000). The short life of Sarah Kane. *The Daily Telegraph*, 27 May.

Simon, R. I. (2006). Imminent suicide: the illusion of short-term prediction. *Suicide and Life Threatening Behavior*, 36: 296–301.

Smith, R. (1981). *Trial by Medicine: Insanity and Responsibility in Victorian Trials*. Edinburgh University Press.

Stanley, M. and Mann, J. J. (1983). Increased serotonin-2 binding sites in frontal cortex of suicide victims. *Lancet* 1: 214–16.

Stevenson, C. and Cutcliffe, J. (2006). Problematizing special observation in psychiatry: Foucault, archaeology, genealogy, discourse and power/knowledge. *Journal of Psychiatric and Mental Health Nursing*, 13(6): 713–21.

Steward, J. B. (1845). *Practical Notes on Insanity*. London: John Churchill.

Strahan, S. A. K. (1894). *Suicide and Insanity; A Physiological and Sociological Study*. London: S. Sonnenschein & Co.

Stockard, J. and O'Brien, R. M. (2002). Cohort effects on suicide rates: international variations, *American Sociological Review*, 67(6): 854–72.

Strozier, R. M. (2002). *Foucault, Subjectivity, and Identity: Historical Constructions of Subject and Self*. Detroit: Wayne State University Press.

Styron, W. (1991). *Darkness Visible: A Memoir of Madness*. London: Jonathan Cape.

Szasz, T. (1971). The ethics of suicide. *Antioch Review*, 31 (spring): 7–17.

(1974). *The Myth of Mental Illness: Foundations of a Theory of Personal Conduct*, Revised edn. New York: Harper Row.

(1986). The case against suicide prevention. *American Psychologist*, 41: 806–12.

(1989). Suicide and psychiatric coercion. *Journal of Humanistic Psychology*, 29 (summer): 380–4.

(1999). *Fatal Freedom: The Ethics and Politics of Suicide*. Westport, CT: Praeger.

Tanney, B. L. (1992). Mental disorders, psychiatric patients, and suicide, in R. W. Maris, A. L. Berman, J. T. Maltsberger and R. I. Yufit (eds), *Assessment and Prediction of Suicide*, pp. 277–320. New York: Guilford Press.

(1995). After a suicide: a helper's handbook, in B. L. Mishara (ed.), *The Impact of Suicide*, pp. 100–20. New York: Springer.

Taylor, C. (1986). Foucault on freedom and truth, in D. C. Hoy (ed.), *Foucault: A Critical Reader*, pp. 69–102. Oxford: Blackwell.

(1989). *Sources of the Self: The Making of the Modern Identity*. Cambridge, MA: Harvard University Press.

Taylor, S. (1982). *Durkheim and the Study of Suicide*. London: Macmillan.

(1988). *The Sociology of Suicide*. Harlow: Longman.

Taylor, T. (1853). *The Life of B. R. Haydon, from his Autobiography and Journals. In Three Volumes*. London: Longman, Brown, Green & Longmans.

Thomas, C. (1980). First suicide note? *British Medical Journal*, 281(6235): 284–5.

Times, The (2005). Dying to succeed: fatal pressure on our children. 4 August. Available online: www.timesonline.co.uk/article/0,,8123–1719921,00.html

Tinker, J. (1995). Review of *Blasted. Daily Mail*, 19 January.

Träskman-Bendz, L. and Mann, J. J. (2000). Biological aspects of suicidal behaviour, in K. Hawton and K. van Heeringen (eds), *International Handbook of Suicide and Attempted Suicide*, pp. 65–78. Chichester: Wiley.

Tuke, D. H. (1892). *A Dictionary of Psychological Medicine*. London: J. & A. Churchill.

Tweedie, A. (1840). *A System of Practical Medicine, Comprised in a Series of Original Dissertations*. London: Whittaker & Co.

United Nations/World Health Organization (1996). *Prevention of Suicide: Guidelines for the Formulation and Implementation of National Strategies* (ST/ESA/245). Geneva: World Health Organization.

University of Manchester (undated). The STORM Project: Training in risk assessment and management of suicide and self-injury. Training package.

Valente, S. M. (1994). Psychotherapist reactions to the suicide of a patient. *American Journal of Orthopsychiatry*, 64(4): 614–21.

van Heeringen, C. (2001). Suicide, serotonin, and the brain. *Crisis*; 22(2): 43–6.

van Hooff, A. J. L. (1990). *From Autothanasia to Suicide. Self-Killing in Classical Antiquity*. London: Routledge.

   (2000). A historical perspective on suicide, in R. Maris, A. L. Berman and M. M. Silverman (eds), *Comprehensive Textbook of Suicidology*, pp. 96–123, New York: Guilford Press.

van Praag, H. (2005). The resistance of suicide: why have antidepressants not reduced suicide rates? In K. Hawton (ed.), *Prevention and Treatment of Suicidal Behaviour: From Science to Practice*, pp. 239–60. Oxford University Press.

Vijayakumar, L. and Rajkumar, S. (1999). Are risk-factors for suicide universal? A case-control study in India. *Acta Psychiatrica Scandinavica*, 99: 407–11.

Wærn, M., Runeson, B. S., Allebeck, P., Beskow, J., Rubenowitz, E., Skoog, I. *et al.* (2002). Mental disorder in elderly suicides: A case-control study. *American Journal of Psychiatry*, 159(3): 450–5.

Watt, J. (ed.) (2004). *From Sin to Insanity: Suicide in Early Modern Europe*. Ithaca, NY: Cornell University Press.

Williams, J. M. G. (1997). *The Cry of Pain*. London: Penguin.

Winslow, B. Forbes (1840). *The Anatomy of Suicide*. London: Henry Renshaw.

   (1860). *On Obscure Diseases of the Brain, and Disorders of the Mind, Their Incipient Symptoms, Pathology, Diagnosis, Treatment and Prophylaxis*. London: John Churchill.

World Health Organization (2000a). *Preventing Suicide: A Resource for Primary Healthcare Workers*. Geneva: World Health Organization.

World Health Organization (2000b). *Preventing Suicide: A Resource for Media Professionals*. Geneva: World Health Organization.

World Health Organization (2000c). *Preventing Suicide: A Resource for General Physicians*. Geneva: World Health Organization.

World Health Organization (2000d). *Preventing Suicide: A Resource for Teachers and Other School Staff*. Geneva: World Health Organization.

World Health Organization (2006a). *Preventing Suicide: A Resource for Counsellors.* Geneva: World Health Organization.

World Health Organization (2006b). *Preventing Suicide: A Resource at Work.* Geneva: World Health Organization.

Wynn Westcott, W. (1885). *Suicide: Its History, Literature, Jurisprudence, Causation and Prevention.* London: H. K. Lewis.

Wynter, A. (1875). *The Borderlands of Insanity and Other Papers.* London: Robert Hardwicke.

Index